Thoughtful Writing

Misunderstanding and Its Remedies

Gene Hammond

State University of New York at Stony Brook

Third Edition

Kendall Hunt
publishing company

Cover image © Kristian Sekulic, 2009. Used under license from Shutterstock, Inc.

Kendall Hunt
publishing company

www.kendallhunt.com
Send all inquiries to:
4050 Westmark Drive
Dubuque, IA 52004-1840

Contents

1

Where Do We Start?

Critical Skills and Attitudes for a Writer

You probably don't think you need a course in writing. Certainly, you'd rather be doing something else than taking this course. After all, you have been reading, speaking, and writing English for most, if not all, of your life. My guess, though, is that despite all the writing you've done, you don't feel very confident when you're asked to write. That lack of confidence needn't be a life-long burden, though. You'll be surprised at how much this course you're beginning can improve your writing, and how much easier it will make writing for you. In the past the tools of the writer were paper, a pen or pencil, and (in the 20th century) a typewriter. Today, fortunately, the universal writer's tool is the miraculous computer. The computer makes writing and revising much easier than they were with any of the earlier writing tools, and as a bonus, through its access to the internet, the computer makes research easier (sometimes deceptively easier) than it has ever been. With this powerful tool, and equally important, with a willingness to give some of the soul and sweat that the student quoted above thought he was unwilling to give, you'll emerge from this course a different person, one who can take writing tasks, and public presentation tasks, two of the activities that psychological studies say that we fear the most, in stride.

In the course of this class you can expect to improve your writing in at least fifteen ways:

1. You'll become more observant.
2. You'll become a skilled collector and user of telling details.
3. You'll learn how to find what you need or want in a library or online.
4. You'll learn how to organize any chaotic mass of information.
5. You'll become confident (if you aren't already) about your grammar.
6. You'll master the use of commas, dashes, semicolons, and colons.
7. You'll learn to make every sentence in your writing count.
8. You'll learn to paragraph in a way that makes reading easier for your readers.
9. You'll learn to link your sentences smoothly.
10. You'll learn how to rethink and revise your first drafts.
11. You'll learn how to write effective introductions and conclusions.
12. You'll learn to write effectively to unsympathetic readers.
13. You'll learn to write with a voice that readers can recognize as yours.
14. You'll learn to write clear essays in class under pressure.
15. You'll learn to use your writing skills to help you with related forms of communication such as photography, video production, or public speaking.

You can accomplish all this even if, like most of us, you don't especially like to write. But there is one condition: that you *want* to improve your writing. If you don't want to learn, you might as well drop the course now, sell this book back to the bookstore, get into another course, and come back another semester when you're ready. You can succeed in this course if you're shaky about your grammar or if you think your writing is awkward. You can succeed if you think your aptitude is not for writing but for engineering or computers. But if you're not curious, if you're not patient, if you're not receptive to our advice, if you're not willing to work hard, or if you're only taking this course because it is a requirement, you may have serious trouble with it. The workload in this course is going to fall not on your teacher but on you. Neither your teacher nor this book can tell you how to write better. You must decide for yourself that *you* want to improve. If you write badly now, it's not because you are not intelligent. It's because you haven't been *attentive* about improving your writing. That attention is where we need to start.

You can't learn to write if you don't want to learn. You also can't learn to write by studying about writing. You learn to write by writing—and by *thinking* while you write. In this class you will try to produce writing that you and your teacher and your classmates can genuinely admire. Much of your progress as a writer will come from practice: repeated application letters that fail to get you a job, repeated memos that are sent back for yet another revision once you do get a job. But you can also practice in this class, with less at risk, by writing assigned papers for your teacher and for your classmates and by doing the exercises suggested in this book.

The exercises in this book have been designed to enable you to practice and develop your writing skills one or two at a time until all the skills become part of your intuitive resources, thus improving your writing performance and giving you greater confidence as a writer. All the assignments, discussions, reading, and writing you do in this course will go into building your writing intuitions—intuitions for how to begin, how to organize, how to make your writing "flow." Writing is a complex task that requires everything from getting your spelling right to making your voice distinctive enough to be heard. Writing any new assignment requires a combination of thought, hard work, and intuition. The more you can rely on intuition, the more energy you have left for thinking about matters that are really new.

In this course you will not simply be delivering enough words and sentences to reach your teacher's page limit. Nor will you be able to write any of your papers the night before it is due. You'll be thinking and taking notes about your subject from the day each of your papers is assigned. Also, you'll be trying to learn much more about writing than simply how to develop a good "style." You'll find that *collecting information, sorting it, drawing conclusions from it, and selecting only the best of your information and conclusions for your final draft, are the most crucial writing skills.* If you learn to present pertinent information clearly, you'll find that you have developed, without even trying to, your own style.

This book contains very few rules. If you think you'll do well in college, or in life, or in writing, by following infallible rules, you're mistaken. There are guidelines for most situations, writing or otherwise, but success lies in making the most of the options you have within these guidelines. Some so-called *rules* of writing were merely fashions which are now as obsolete as top hats or dress gloves—"Never begin a sentence with *and* or *but*," "Never end a sentence with a preposition," "Never split an infinitive." Other "rules" of writing—"Grab the attention of your readers," "Outline everything you write"—are more precisely rules of thumb. They are useful in many cases, but not in all. The key to good writing is not learning to follow rules but learning what your choices are—choices in tone, in words, in paragraphing, in punctuation. As this course progresses, you'll learn new options from your teacher, from your classmates, from me, and from your own increasingly good judgment. Think carefully about our choices. But take seriously your own preferences too. Your progress in developing both writing ability and confidence will be gradual but substantial.

Throughout this book, I'll stop talking to you as often as possible to give you time to try exercises that will help develop your thinking about writing. You may interpret the exercise numbers that introduce these exercises as invitations to skip over to the next regular reading. If you do, though, you'll be wasting much of the money and effort you've invested in this course. My thoughts about writing may stay with you for six months (an optimistic estimate). But your thoughts about writing, as you discover them for yourself in these exercises, will stay with you for life.

Assessing Your Current Writing Ability

Exercise 1-1
on your own or in class

All of you are starting this course with different writing strengths and different writing weaknesses. So before we can begin sensibly to work on improvement, we have to find out what your current writing abilities are. Perhaps you feel confident about your writing; more likely you do not. To let your teacher know your strengths and your weaknesses, *write a page or two about your training in English to this point and about what kind of writer you now are as a result of that training.*

- Be as specific as possible.
- You may write about just a single English class if you prefer.
- Cross out and revise as much as you wish. Don't worry about neatness.
- You might want to stop for a few minutes and take a few notes before you begin.

Writing Priorities Survey

Exercise 1-2
in class

You undoubtedly have noticed, and probably been frustrated by, the fact that the various writing teachers you've had so far in your life have had different standards for what is good writing. We have the same disagreements about movies, about politics, and about religion, so it shouldn't be too surprising that we have these differences about writing. The differences that even experts have in evaluating writing are most often due to differing standards of what is most important when judging writing. So before we go too far in a writing course, we should try to find out what our standards are. Look at Table 1-1 that follows, which lists priorities it is possible for teachers and students to have in a writing class:

1. Mark with an H the five items that you think should have highest priority in this writing class.
2. Mark with an L the five items that you think should have lowest priority.

Table 1-1   Priorities: A Survey of Opinion

Writing Class Priorities	High-Rated			Low-Rated		
	Self	**Group**	**Teacher**	**Self**	**Group**	**Teacher**
1. Writing accurate thesis statements	✓					
2. Writing argumentative topic sentences						
3. Using supporting details			✓			
4. Avoiding sentence fragments				✓		
5. Learning precise verb forms and subject-verb agreement						✓
6. Spelling correctly				✓		✓
7. Punctuating correctly						
8. Drawing inferences	✓					
9. Writing introductions						
10. Writing conclusions						
11. Developing a distinct tone of voice			✓	✓		
12. Observing one's subject carefully	✓					
13. Writing logically						
14. Connecting sentences coherently						
15. Being concise						
16. Using words precisely						
17. Paragraphing clearly						
18. Planning before writing						
19. Revising drafts	✓					
20. Becoming aware of one's readers			✓	✓		
21. Learning to read more critically.						
22. Knowing correct manuscript form				✓		✓
23. Learning to judge one's own work	✓					
24. Other (specify)_____						

When you've finished marking your highest and lowest priorities, your teacher can survey the results in your class so you can mark those results on this chart alongside your decisions. Your teacher will also tell you his or her current opinion. Note the totals, and compare your teacher's and the group's opinions with your own. Some of my own H's the last time I took the survey went to "using supporting details," "developing a distinct tone of voice," and "becoming aware of one's readers." My L's went to "learning precise verb forms," "spelling correctly," and "learning correct manuscript form." Looking at my L's reminds me that I consider even these items important, though not as important as the others. In this course we'll be working on everything. You may, though, want to focus on weak areas while building up your strengths in all.

What we'll be learning in this course is called nonfiction writing. Nonfiction writing is often considered to be the opposite of so-called creative writing. But seeing an opposition here is absurd. All writing, not just fiction and poetry, is creative. The nonfiction you'll be writing in this class will never be a simple mirror of reality. It is always a *version* of ideas or events, of which there are many other possible versions. Nonfiction, no less than fiction, requires creative, thoughtful decisions about selection of material, interpretation of material, arrangement of material, tone of voice, and the best way to persuade our readers.

You, and all your new classmates, will be writers, thoughtful writers I hope, in the professions you take up when you graduate. Because writing is private work, though, and so we rarely watch people do it, you may not yet realize how much of your time as a professional is going to be taken up with writing. Lawyers in television series spend their time in court. Police officers in television series spend their time making arrests. But Chicago lawyers and Detroit police officers and Los Angeles sales managers spend much of their time writing. Job announcements even for routine work often ask for written-communication skills. And promotions beyond college-exit jobs are almost always dependent on your communication skills. Schools and departments which test you exclusively through multiple-choice tests are (unintentionally) misleading you about your future. There are no multiple-choice tests after college. Whether you plan to be a teacher, an engineer, a market analyst, or a computer programmer, surveys show that you're likely to spend at least 25 percent of your working hours writing or planning writing—letters, reports on research, budget reports, grant proposals, business forecasts, press releases, speeches, management briefings, equipment justifications, technical bulletins (Faigley and Miller 560–61).[1] Much of the time you are not writing, you will be

---

[1]In this book I will acknowledge my sources, as I recommend that you do, by following the guidelines of the *Modern Language Association Style Manual* (2009). Whenever I quote or paraphrase material from another source, I'll add in parentheses at the end of my sentence the author or authors and the page or pages that I've borrowed from. Then I'll put all the details about the source in my Works Cited list on pages 227–230. Check my Works Cited list right now for the information about Faigley and Miller's article, so you can see how this reference system works, and then master it yourself for your own writing.

trying to be informative and thoughtful in other ways. What you learn in this course about writing will often help you to conduct business in person or over the phone. It will also help you to talk more clearly and specifically with your family and friends. Even if you never write for the rest of your life (an unlikely possibility), you'll find the thinking, research, and organizational skills in this course useful in all the ways that you interact with other people.

This book is shorter than some writing course texts because in this course *you* are going to have to do most of the work. Newspapers, your city council, your local courtroom, a person whom you choose to interview, the internet, and your library's books, magazines, and CDs will all expand this textbook. At the end of this course you won't carry away a fund of propositions or rules. You'll leave with a willingness to work hard and a good set of writer's intuitions that will make you confident in attacking college and professional writing assignments.

HUGE HINT: The best way to learn from this book is to complete most of the exercises in it, and to write and turn in to your teacher a one-sentence-per-paragraph outline of what you've read each time your teacher assigns you to read a chapter or other portion of this book. Those outlines will ensure that your mind is fully alert as you read.

2

Telling Details

George Bernard Shaw once said that as he grew older, he became less and less interested in theory, more and more interested in information. The temptation in writing is
just the reverse. Nothing is so hard to come by as a new and interesting fact. Nothing
is so easy on the feet as a generalization.

JOHN KENNETH GALBRAITH

Lloyd George, Prime Minister of England during World War I, was convinced that if
the war could once be described in accurate language, people would insist that it be
stopped.

PAUL FUSSELL

Telling Details: The Basis of All Effective Writing

On March 14, 1983, Ruben Zamara, a negotiator for a coalition of five
guerilla groups in El Salvador, complained about the progress of talks between
the guerillas and the Salvadoran government: "Let's use fewer adjectives and
more facts" (Hall B1).[1] If adjectives like "communist" and "imperialist" and
"terrorist" were preventing communication from taking place in the 1983 El
Salvador peace talks, so also do adjectives like "boring" or "interesting" or "different" hinder genuine communication when we write. Which of the two statements at the top of the next page, each taken from a student's paper about
adjustment to college, tells you more?

---

[1]Here is my second parenthetical reference to the Works Cited list on pages 227–230 where
you'll find the complete details about this article. Again I've listed in my parentheses the author's last name and the page number that the quotation appears on. This page number
looks different because it's from a newspaper with pages numbered by section, A1–A20,
B1–B14, C1–C16, D1–D12.

- So far I haven't had as much of a problem adjusting to college as I thought I would have. I have met some interesting people, and some not so interesting people.
- I share a dorm room 9 by 18 feet with two desks, a sink, a set of bunkbeds, and a 6-foot, 4-inch roommate from Buffalo. It's the most space and the most privacy I've ever had.

Fortunately for us, photographers and filmmakers don't have adjectives like "interesting" at their disposal, so they work hard to find facts that make their points. The photograph below, using a "telling" fact, could replace many a written editorial. Every film you see is a continuous series of telling photographs and incidents. Since most films try to tell, in two hours, stories which would take twenty or thirty hours to read, they focus on crucial incidents. In *No Country for Old Men*, the director lets us come to our own conclusions about the subtle cruelty of Javier Bardem's character when he shows us Bardem flipping a coin in front of a convenience store clerk to decide whether he will spare his life. In *Hustle and Flow*, when the Taraji Henson character quietly complains that the other characters in their small home are waking up the baby she has just put to sleep, and they don't even stop talking to listen to her, the director has "told" us how little power she has in her own house.

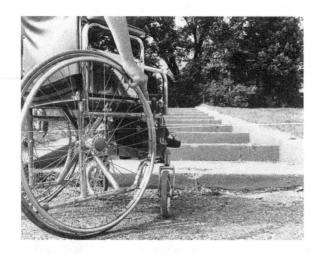

Published statistics are another familiar type of telling fact. *Harper's* magazine has for many years now published a page of facts like the following at the beginning of every issue:

- Number of Iranian tanks that Iraq has captured and sold back to Iran during the Iran Iraq war in 1986: 150
- Total U.S. aid to Iowa farmers in 2006: $3,700,000,000

- Percentage of Americans who have smoked at least one whole cigarette before they were 13: 14%
- Percentage of visits to doctors' offices that concern stress-related ailments: 75%
- Portion of immigrants to the United States who settle in California: $\frac{1}{4}$
- In 1844 there were 13 colleges in the state of Ohio. All 13 were sponsored by the United Methodists.
- One out of every eight couples who married in 2006 met online.
- Number of cheerleaders in the United States: 600,000
- Percentage of recruited student athletes at Division 1 NCAA universities who graduate: 67%
- Percentage of all students at those universities who graduate: 59%

We shouldn't be *too* easily persuaded by such telling statistics. We might not understand the entire context from which they were taken. But they undeniably provoke thought and by doing so encourage both writer and reader to look more deeply into the matter being statistically described.

Readers, no less than filmgoers or statistics collectors, appreciate facts that carry a clear message. Ken Macrorie calls these "telling facts" (32).[2] Others call them "telling" or "revealing" or "significant" details. If you become able—after this chapter, or by the end of this course—to find telling details and use them in your writing, you will have mastered one of the most difficult skills (and the one requiring the most thought) in the art of writing. Decide now that you're willing to spend the time necessary to understand, collect, and use these telling details. Here's a start.

Recalling and Writing Telling Details

Exercise 2-1
on your own

Think back to the home you grew up in. Write down some detail from your kitchen or attic or basement that would, by itself, give your teacher and class some idea of the character of either your father or your mother. Your response might be a single sentence, or two or three. In class, compare what you come up with with the attempts of your classmates.

Have some of you succeeded in using a fact or detail to give us an idea of a parent's character? Be strict in your standards—you have nothing to lose if you don't succeed

---

[2]My second parenthetical reference in this chapter contains only a page number, not the name of the author, because I've already mentioned the name of the author in my sentence. Full details of the Modern Language Association guidelines for parenthetical references and for making up a works cited list are given in Chapter 10, "Research on the Internet and in the Library."

now, but you have everything to lose if you don't learn through your mistakes. Here are a few successful examples:

- One corner of our basement is a large paneled room with three fluorescent lights hanging from the ceiling and plenty of three-pronged outlets.
- As you walk through the living room into the kitchen, immediately you see the table fully set with four places. It's only 3:30 in the afternoon.
- On the top shelf of the refrigerator are full and not-so-full cans of Miller Lite and Diet Coke. On the next, there are ten or fifteen plastic containers that offer yellow or green fuzz if you peek into them. Hamburger expected to be cooked for dinner nights ago sits on the shelf slowly turning brown. The freezer looks like a perfect place for cross-country skiing.

This kind of success is rare. You'll undoubtedly find as you read each other's samples that details haven't come easily, and they haven't come easily because there are two easier, less effective ways to describe things that come to the mind and to the pen much more readily.

There are three ways to describe a person or a place: by giving a *detail*, by making a *comparison*, or by stating a *quality*. Details consistently give a reader something to think about. The second way to describe, offering a comparison, *can* be helpful. The cross-country skiing comparison above gives us a vivid picture of a freezer in trouble, but comparisons do not always convey a clear image to a reader, as in the following examples:

- As I entered the basement, I felt as if I were entering a dentist's office.
- Our kitchen is a riot.

The third way to describe, stating a quality (through an adjective) comes most easily to us, but it is least helpful to our readers:

- The kitchen in my present house has a tendency to be a bit *sloppy* by the end of the day.
- I have always been overwhelmed by the *strong and dictative* atmosphere that the basement of my house possesses.
- Our attic is *weird*.

The value of almost any piece of writing depends not on its comparisons or on its assertions of qualities but on its details. A good letter of recommendation, written for you, for example, will make a much better impression with details about your performance—"Matt grew impressively as an oral interpreter and actor of Shakespeare, starting out with modest roles like Rosencrantz and Bardolph, but eventually gaining the confidence to effectively portray Antony and King Lear"— than with adjectives like *intelligent, serious,* or *sensitive.* Every fact included in such a recommendation reflects the writer's interpretation of your character (since it is selected from hundreds of brief encounters you've had). But readers get a much clearer picture when they're given facts, and they enjoy drawing their own meanings from them. Facts are therefore more persuasive than opinionated adjectives. Comparisons help if carefully selected, and qualities are sometimes a useful shortcut when we're in a hurry, but by far the most effective communication is achieved through details.

Qualities, Comparisons, Details

Exercise 2-2
on your own or in class

Look at the following notes (not yet complete sentences) toward a description of a neighborhood. Which notes are statements of quality, which are comparisons, and which are details (or telling facts)? Which do you find most effective, and why?

Every kid should be raised in a ghetto. Predominantly white, Irish-Catholic neighborhood with a sprinkling of a few black-haired, tanned-skinned, Italians. Something out of an Irish Soap commercial. A Black, Oriental, or Jew nowhere to be found and Protestants treated like illegal aliens. One-way street so narrow one could spit across it (popular game). Stick ball, wise ball, half ball (called hemisphere), step ball—city games—make do. 23 row houses attached one to another on both sides of a 1-way street. Unread pages of the *Philadelphia Bulletin* blowing up and down the street making the ordinary trash somewhat more intellectual. Not unlike the floor of the N.Y. stock market during a bull market. 45 good Catholic families who have littered the street with over 150 children. Chalk designs on the street, crying babies, fighting children while parents do some city socializing on front steps. Ice Cream and Water Ice Trucks make their respective ritualistic appearances at 9:07 and 9:35. The sound of horns blowing accompanies the youth's shouts for the money from parents. The only universal sound emanating from households is the sound of the radio's baseball broadcast.

The evening ends with the last out of the ninth inning. The final roundup of camaraderie and community of purpose or maybe plight. Young and old. Sporadic crying, yelling, laughing, and coughing. No air conditioning. The heat which for 12 hours bakes the city's concrete carpeting. A night with little promise of relief.

One more point. Not all details are telling. If I were to describe the room I usually teach in by saying, "The room is painted light green," I wouldn't have told you much. You'd have a much better picture if I noted, "The ceiling is covered with water stains, and the exposed pipes rattle every time a toilet is flushed upstairs." Telling facts are facts that *tell* a reader something. They imply more than they say.

Coming Up with Telling Facts

Exercise 2-3
In class

Take five or ten minutes to try to write some telling facts about any subject. Once you have a list, offer your attempts to the class to see what they think. Are the facts offered telling? Or ho-hum? If, after hearing from others a few successful telling facts, you decide that one of yours is clearly unsuccessful, offer it to the class as an unsuccessful attempt and see whether you can explain why it doesn't succeed. You can often learn more, at this point, from failures than from successes.

Here are a few effective telling facts that students have come up with in completing the exercise above.

- She slogged through the mud path across the main quad to her next class. (*Implication: Students don't stay on the sidewalks and the college doesn't take care to pave the most convenient student routes.*)
- My father got out of his car, stopped to pick two daffodils in the front yard, and stepped into the house. (*Implication: He has not surrendered to the pressure to rush, rush, rush through life.*)
- When the grease that coats the top of the stove is splattered, it hits all four walls of the kitchen. (*Implication: The room is small, and its cooks are sloppy.*)
- He begrudgingly agreed to lend her $2 but then found that the smallest bill he had was a twenty. (*Implication: The more money a person has, the less likely he'll be generous.*)
- When he was introduced, his handshake was firm, but his palms were damp with sweat. (*Implication: He was nervous, though pretending not to be.*)

Of course, our efforts are not always so successful. Here are a few attempts that the class decided were inadequate:

- As he walked down the street, the beer and ale called out to him from the passing restaurants and bars. (*Not a fact.*)
- Giant "Eiffel Tower" steel electric-generators stand on a sweep of smooth bright grass. (*Not focused. What implication is intended?*)
- After two drinks, she could dance a fair polka; after three drinks, she was Polish. (*The second half is not a fact.*)
- The professor's desk was piled high with dusty books and papers. (*Perhaps a telling fact, but one used so often that it has become a cliché.*)

A common type of attempt at writing a telling fact follows:

- In the attic of the house I grew up in was a box placed so high I could not examine its contents until I was 8 or 9; then I discovered it contained dozens of letters, yearbooks, corsages—all sorts of artifacts from my parents' lives. They must have kept everything!

■ My mother uses her own set of kitchen knives and keeps her knives in a special drawer so that no one else can use them. To her, the art of cooking lies in the right way of cutting.

In both cases above, a strong telling fact in the first sentence is weakened by a lame explanation or comment in the second sentence. Try, for now, to resist the urge to explain. In your writing later, you will, of course, be commenting on the facts you've selected. But that commentary is relatively easy, while finding facts that can convince is much more difficult. If you want to learn to be a good writer, you have to learn to *earn* the right to make a comment by starting with well-chosen details.

Writing Telling Facts from Direct Observation

Exercise 2-4
on your own

Coming up with a telling fact is difficult—getting yourself to think using specifics is difficult—it requires clearing out the cobwebs that naturally gather in all of our minds. But it's also difficult because so far you've been trying to recall telling facts rather than to write them from observation. *Telling facts are easier to collect than to recollect.* So for homework for the next class, stop somewhere to observe for a while—allow yourself at least an hour—and write out five telling facts to bring to class. (It should be clear by now that the word *fact* is not limited to statistics; a fact is anything that can be observed.)

You can check your ability to find these telling facts by comparing yours, in your next class, with those of your classmates. One effective way to compare notes is to divide into groups of three or four in which you decide on the group's best five and worst five telling facts. Once a group has come to a decision, it can rejoin the class and read the facts chosen randomly. The class may then vote whether each example is or is not a telling fact. The class should vote the facts "telling" (when they have clear implications) or "boring" (when they call forth only a "so what" response). Finally, you might hand your facts in to your teacher to get a more experienced opinion. When your teacher and the class disagree, think about why that can happen.

Writing is never excellent or weak except in relation to whom we're writing for. Therefore, deciding whether a fact is telling or boring will always vary somewhat from person to person. Our response to any writing is colored by our past experience and our past reading, and in no two cases will that experience be identical. In the most extreme cases, some of us may miss the point of a telling fact because we're not at all familiar with the subject. But the experience of people living in the same culture is usually similar enough that your class will reach consensus about which facts are telling and which are not.

Many facts that a writer uses do his work (like supplying useful background information for a reader) without calling attention to themselves as telling facts. But telling facts are always worth striving for. The quest for them will keep any writer—a professional writer, a student A-writer, or a student D-writer—challenged while working on any writing assignment. Every paper, whether a story, a description, a textual or artistic analysis, or a researched argument, needs strong details to support and explain its purpose. *No amount of correct or clever writing can substitute for a mass of telling facts in helping a writer achieve his or her ends.* If you didn't come up with five good facts the first time you tried for homework, try the same exercise again until you're more comfortable with, and more skilled at, selecting and writing them. Force yourself to sit quietly in a busy place and observe. Once you get the knack for finding telling facts, all your writing will be easier and more effective.

Taking Pains Not To Write without Details

When we prepare well for writing, we first gather facts from observation (of places, people, books, newspapers, films) and then come to interpretations of the facts we've gathered. When we're rushed, though, we write because we already have an interpretation, or opinion, that we want to get across. In such a case, we too often rely on our memory rather than firsthand observation to back up our opinions. And our memory offers, again too often, only vague recollections, as in one of the sentences that introduced this chapter:

■ I have met some interesting people, and some not so interesting people.

We can't let sentences like that quit. They remain opaque to the reader, and three or four in succession, or six out of eight, will put the reader to sleep.

Exercise 2-5
on your own or in class

Search the following passage for genuine details. Note where the writer has allowed herself to be satisfied with vague recollections.

Some girls join sororities to increase their social interests, but a smart girl joins for a chance to better herself. She comes to the sorority to escape the anonymity of a large university. She works to become a person, an identity with feelings, instead of number 000-11-7777. Living with a large group of girls, she becomes more aware of others' wants and needs. By working with others, she learns to express her ideas and interests and become a leader. The sorority gives her the opportunity to work with the underprivileged and the disabled, helping her to grow mentally. As she works to become a part of the sorority, she grows stronger as an individual. With the support of the other members, she is fulfilled by the increase in her self-image.

There's a lot of feeling in this passage, but the message that gets through to the reader is muddy. We still don't know after reading this passage what this girl or her sorority actually does. Don't let yourself be satisfied with such careless, lacking-in-detail, writing.

To see how you can build an essay out of specific details, you might try, at this point, to write a description of a place in your experience that you'd like your classmates to know about. When I say "description," I don't want your mind to leap immediately to "beauty." There's no point in writing fantasy like the following:

> My first glimpse of the beach was from a distance. I was standing on a hill gaping at what seemed to me the perfect beach. The scenic view looked like it belonged in a travel agency poster. There was a thick grove of coconut palms and a strip of virgin white sand that separated the trees from the deep blue Caribbean Sea.

You'll miss the whole point of describing a place in writing if you aim for beauty. When you try to describe something, you should be aiming *not for beauty but for honesty.*

Description	≠	Beauty
Description	=	Honesty

What is your place really like? What makes it distinctive? How do people use it? Places are distinctive—and thus worth writing about—only because people have made them so. People have conceived them, built them, and perhaps neglected them. Now other people frequent them, or pass by them as quickly as possible. How? Why?

Your raw material for any description will be telling facts that you collect by observing, patiently observing. Here is part of what one student saw when she took a pencil and notebook to the back room of a veterinarian's office where she had formerly worked as a receptionist:

> The back room is filled with cages lining all four walls, stacked three and four cages high. The "E. E. box" (excremental exercise box), otherwise simply known as "the box," takes up most of the area in the middle of the room. Looking into the box, you can usually see one or two dogs curiously sniffing the urine-soaked newspapers. In one corner of the room, between two walls of cages, is a stack of donated newspapers that are constantly in use. Another corner has three steps leading up to the rear exit. Next to the rear door are stacked cases of various prescription dog food, sometimes stacked 6 to 7 feet high. At the bottom of the steps is a trashcan used to

hide euthanized animals, each one placed in a trash bag, until they can be properly disposed of. In a third corner is a bathtub for bathing cats and dogs. Sticky jugs of flea shampoo are placed at random on the floor around the tub. Behind the tub is a concealed lavatory. The door to this 4- by 5-foot room rests on its lower hinges. Inside the lavatory, a dusty toilet with a cracked seat and no lid is camouflaged by more cases of prescription dog food, as well as cat food. A window fan, in the same tiny room, slowly rotating in a breeze of muggy summer air, is temporarily placed in the window above the toilet.

The writer's fresh interpretation of these details and others will of course be an important part of the paper she finally writes. But her interpretations will fall flat for the reader unless she has amassed many details like these to begin with. As we collect these telling details, we come to recognize meaning in the most ordinary details of our lives. When we include them in our writing, we offer the same pleasure of recognizing that meaning to our readers.

This habit of observing patiently, of respecting what facts can tell us, and of seeking out the facts that resonate most, will make all your paper writing more successful. Observation, after all, is not only useful in describing objects. When we read a book well, we underline or circle various words, sentences, and paragraphs. By doing so, we implicitly acknowledge that these are telling words, telling sentences, telling paragraphs. These particular words express, in miniature, much more than they actually say. If you were writing a paper on, say, Alice Schroeder's *Warren Buffett and the Business of Life* (2008), you'd want to look back at your carefully observed underlined passages to find telling quotations to use in your review. If you were to interview a woman in a nursing home, you would observe carefully how she acts and what she says. Some of how she looks would be telling; you'd be sure to include those details. Some of what she says would also be telling; you'd of course include that too. If you were writing a paper on secrets our government has kept from the people, you would note the most policy-changing secrets that you found in your research and the most surprising behavior of public officials that helped keep those secrets secret. By seeking out telling facts and then drawing responsible inferences (conclusions) from them, you would be likely to write a fresh, honest, thoughtful paper.

Research of all kinds, then, is a form of observation, selected observation. The same keen observation, the same research methods, apply in analyzing a place, a person, a book, a table of statistics, a film, a magazine, a newspaper, a public issue. It takes practice in each form of observation to look through the raw material and find what's significant, what's thought-provoking, what's of human interest. It takes practice in each to find the telling facts, and to determine the meanings that those telling facts reveal. Collecting information of any kind requires patience. You don't always find what you want right away. But the patient exploration the writer goes through each time follows the same pattern. And once you're confident that you can find evidence, you'll never again have to sit at your desk for hours staring at a blank screen and worrying about how you're going to fill it.

Work at noticing telling facts until you can select them almost instinctively. Our ability to write telling facts is a reflection of our ability to discriminate, to select, to distinguish meaning from the lack of it. Telling details are the foremost tools of photographers, filmmakers, fiction writers, informative writers, persuasive writers, thoughtful writers—anyone who wants to get a point across economically and vividly.

3

Facts, Inferences, and Theses

As in other sciences, so in geography, careful, systematic, direct observation and description are preliminary to, and necessary for, any classification and explanation that may follow. The geographer in his study of any region, therefore, first of all systematically observes and records, usually onto a map, the patterns and arrangements of natural and cultural features. The second step, following observation and description, is the search for explanations as to why the region is as it is.

VERNOR FINCH AND GLENN TREWARTHA

Most people would rather die than think, and most people do.

BERTRAND RUSSELL

Exercise 3-1 Review
on your own

Before starting this chapter, write out brief answers to the following questions:

1. What is an inference?
2. What is the difference between a fact and an inference?
3. What is a thesis statement?

You'll remember better the principles of this chapter if at the end of the chapter you come back and check what you've learned against these original impressions you had.

Inferences

As much as I have emphasized facts so far, I don't mean to suggest that facts are to be used by a writer without analysis, without commentary, without conclusions or judgments that the writer draws from those facts. (It is an insecure lawyer or manager who stuffs a chaotic pile of facts into a brief or a report in the hope that some of the facts might convince.) We build a paper out of facts, but the resins that hold a paper together are the *inferences* that we draw from these facts. Inferences, I know, is a word that you either haven't heard before or are a little fuzzy about. You don't hear it much in everyday conversation—we take inferences for granted. But drawing careful inferences is crucial to becoming a good writer.

An inference is a judgment based on at least one fact. You drew inferences in Chapter 2 whenever you decided what you thought each telling fact "meant." *Inference* is very closely related to a much more commonly used term, *implication*. When a writer uses a telling fact—"In 2004 there were 604,200 African-American men enrolled in higher education in the United States, and 757,000 in federal, state, and local prisons"—she is *implying* that there is some injustice here. When you or I read the same telling fact, we are likely to *infer* that there is some injustice. We're both going in the same direction—*from* the fact *toward* the idea of injustice—but the word used to describe the writer's action is *imply*, and the word used to describe the reader's action is *infer*. This chart may help:

S. I. Hayakawa, in *Language in Thought and Action*, has explained inferences so clearly that I'll call on him here to help me (41):[1]

> An inference . . . is a *statement about the unknown made on the basis of the known*. We may *infer* from the material and cut of a woman's clothes her wealth or social position; we may *infer* from the character of the ruins the origin of the fire that destroyed the building; we may *infer* from a man's calloused hands the nature of his occupation; we may *infer* from a senator's vote on an armaments bill his attitude toward Russia; we may *infer* from the structure of the land the path of a prehistoric glacier; we may *infer* from a halo on an unexposed photographic plate that it has been in the vicinity of radioactive materials; we may *infer* from the sound of an

---

[1]Now that you're in the habit of checking the Works Cited list on pages 227–230 when you see a number like this in parentheses, I'll stop offering you reminders. This is your last footnote.

engine the condition of its connecting rods. Inferences may be carelessly or carefully made. They may be made on the basis of a broad background of previous experience with the subject matter, or no experience at all. For example, the inferences a good mechanic can make about the internal condition of a motor by listening to it are often startlingly accurate, while the inferences made by an amateur (if he tries to make any) may be entirely wrong. But *the common characteristic of inferences is that they are statements about matters that are not directly known, statements made on the basis of what has been observed.*

Drawing inferences responsibly is a very important thinking skill. In this chapter, you'll practice "drawing" several kinds of inferences from several different kinds of facts.

Geologists and archaeologists are masters at drawing inferences. Most of the European world in the eighteenth century believed that Noah, about 3000 B.C., had built an ark and survived a forty-day flood. Then geologist James Hutton in the 1780s discovered clam fossils embedded in the granite of the mountains of Scotland. Thinking about the fact of the embedded fossils, Hutton inferred that much of Scotland was at one time under water—not 5000 years earlier, as the biblical story of Noah suggested, but perhaps 6 million years earlier. Hutton's inference was a bold one in 1785, but much evidence discovered since his time has supported his claim (McPhee, *Basin and Range* 91–108). Geologists' professional work is to look at surviving artifacts from millions of years ago and try to interpret them, try to draw reasonable inferences from them.

Archaeologists work the same way. They sift through the remains of more recent times, the times since we humans made our appearance. Their method of working is well described by Craig Stoltz (3):

> Professor Joe Dent arrives to the first meeting of "Archaeology 451" with a plastic trash bag slung over his shoulder. He grabs the bag by the corners and shakes its contents onto the floor: several institutional memos, a Mozart Festival brochure, a Coke can. A small paper envelope imprinted with the name of an English industrial archaeology museum, a "Dear Friend" direct mail piece from an historical society, a black plastic canister the size of a thread spool. A cellophane pipe tobacco packet, a twisted pipe cleaner, flecks of charred tobacco, and a scattering of papers, some handwritten, others typed, a few dittoed. Some are balled up.
>
> "This," says Dent, spreading the mess around with his foot, "is what archaeologists deal with—garbage." He's dumped onto the teacher's platform what has accumulated in his trash can since 7:30 that morning. The students of Archaeology 451 don't say much, but just look at the trash, their pens poised at their notebooks. They had planned on merely taking notes. "So what does this garbage tell us?" Dent asks. "Anything?" We begin to speculate, carefully at first. That Dent doesn't like classical music. No, that he doesn't like Mozart. Maybe he doesn't read brochures. Well, maybe he *reads* them but doesn't keep them. He's literate, we guess. He has a mild addiction to caffeine. No, practically everybody drinks Coke.

At least he's not a health nut—he smokes. But a pipe. A clean pipe. *Was* dirty, though. Probably a tourist type, with a decent camera. Those balled up papers— he has a temper. Or was bored. Maybe shoots baskets. Maybe shares an office. Or someone else put that trash in his can.

We continue for twenty minutes or so, leaping from fact to rickety inference, back to solid fact, on to other facts. Valid inferences, we find, are hard to draw: each must be checked in relation to other facts and inferences. After twenty minutes of pawing and grabbing, we know little about the man behind the garbage. Even this morning's trash, it turns out, doesn't yield many answers.

Archaeologist that he is, Dent has also brought in some "real" artifacts—the kind we'd planned on taking notes about. One is what we call an "arrowhead" of brown stone (later, we'll learn to call such things "projectile points"); another is an axe head the size of an open hand, a smooth finger-wide groove dividing it in two. Dent claims these are garbage too—cultural discards—but harder than fresh trash to draw inferences from: there are no other items with which to associate them. There is also a rectangular stone slab a-foot-and-a-half long and three-inches thick, half of its top face chipped an inch deep. This artifact has proved very difficult indeed to make assumptions about, Dent reports—to date, nobody has been able to figure out what it might have been used for. Such an item is known in archaeologist parlance as a "FRGOK": Funny Rock—God Only Knows.

"The archaeologist's real problem," Dent says, nodding back at the fresh trash scattered on the floor, is that "over time, almost everything disappears." If this trash were dumped outside, the paper and tobacco would decompose in a month; the plastic and metal would get kicked around, eventually buried, and biodegraded within a few hundred years. Even the gray plastic trash bags, always a target of angry environmentalists who complain that plastic lasts forever, would disintegrate within a millennium or two. So when archaeologists apply what may seem absurd scrutiny to chunks of stone, says Dent, holding the Funny Rock in his arms, it is not because they think these are the most telling cultural remains. They are not. It's because, most of the time, that's all a prehistoric culture has left behind. The rest has rotted away.

Drawing Inferences from Observed Facts

Exercise 3-2
in class

Your teacher may not be so accommodating as to bring in the garbage, but a memorable way to practice drawing inferences is to draw them from the objects on your teacher's office desk, or from the notes on his or her monthly calendar, or from the contents of his or her pockets, purse, brief case, or bookbags. Every item you note (e.g., an American Express card) is a fact from which you may draw a timid inference ("she doesn't like to carry lots of money with her") or a bold inference ("she's rich") or even—we hope—a responsible inference somewhere between those two.

It will help you sort things out in your mind when doing this exercise if you make a list down the left-hand side of a piece of paper of the items you've observed. For example, let's assume you've seen, from your teacher's bag:

- a Walmart receipt
- a note reading "return mother's salad bowl"
- cough drops
- a small bag of dog treats

Then, as you draw inferences, list your inferences opposite the facts you drew them from, with arrows between them:

- a Walmart receipt → cheap
- note about salad bowl → recently had a party
- cough drops → has a sweet tooth
- bag of dog treats → her mother has a dog

When you draw these inferences, do you have full confidence in them? What other facts would help you feel more sure?

At this point you should be noting that some of your inferences are timid and some are bold, that inferences with several facts behind them are more secure, that the inferences you can draw will differ from those of others because you start from different assumptions or you know more about a given subject. Most important, though, you should feel in your bones that from now on you can distinguish a fact from an inference. If you're ever confused in the future, all you have to remember is that *all those objects your teacher carried were facts. All the conclusions you came to, to the right of your arrows, were inferences.* When you've exhausted your teacher's patience with your "bold" inferences, do the same exercise with a volunteer student's backpack, or pair off with another student in the class and see how well you can infer things about each other using the objects each of you carries around.

Drawing Inferences from Statistics

Exercise 3-3
in class

After this brief skirmish with drawing inferences, try the same move from facts to inferences with a more revealing (or is it a less revealing?) kind of fact—statistics. The following is a breakdown of types of ads in four different magazines. Use Tables 3-1 through 3-4 (one at a time) to draw as many inferences as you can about the audience—in terms of age, gender, marriage status, interests, and occupations—at which you think the magazine is aimed. Compare your results with those of the rest of the class, note what

Table 3-1   Magazine #1 May 2009   *Adult/Senior College Students*

Types of Ads	1/2 or Full Page Ads	Ads 1/4 Page or Smaller
Food	2	1
Cleaning Products	7	
Self Improvement Books and Software	2	10
Treatment Centers	1	5
Medicine	10	2
Education	5	27
Health Products	3	10
Pet Products	1	
Music/Music Products	1	
Home Improvement Products	1	2
Websites	2	4
Astrology and Psychics	1	7

Table 3-2   Magazine #2 May 2009

Types of Ads	1/2 or Full Page Ads	Ads 1/4 Page or Smaller
Trucks/Tractors	2	1
Car Products	2	
Medicine	5	1
Home Improvement Products	12	16
Television Shows	1	
Hardware Stores	3	
Websites	4	
Health Products	1	
Furniture	2	
Computer Hardware or Software	2	
Tools	5	4
Self Improvement Books and Software	2	
Vacations	1	
Clothes	1	1
Magazine	2	
Hobbies		1
Music/Music Products	1	1
Insurance	1	

Dads

Table 3-3 Magazine #3 October, 2008   Women (40-50)

Types of Ads	1/2 or Full Page Ads	Ads 1/4 Page or Smaller
Skin Care	30	2
Clothes and Shoes	80	16
Jewelry	14	
Cars	1	
TV Show	1	
Health Care	4	
Alcohol	1	
Credit Cards	1	
Cleaning	1	
Health Foods	1	
Music	1	

Table 3-4 Magazine #4 Feb. 11th & 18th, 2009

Types of Ads	1/2 or Full Page Ads	Ads 1/4 Page or Smaller
Cars	7	1
Clothes and Eyeware	5	3
Energy Co.	1	
Jewelry	2	2
Movies and TV		2
Investing	4	
Alcohol	2	
Food	1	
Computer Hardware or Software	1	1
Books	1	10
Hotels	2	2
Health and Insurance	1	2
Art and Music	2	3
Travel	6	3
Home Accessories	1	4
Education	1	7
Mental Health Retreat		1
Weight Loss		1

Women (20-30)

assumptions or background information led you to your inferences, and note whether your inferences tend to be bolder or more timid than those of your classmates.

After completing this exercise, you might want to guess what each magazine was: the answers are at the beginning of Chapter 14. Completing these exercises, you will have noticed again that some inferences made by your classmates are bold, some timid. Those who tend to draw timid inferences should try to take greater risks, to think a bit harder before writing. Those who tend to draw bold inferences need to seek out more evidence to justify the leap that they are asking their readers to make.

Combining Inferences into a Thesis

Exercise 3-4
in class

For more practice in drawing inferences, this time noting how they can enable you to structure a paper, take a look at the photographic composite on the opposite page. As a class, examine the photo in detail, and begin to list details—not judgments—about the picture along the left side of a sheet of paper. Once the class has noted ten or fifteen details, put on the right side of your paper, opposite each detail, any inferences that you feel the detail might justify. Again, you're drawing inferences from the facts (details) you've noted. Once the right side of your paper is pretty full, describe at the bottom of your sheet the overall impression that you think the photographer of this picture was trying to get across. What do you think the purpose of the photographic composite was?

You'll find, I think, that your interpretation of the photographer's purpose (i.e., your thesis) will be some kind of summation, or summation with qualification, of the inferences that you've listed on the right side of your paper. If you were to write out an analysis of this picture at this point, it would most naturally begin with a sentence stating the purpose of the picture, and that sentence would be substantiated by a listing (probably with some explanation added) of some of the details you first put down on the left side of the page.

This exercise should help you see how most papers take shape. Your research begins with an examination of details from which you gradually, via your inferences, arrive at a thesis. Just to make things difficult, your papers are expected to begin at the opposite end of the fact-inference-thesis sequence, with a summary of your inferences—a thesis. Your inferences then follow in the form of topic sentences, and your details follow those topic sentences as the evidence to support those topic sentences. The most difficult skill for most writers to acquire is to learn to place your thesis, which you have arrived at late in the writing process, way back at the beginning—the end of your introductory paragraph—as a service to your reader.

Image © DUSAN ZIDAR, 2009. Used under license from Shutterstock, Inc.

Drawing Inferences and a Thesis from a Text

Exercise 3-5
in class

You have practiced drawing inferences from objects you can see, from statistics, and from details in a photograph. Now you'll practice on the most common type of information that writers draw inferences from—writing itself. Read the following advertising flyer found on a car windshield in a shopping mall parking lot.

Your goal in this exercise is to come to some judgment about what kind of a person you think Sister Rebecca is. To prepare to make that judgment, draw any inferences about Sister Rebecca that you can from this flyer. Either circle your evidence and draw an arrow to the margin where you write your inference, or make a list like those you've been making in earlier exercises, with facts (in this case, words) on the left and inferences opposite on the right. Then, after looking over your facts and your inferences, write a sentence-or-two conclusion—your thesis—giving your judgment of Sister Rebecca's character.

Always caps Name, must be important

■ ■ ■

ESP Spiritual

Reader and Advisor
Religious *Sister* Rebecca   *switches POV, unprofessional*

I will tell you your troubles and what to do about them. Don't let other people confuse or mislead you. God helps all those who want to help themselves. Through SISTER REBECCA all things are possible with God's help on earth. I will show it to you! Advice on all affairs of life.

conclusion

The Religious Holy Woman healer, God's messenger who will heal the sick and the ailing, and remove all suffering and bad luck from your body. She will call your enemies by name and tell you who to keep away from. She is a religious and holy woman who will show you with your own eyes how she will remove sorrow, sickness, pain and all bad luck. What your eyes see your heart must believe. The touch of her hand will heal you.

SISTER REBECCA has the God-given Power to Heal by Prayer. Are you suffering? Are you sick? Do you need help? Do you have bad luck? Are you unhappy, unlucky, and unable?

See SISTER REBECCA today. She guarantees to reunite the separated and solemnly swears to heal the sick, and help all who come to her and remove all evil spells. *She restores lost nature.*

She guarantees to cure you where others have failed. Will take the sickness and pain away from you. One visit will convince you that she is God's messenger on earth. SISTER REBECCA has helped thousands and thousands and guarantees to help you, too. SISTER REBECCA removes all pain. This religious healer will help you where others have failed. If you suffer from alcoholism and cannot find a cure, don't fail to see this gifted woman who will help you. *poorly phrased sentence → low education*

If you have done this exercise carefully, you should be able to imagine how you might paragraph an essay about Sister Rebecca. The body of your paper would consist of several paragraphs, each emphasizing one of Sister Rebecca's character traits—her religious views, perhaps, her business sense, her intelligence, her own emotions, and her sense of the emotions of her readers. The topic sentence of each paragraph could be the most thoughtful inference you could come up with in each of those areas, and each topic sentence could be followed by several sentences quoting passages from the flyer which serve as evidence for your inference. With an introduction that speculates about why such businesses exist in our society (and most others) and a conclusion that shows some concern about the lives of both Sister Rebecca and her clients, you would have an excellent paper, solidly researched, and very well organized, based on just one page of evidence.

Fact-Inference Pairs as a Research Tool

Exercise 3-6
in class

The pattern of moving from facts to inferences to a thesis applies to the investigation of any kind of raw material. In this exercise, we will practice fact selecting, inference drawing, and thesis forming using newspapers as data. Have someone in the class pick up twenty to twenty-five copies (one for each member of the class) of some newspaper that you're not familiar with. Read through your copy of the paper, thinking of yourself again as an archaeologist. Collect twenty telling facts about the paper—not the telling facts chosen by reporters to tell their stories, but facts *about* the paper itself that tell us something about the paper's intended readers. Look for evidence of at least five different kinds: (1) facts about ads or the numbers of ads; (2) facts about the types of articles included; (3) facts about the arrangement of material—articles, pictures, statistics, ads—in the paper; (4) facts about the language used in the paper (that will lead to inferences about the assumptions, style or tone of voice preferred by readers); and (5) facts about the newspaper's own use of facts and inferences—what kinds do they use? in what proportion? Look also at the issues addressed on the editorial pages, the issues addressed and the tone of voice of the letters to the editor, or at anything else that strikes you about the newspaper. Your evidence is much more varied here than in any of the exercises above. If, at first, nothing "strikes" you, compare this newspaper with one with which you are more familiar, and you'll more easily see distinctive features. Again, place distinctive facts about the newspaper along the left side of a sheet of paper, and put your inferences about the paper's readers opposite on the right. Here are some examples:

Facts	**Inferences**
The *Seattle Post-Intelligencer* prints a story of an explosion that injured three workers in an Ilwaco factory on page A-11 and reports the story matter-of-factly.	Readers probably are more proud of industrial productivity than they are alarmed about industrial accidents.
A *Baltimore Sun* headline reading "Politicians' Egos on the Line" is set in special type.	The *Sun's* readers are interested in politics, but only superficially—in things like the psyches of politicians.
All the *Village Voice* ads for beer and wine are for foreign brands.	The readers have expensive tastes and are snobbish about what they drink.

The *Village Voice* contains no reference to children or schools except a full-page ad for the Macy's parade and a small ad for a dance class.	The *Voice* is not a family newspaper. The Macy's parade must be an "in" event. If readers have children, they are precocious.
The *Village Voice* contains very few furniture ads but four full pages of ads for music.	Readers take their music seriously but don't have much furniture.
The *Rutland Herald* publishes elaborate, detailed obituaries of people from all social classes.	Many readers probably know each other. It's a close-knit community.

The first list like this that any of you make is likely to have some strong elements and some weak ones, so to get help in setting standards of quality for yourself, bring your first list to class, get in a group of three or four students, and decide what are the ten best fact-inference pairs you've come up with among you. The "best" ones will include facts not everyone would have noticed and inferences not everyone would have thought of. Now that you see more clearly what constitutes "quality" in fact-inference pairs, go home and upgrade your list, keeping your best pairs and adding new ones until your list reaches twenty-five. When you come to class again, look over your list, and write out a thesis statement (a summary of the points you'd like to make) for a paper you could write if you were asked to characterize the newspaper or its audience.

Here are some sample theses:

- The Friday, September 24th, issue of the *New York Post* seems to indicate that it hopes to attract a wide variety of working-class people who are delighted with controversy, who are not politically knowledgeable, and who probably commute to work.
- The *Rutland Herald* addresses a group of rural, middle-aged, middle-class readers interested not only in local news but in international conditions. The majority of the readers are probably white and Protestant, and American by birth.
- The readers of the *Village Voice* see themselves as an exclusive, "in-the-know" group. They also see themselves as the champions of minorities and as politically savvy. They are most likely not your average New Yorkers, nor would they want to be considered so.

How did these writers come up with their theses? How did you come up with yours? They noticed the kinds of inferences that they drew at least two or three times, and their theses were summaries of those inferences.

Compare your thesis with the theses of the other students in the class. You'll be curious to see not only how your judgments differ but how complex the theses are, how specific, how clearly thoughtful.

Next, ask your classmates how they would support their theses. Tell them how you would support yours. Now you should be able to see more clearly (1) how a thesis statement should be arrived at, after consideration of the evidence, and also (2) how to use evidence to support a thesis.

Paragraphing with Facts and Inferences

Fact-inference pairs can be used not only to arrive at a thesis that you can substantiate but also to help you paragraph your paper. Any inference that you've made three or four times could serve as the topic sentence, or main point, of a paragraph. Look at your list of fact-inference pairs, and collect a group with the same inference, or similar inferences. See whether, by listing all the facts together, you can make your inference more complex or thoughtful, as did a writer who was studying a copy of *The National Enquirer*:

Facts	Inferences (in Sum)
Eleven articles about general health issues (arthritis, asthma, cancer, stress, high blood pressure, weight loss, "beating the blues," digestion, hypnotism to treat health problems)	Readers very concerned about health problems. Apparently more given to worry than to action. Especially concerned with weight loss and energy. Very sedentary. Not willing to make major changes in their habits, although perhaps willing to make minor modifications. More oriented toward cures, especially miracle cures, than prevention. Not very skeptical of inflated promises for instant relief.
Cover article is "Top Experts Reveal Easy Way to Lose Weight While You Sleep"	
Eleven ads for diet and pep pills	
No articles about exercise or nutrition (or ads for health spas or exercise programs)	
Three ads for vitamins	
Ad with the heading "Lose Pounds Fast, Lose Bulges, Bumps and Inches Instantly"	
Ad with the heading "Instant Relief for Tired Aching Feet"	
Five cigarette ads, all for light cigarettes (Virginia Slims, Golden Lights, Barclay, Marlboro Lights, Raleigh Lights)	

This writer now has a point to make (the inference) and facts to substantiate that point that will make up a solid paragraph or two.

Distinguishing Facts, Inferences, and Comparisons

Exercise 3-7
in class

To see how every word you use can be classified either as a fact, an inference, or a comparison (and that occasionally these categories overlap), look at the following short explanation of how a sewing machine works from David Macauley's *The Way Things Work* (1988). Put a rectangle around all facts, a circle around all inferences, and a triangle around all comparisons (in the form of metaphors, similes, or personifications):

> The sewing machine is a marvel of mechanical ingenuity. Its source of power is the simple rotary movement of an electric motor. The machine converts this into a complex sequence of movements that makes each stitch and shifts the fabric between stitches. Cams and cranks play an important part in the mechanism. A crank drives the needle up and down, while two trains of cams and cranks move the serrated feed-dog that shifts the fabric.

Once you've marked up the whole passage, compare notes with your classmates on any disagreements and about where you can't be quite sure.

The Vulnerability of Inferences

Inferences that we draw, unlike facts that we observe, are never wholly reliable. You'll note that even when the members of the class are all investigating the same newspaper, each member arrives at a slightly different (in some cases even a wildly different) thesis. Using the same newspaper and the same facts, some students will label the paper conservative, and others will label it liberal. Facts, even telling facts, can't yield 100 percent certain inferences. All inferences are personal—valuable, and yet vulnerable. Nevertheless, all inferences can be made more persuasive with the help of company. An inference substantiated by five facts is more reliable than one substantiated by only two. That's more reason for us to develop our ability to seek out the most pertinent, most telling facts.

As we learn to draw inferences, we must learn to draw responsible inferences. We cannot complacently assume that a single fact we've presented justifies the inference we'd like to draw. Occasionally, people will come up confidently proud with a telling fact that is implicitly racist:

- My Chinese roommate never goes out to party and expects me to be in bed by midnight.
- Our cleaning lady can hardly speak English.

As human beings, we are drawn to making such observations because we already feel sure of what they mean. But one fact does not, of course, justify a conclusion. A single fact is always at least slightly unstable: from any fact, several (more or less probable) inferences can be drawn. Since several inferences can be drawn, we see the need for additional facts to limit the number of possible inferences. If the paint on my classroom wall is peeling, for example, it could be the maintenance crew's fault, or it could be the state legislature's fault. The added detail that state funds for the university have been cut back 10 percent per year for the past seven years might help to fix the inference and the blame. The quality of an inference depends, too, on the expertise of the person making it. A crack in a basement floor means more to a groundwater geologist than it does to a new homeowner:

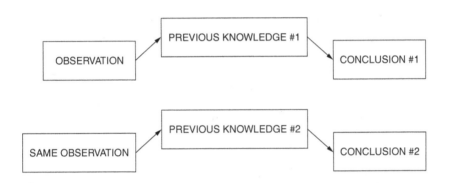

Since expertise is for the most part a matter of mastering more facts in a given area, we should be making a lifelong effort to become more expert in as many areas as possible so that we will be better able to interpret the new facts we face every day.

Just as knowledge differs from person to person and influences the inferences we draw, so do our assumptions. If, in the pocket of a married man in Exercise 3-2, three people saw a $98.00 grocery receipt, one person might infer that that man enjoys cooking, a second that he shares the grocery shopping with his wife, and a third that his wife made him go shopping this week. The first inference results from an assumption that husbands who grocery shop are comfortable doing work that was traditionally expected of women. The second results from the assumption that the most shopping a husband might do is half of it. The third results from the assumption that all decisions about shopping in a marriage are made by the wife.

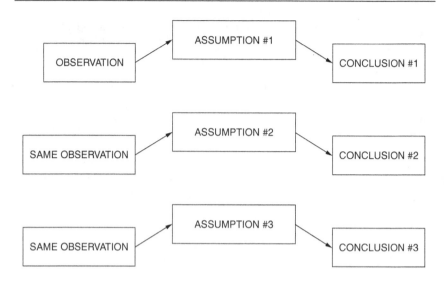

I mentioned in Exercise 3-4 that *a thesis is a summation, or summation with qualification, of inferences you've drawn about a body of material*. The qualification I mentioned there is often necessary because our inferences, like all inferences, are vulnerable. There may be evidence we haven't found yet that contradicts them. And of course there may be evidence that we *are* aware of that contradicts them, but we're inclined to hide it because we are not willing to face the implications of that evidence.

Qualifying Inferences

Exercise 3-8

in class

To remind yourself of the vulnerability of inferences, read the following five facts collected by a student preparing to write a paper about the year in which he was born:

1. In January 1986, Mikhail Gorbachev proposed total nuclear disarmament by the year 2000.
2. The Central Committee of the Soviet Union's Communist Party passed a broad economic reform package in June 1987, giving up much of its total control over the Soviet economy.
3. Gorbachev took a number of steps in 1987 toward greater democracy and freedom of speech in the Soviet Union.

4. Gorbachev signed an Intermediate-Range Nuclear Forces (INF) agreement with the United States in December 1987 to destroy all intermediate-range nuclear missiles in Europe.
5. While he was in the United States to sign the nuclear missile treaty, Gorbachev agreed to release forty to fifty dissidents.

What inference, what interpretation, would we be inclined to draw from these facts? Should we be willing to write a paper using just these facts as evidence? What kinds of facts should we look for to more fully support our interpretation?

What if, as we search for more support, we also find evidence to contradict our interpretation? For example, that:

1. Intermediate-range missiles constituted only 4 percent of the world's nuclear arsenal in 1986.
2. The Soviet Union still had tens of thousands of dissidents that it would not allow to emigrate in 1986.
3. The Soviet occupation of Afghanistan continued until 1989.

What should we do about this evidence?

Often, when you have accumulated fact-inference pairs and you are eager to start drafting your paper or even to turn your paper in, you'll realize that your inferences are still vulnerable and that your integrity and your desire to write a well substantiated paper demand that you search out a few more facts. Honesty is *usually, but perhaps not always,* the best policy in life; it is *always* the best policy in writing. If you concede that some evidence exists that complicates your position, your readers are much more likely to respect your position—and your intelligence—than they are if you naively or deliberately ignore opposing evidence. When you qualify your inferences in writing and acknowledge that not all the evidence is on your side, you win more readers over because you've responded to your readers' questions before they can get upset and raise those questions themselves.

Substantiating Assertions

You should see easily now that every assertion that we make imposes upon us a responsibility to substantiate it. When we make any assertion— *Tanya is a liar,* or *nuclear reactors are dangerous,* or *Robert Mugabe is a dictator—* we usually make it because we've heard someone in our family, or on the news, make the same assertion. Too easily, we accept these assertions, these inferences, as facts. But any written assertion is incomplete (and in most cases ineffective) until it is substantiated by facts. Substantiating our assertions is an acknowledgment that justice is a standard more to be respected than that of our particular desires.

Exercise 3-9
in class

Look, one at a time, at the following list of reckless assertions. As a class, try to find four or five specific examples, specific details, that would substantiate these assertions so they would look less reckless. Note that when extreme assertions are made, evidence can easily be found both for and against them.

1. _____ is a racist campus.
2. There's no racism any more at _____.
3. The automobile is wrecking American life.
4. The automobile, more than any other technology, increases the quality of people's lives.
5. Men don't do their share of work in this society.
6. Men have far more responsibility than women in this society.
7. Young people are more ethical than old people.
8. Young people should learn from their elders.
9. *Eternal Sunshine of a Spotless Mind* (or a movie of your choice) was a great movie.
10. *Eternal Sunshine of a Spotless Mind* (or a movie of your choice) was a terrible movie.
11. Living in the suburbs is like not living at all.
12. The best American life is to be found in the suburbs.
13. Criminals commit crimes not because they are bad but because they've been injured by their families or society.
14. Criminals should be shot.

We're all familiar with reckless assertions. Now you can think of them as insufficiently substantiated inferences. Through this exercise you'll be learning to reveal yourself less recklessly in your own writing, and perhaps, too, in your everyday life.

Facts and inferences are the building blocks of our writing skills. Any set of facts will yield at least slightly different inferences to every different writer. No two of us have the same experience, and our experience colors all our inferences. Nor do we share the same assumptions, which also color our inferences. We can thus *guarantee* that anything anyone writes—unless it copies both facts and inferences from another writer—is original. So don't waste any time worrying about whether or not your writing is original. At the same time, it will be pretty clear to others—to your teacher, and to your classmates—if you steal the inferences of someone else (whether a parent, a friend, an expert you know, or an internet or book author). The inferences of others don't carry your voice. They won't *sound like* your inferences. You will immediately be suspected of plagiarism. As a rule of thumb, we can feel free to borrow one or two facts, but if we borrow more than two, or if we borrow even a single fact that a writer has worked hard to find, we must cite our source and thus acknowledge who helped us. With inferences, however, not even a little bit of borrowing is allowed. The inferences we make must remain our own. What we call intelligence in a person consists primarily of the thoughtfulness of the inferences that he or she consistently comes up with. The intelligence you show in your papers must be yours.

We are often advised by textbooks to write by starting with a subject (say, the automobile), trying to decide on an idea about the subject (say, "The automobile is harming American life."), then "factoring"—as you do an equation—that idea into at least three parts (say, "The automobile is harming American life by polluting our cities, by distracting our 16-year-olds from their studies, and by distracting all of us from walking through our neighborhoods and talking to people."), and finally trying to substantiate each of those ideas with facts and examples. This method of finding a thesis and then a factored thesis is a good place to start if we are writing an essay exam, the purpose of which is to show someone what we already know about a subject. But if we're examining any subject seriously, we're on very shaky ground when we start to write with "ideas." Most often, our ideas on gender roles, dorm life, gun control, immigration, and other such issues are half-baked (more often quarter-baked) and based on the reflected opinions of parents and newscasters. The "ideas" we write down are surprisingly seldom our own, and surprisingly often contrary to our own feelings or to a substantial part of our experience. Thesis statements cast in stone before a writer begins research and writing are dangerous invitations to muted or biased observation. And so we shouldn't allow ourselves to write "ideas," or theses, until they are earned with sufficient evidence. The first step in any assignment—whether an autobiography, a speech, an analysis of a short story, or an argument on an issue of our choosing—should be a search for the facts, the pertinent facts, the telling facts. Every fact you write down triggers an inference, which in turn may remind you that you have other facts at your disposal or others you need to search out. And then the implications of those facts, in sum, will lead to an idea, a thesis, a proposition, that will always be more responsible than one arrived at through a deskbound search for an appropriate "topic" for a paper.

I'll be giving you a great deal of advice later in this book about what you should take *out* of your prose. From this chapter and the previous one, though, you now know *what you should put in: carefully selected facts and sound, thoughtful inferences.*

As you think further about facts and inferences, you might find the following charts helpful:

Synonyms and Near Synonyms for "Fact"	**Synonyms and Near Synonyms for Inference**
detail, example, experience, evidence, observation, sensation, result	claim, idea, moral, reflection, implication, assertion, conclusion, judgment, insight, interpretation, explanation, contention, generalization, analysis, hypothesis

Kinds of Facts

measurements
experimental tests
quotations
anecdotes or oral testimony
observed events
remembered events
works created by us
contexts for such works
details of arrangement or format
omissions

Kinds of Inferences

classified by organizational effect:
—causal, classifying, defining, comparative
classified by the inferer's role:
—evaluative, explanatory, predictive
classified by the inferer's world view:
—ethical, legal, religious, communist,
patriarchal, feminist, capitalist
classified by strength:
—timid, bold
classified by focus
—e.g. in a written work: on the writer,
on the reader, on the words, or on
the cultural context
e.g. in a court of law: on motive, on
character, on degree of guilt

4

Writing for a Reader

A reader doesn't read from an insatiable need to applaud.

SOURCE UNKNOWN

I now think more about the people reading my paper and try to make it so that it would sound clear to them. Before I used to write unspecific things because I expected people to know already what I was talking about.

STUDENT

The most important thing I learned in this course was not to be a "selfish" writer.

STUDENT

A good piece of writing closes the gap between you and the reader.

LINDA FLOWER

Exercise 4-1   Review

on your own

Your interest in the issues raised in this chapter will be greater if you take a few minutes to respond to these two very different requests:

1. Describe two or three examples of a tone of voice that gets on your nerves.
2. List anyone who has ever read anything you have written.

Developing an Honest and Recognizable Voice

At least half the time that we pick up a book, we soon wish we hadn't bothered, as we are forced to try to digest statements like this one at the beginning of a book I bought to learn more about China:

> Disbelief and hostility or unreadiness to think or listen one can comprehend. It is part and parcel of a more or less coherent lengthy process of ideological socialization (Worsley 15).

Unfortunately, it is easy to see how such books come into being. We don't often master the lesson in our writing classes that we need to work, work, work to be specific. The first drafts of student papers are all too often no more helpful than the sentence above:

> Stacey is my roommate at my dorm Queen Anne. I thought I would write about her because she is a wonderful person. We have a great deal of fun in anything we do. We help each other out if we have any problems. Our study habits are about the same. Stacey and I have the same taste in just about everything. It's a nice feeling when you can relate and trust a person as I do Stacey.

Even when we write about a subject we know well, we often do no better than the description of Stacey above:

> The general notion of gymnastics brings to mind flips and swings on various apparatus. There exist various imposed requirements within men's and women's gymnastics which reflect the differences of these two sports. It is these requirements which make up the very essence which separates men's gymnastics from women's gymnastics. The difficulty of a woman's routine is set by a minimum requirement of one superior and two medium skills. Other skills are required for a routine, but they hold no difficulty value. The context of men's gymnastics is emphasized by the philosophy that a man will be strong, forceful and fluid. The framework of men's gymnastics is built on these concepts and dictates a design such that the aspects of strength and swing can be stressed. These differences go beyond the superficial individuality of each event, and we can see that each sport seems to stress different points. It is this concept which indeed accounts for the wide differences between men's and women's gymnastics.

As Faulconbridge complains early in Shakespeare's *King John*, "Zounds, I was never so bethumped with words" (2.1.466). These passages fail, I'm afraid, to meet the standard for good writing established by the British Admiralty Pilots during World War II: "It should be intelligible to a tired man reading in a bad light."

Ken Macrorie has called the type of writing in the above examples "Engfish." One of my students who misheard the term calls it "Inkfish." Either is a good name for murky, bloated, pretentious language that results when a writer hasn't remembered that the job of a writer is to communicate. Swamped by writing like this, no wonder professors as well as students sometimes despair over the future of the written word. Writing like this keeps authors busy and paper companies solvent, but it communicates very little, and it enhances our lives not at all. When a television show doesn't tell us anything, we often sit and watch anyway because we like the characters and the HD picture is attractive. But when a writer doesn't tell us anything, we drop the book and fall asleep, because a printed page, as a printed page, is tiring. Many of us have self-destructively given up on books, not because books are incapable, even in this computer and television age, of entertaining us, informing us, and making us more human, but because we're not careful enough to be selective—to read only the best, and to avoid books published because an issue is temporarily popular or because (in school) a certain body of material, say, introductory psychology, needs to be "covered." Writers who provide these "demand" books often don't write their best because they don't have enough time to think through their subject carefully. And when, as readers, we look into three or four dull books (often textbooks) in a row, we sometimes too easily give up on books in general.

In this writing course, and after it, try to avoid adding to our pile of unreadable writing. Take your time when you write; give the reader something for her money, something for her time, something for her effort. That something is information, news, something she didn't know before, something that will help her live the rest of her life in a better way than she has to this point. That something is not just information (facts) but also your interpretation of the information (your inferences). The reader may disagree, but she can only disagree if she knows what you think and if she knows the facts that have led you to think as you do.

Writing that stands out from the morass of words like those on the previous page is writing that sounds like it is being spoken by someone. Nevertheless, most of us hold back our personalities as we write. Some of our teachers have told us to keep our selves out of our writing. But even without that advice, we often write in voiceless language out of fear of revealing too much. We don't want people to recognize what we perceive as our ignorance or our lack of confidence about what we're writing. Our caution is not without reason. When we write (or talk), we do give our readers and listeners evidence (language) that they will use, whether we like it or not, to draw inferences about us. But the only way we can improve our voice, our intelligence, our writing, to the point where we'll be proud of it, is to practice, practice, practice—to write, write, write.

Drawing Inferences about Writers

Exercise 4-2
in class

To best understand how others will draw inferences from your language, practice drawing inferences yourself about the speakers and writers of the following passages, using only their language as evidence. I suggest that you circle the words or phrases that you find telling about the authors and draw arrows to some free space where you can write your inferences.

1. C-130 rollin' down the strip. *Slang could imply lack of education or care*
   Airborne Rangers on a one-way trip.
   Mission unspoken, destination unknown,
   Don't give a damn if they ever come home.
   Locked and loaded, ready to kill,
   Always have and always will.
   Squeeze the trigger and let it fly,
   Hit the bastards between the eyes.
   Before he died, I heard him yell, *has no filter, maybe offensive*
   "Airborne Rangers are bad as hell."
   [U.S. Army Ranger chant (Harris 4.1–4.2)]

2. *holds grudges* *too self confidence* The ultimate revenge in this life is to come back to your high school as its commencement speaker. Imagine. Me. Not the president of my class, not the former chairman of the Latin Scrabble Club, not the head of the Keyettes. But me, from the very bottom of my class. [Carl Bernstein, coauthor of *All the President's Men*, speaking at a high school graduation (5)]

3. *a little condescending* *probably upperclass* I have never been in a strike before. It is like looking at something that is happening for the first time and there are no thoughts and no words yet accrued to it. If you come from the middle class, words are likely to mean more than an event. You are likely to think about a thing, and the happening will be the size of a pin point and the words around the happening very large, distorting it queerly. It's a case of "Remembrance of things past." When you are in the event, you are likely to have a distinctly individualistic attitude, to be only partly there, and to care more for the happening afterward than when it is happening. That is why it is hard for a person like myself and others to be in a strike. [Meridel Le Sueur, "I Was Marching" (229)]

4. *pretentious* *doesn't say much, classic politician* On January 1, 1967, the Supreme Court of Arkansas will for the first time in a century seat four new judges, all at once. A majority of the seven. This impending influx of the uninitiated led me, some months ago, to turn from the question I so often put to myself, "What can my country do for me?", to a different question: What can I do for these novitiates who are about to outnumber me? That reverie led to this primer. I have decided, not without diffidence, to try to say to you four the sort of thing that I wish my late colleague, Judge Frank Smith, then in his thirty-seventh year on the court, had said to me when as an infant of only thirty-seven years all told I became his devoted associate on the bench. [George Rose Smith, introducing "A Primer of Opinion Writing"]

Compare notes with your classmates about what you infer the characters of these writers might be.

Writing reveals our charm, our goodwill, our intelligence, but it also reveals our anger, our snobbery, our sexism, our racism. Still, you can't write well if you're afraid of what your writing will say about you. You want to write more than just gradable noise on paper. You want to get used to your voice. You want to see what your voice reveals and then—during revision—make whatever modifications you feel are necessary. Only by practice, that is, by trial, and error, and criticism of our errors, can we develop confidence and get away from the voiceless writing that plagues both student and professional writers. But the payoff is generous. Checking on and working on our voices is one of many ways in which learning to write better helps us to become more generally mature, more aware of how we fit in with others.

Rewriting Pretentious Prose

Exercise 4-3

in class

In the following letter I found in the files when I took over my current job, the writer has resorted to "Inkfish" rather than communication. See whether you can repair the damage.

Dear Dr. Washington:
Receipt of your letter of August 2, 1974, with reference to the offering of English 103 and/or 171 to Susan R. Trowbridge is hereby acknowledged.

In view of the fact that she is currently out of the country and is not expected to return until after August the 20th, pursuant to my telephone conversation with your secretary, Ann Allen, I am requesting that the deadline for my daughter be postponed until after her return to enable her to exercise her option of taking either of the courses being offered.

Thank you for the courtesies extended and for your propitious consideration of this request!

Sincerely,
George Trowbridge, Consulting Psychologist (A concerned father)

What do you think of the writer of this letter? Rewrite the letter. Show Dr. Washington that you are indeed a "concerned father" and not just a consulting psychologist trying to show off your importance.

[handwritten margin note: We saw the course offerings, but my daughter is currently on vacation. She can't make a good decision about her education like that. Can you extend the deadline. T. Hanks]

Since I've made you so self-conscious about voice in this chapter, you're probably concerned now about what voice is your natural voice. You can't achieve that natural voice by consciously trying to achieve it, so let's get at it another way.

Timed Writing

Exercise 4-4
in class, then for homework

Take out your notebook, begin on a new page, and write for ten minutes without stopping. You can write on any subject at all, but don't let your pen stop. Consider that attempt a warm-up. Now write again for ten minutes without stopping, again writing on any topic at all. For homework this evening, write three more of these timed ten-minute writings, either on paper or on your computer, and see what you come up with. After the writing, make a note of anything that surprises you about what you wrote. Your teacher may want to look over and comment on one of the five timed writings that you've done.

You probably feel pretty awkward at first writing these timed writings. But as you practice them more and more often, you will find that they do several things for you. First, they show you that even when you're afraid that you have nothing to say you are never without words. Second, they help you realize what your natural voice is. Third, they help you realize that writing can be used as a thinking technique: when you force yourself to keep typing, you'll find thoughts coming to your mind that you had not realized were on your mind. (When you stop to take time to write, you have stopped to take time to think.) Finally, timed writings remind you that the first words off your pen are often not the best you can do and therefore that revision is a step in writing that should never be ignored. This timed writing doesn't often result in a final version that you'd be proud to hand to a teacher, or to anyone. But it can form the *basis* of a final version that can be handed in. Once you have something written down, you can begin to *choose* what you want to include in a paper. These choices you make, much more than the words you put down the first time, will determine your success as a writer.

Of course, your voice will not sound the same every time you write. Sometimes you're trying to soothe the feelings of the person you're writing to. Other times you're trying to move people to act or think more like you do. A variety of (honest) voices is at your disposal. Imagine describing your first week of college to a friend, to your parents, and to your writing class. Each description (if it's good) will sound like you, but each will select different facts, make different comments, and use different language. Similarly, your history papers, your chemistry lab reports, and your ethnographic studies in psychology will all sound something like previous work in each of those areas, but they should also sound (if the professor is to take any notice of you) something like you. We are assigned many roles to play in life, but our success and our integrity depend on our ability to give each of those roles the special stamp of our own character.

Many beginning writers, afraid of their own voices, feel that they could add some pep to their writing if they could just add some kind of "style," although they don't know quite how "style" is achieved. They sometimes guess that style can be acquired through a thesaurus. But you can't rush the steady climb toward a style you're proud of. Your style develops as your voice develops. And your voice can be only as sophisticated as you are. The more you learn, the more experience you acquire, the more you will have to offer in your voice. In a sense, your voice is dependent on your entire education, in and out of school. The more you learn, the more confidence, authority, and life your voice will carry.

In the meantime, we can achieve the best voice we're so far capable of not by adding some sort of style to our writing, but by subtracting elements in our writing that we share with everybody else. This is why we've been told so often by writing teachers not to use clichés like "hit the nail on the head" or "avoid him like the plague." Our use of a cliché tells readers that we understand life as well as most people do, but it doesn't tell readers our particular point of view on life.

Conventional phrases we've seen in other student papers are another form of clichés:

- This paper will discuss . . .
- As I mentioned earlier . . .
- In today's world . . .

Many of the words and phrases which come most easily off the pen are the words that we all share, the ones that are not distinctive. Pruning these clichés from our drafts leaves us with the word combinations, and the fact-inference combinations, that are our own. Such pruning is, of course, more than verbal: it includes cutting out the comfortable, conventional repetition of ideas that often passes for thinking. The conventions are comfortable, but though we have come to expect conventional prose, we are quietly disappointed every time we read it.

Using conventions is the easiest way to get through life. If we get married too young, for example, we are likely to *imitate* fatherhood or motherhood instead of being good fathers or mothers. When we imitate, we tend to imitate only the surface features of fatherhood or motherhood. There is much to be learned, to be sure, from the way others have been fathers or mothers. But if we want to be distinctively good parents, we have to do what we think is best, adjusting our behavior regularly by checking with the established patterns. The same strategy results in effective writing. We should start writing by noting what we see and by writing what we think ought to be said. Later we can adapt our observations and thoughts to respect one of the many conventional forms that writing takes so that readers can make use of what we've learned. But if we start with a model in our minds and not with what we want to say, we are condemned to repeating old truths and to writing voiceless papers.

Robert Pirsig, in *Zen and the Art of Motorcycle Maintenance*, describes how writing became possible for one of his students only when she came to the seemingly simple recognition that she was free to start afresh. When asked to describe her college town, Bozeman, Montana, she at first couldn't think of anything to write about:

> She was blocked because she was trying to repeat, in her writing, things she had already heard. . . . She couldn't think of anything to write about Bozeman because she couldn't recall anything she had heard worth repeating. She was strangely unaware that she could look and see freshly for herself (186).

Edward Hyams, in *The Changing Face of Britain*, looked freshly at a 50-square-foot creature, "automan," which rolls past each of us hundreds of times daily but which few of us have taken the trouble to think seriously about:

> The cheap, private motor-car is a great boon: it gives the ordinary human being seven-league boots: in the power of movement overland he becomes a giant; but giants, of course, take up more room than people of human size. A man in movement on his feet occupies, at any given moment of time, about four square feet of surface; but an automan—that man-motor-car creature which is more or less the typical inhabitant of a modern industrial country—at any given moment occupies something like fifty square feet.
>
> To cope with the motor car explosion and its growing place in our lives we are forced to modify the shape of our cities to suit not man, but automan . . . and a town designed for automan cannot become a community of men, like a village or a small town (228).

The various subjects we take while in school often ask of us the same freshness. They want us to relook at everyday items that we have come to take for granted. For example, a physics textbook asks its readers to look freshly at a fountain:

> Streams of water form graceful arches as they rise and fall into a pond at the base of a fountain. Some streams rise steeply and fall sharply back to the pond. Other streams arch gently, do not rise as high as others, but fall farther away from their sources. You can easily understand these motions if you think of all curved motion as being simply straight line motion in two directions at the same time (Murphy 108).

Writers willing to look freshly and tell truths are not condemned to re-hashing the same old stories, the same old issues. We have been given plenty of working room by our writing and our nonwriting ancestors. Our bookshelves (even in the so-called nonfiction sections) teem with fictions. As a nation, as human beings, we get very much used to the fictions by which we live—fictions about the family, fictions about good and evil, fictions about government, about race, about sexuality. When we write, unfortunately, we slip more readily into those fictions than we do into truth.

If we ask our readers what they want from our writing, their answer will seldom be *style* or *elegance* or even *clarity* but, rather, *likeness to the truth*. When a student reads his writing class a paper about the Olympics becoming an advertising event for the "official shoes," the "official beer," and the "official deodorant" of the games, the class gives the paper high praise, and when asked why they like it, they say, "Because it's true." Such praise is praise worth aiming for. Telling the truth is a service to other human beings trying to make sense of the world. For telling the truth, they'll call you original, and they'll marvel at your thoughtful, distinctive voice.

Becoming Conscious of Our Readers

Through the discussion of voice that has introduced this chapter, you're beginning to see, I hope, that writing succeeds or fails not because of its elegance but because of the way it affects a reader. When you write, you are not showing off; you are performing a service for a reader. When you think of yourself as trying to talk to someone as you write, then you will be likely to sound like someone when you do write.

One way to begin to think more seriously about your readers is to do some analyzing of groups of readers. You can infer, for example from the way a website is written and from the kinds of ads that it includes, what kinds of readers that website is aiming at. You can make some reasonable guesses about those readers. But your guesses are of course only inferences, and the website in fact will have had many readers that you did not imagine. (You know from your own reading experience that the readers envisioned by many of the writers you've read did not include yourself.)

If we use the results of such a reader analysis carelessly and assume that the group that will read our writing is homogeneous (all alike), we can easily damage both the integrity and the quality of our writing. Because when we write for a stereotyped group, as television writers guided by Neilsen ratings often do, we too easily assume that we have to write *down* to that group. Although we claim in this country to believe in democracy, as writers we easily fall into the habit of looking down on our readers, of distrusting them: "We forever hold back, on the theory that our neighbors are not so wise or remarkable as we are" (Mitchell C1). It's easy, once you've defined your readers as "college freshmen," for example, or as "university professors," to develop contempt for that group as a whole. But if you remember that every individual in that group will be very different and that any individual in that group might be you, you will be much more likely to write well. You will write *to* people, not *down to* them. To write well, we must learn to picture a reader—not a lump of readers, but one reader (at a time) in a large and diverse group.

Readers and Overhearers

You can improve your sense of readers substantially if you reflect for a minute on your experience reading any older newspaper article your teacher has assigned you to read for this class. You yourself, as you were reading, were not, probably, the type of reader that the writers of the articles had in mind while they wrote. If we leave the title "readers" to the original readers of the news articles, your role might be better titled "overhearer." You are reading, but you're also overhearing and judging the whole process of writing and reading.

In many papers you write for a writing class, your teacher plays a very similar overhearing role. In writing a proposal paper, for example, you are supposedly writing to someone with the power to make the change you propose, yet your teacher is overhearing and judging the whole transaction. Similarly, in a persuasion paper, you may well be assigned to write to a classmate whose views you want to try to change. But again your teacher is overhearing. (Having an overhearer is not just a characteristic of writing in school: every time you write a business letter, your boss will be a quiet, or sometimes a not so quiet, overhearer.)

Teachers are not only overhearers, though. They are often cast in the role of being readers and overhearers at the same time. When you write a place description or a newspaper analysis or a research paper or a literary critique, you are writing to your teacher both as a reader (someone who wants to enjoy reading) and as an overhearer (someone who judges the quality of your writing). When other students read your work on draft review days, they take on the same dual role. (Even this role, though, is not unusual in life. The recipients of your business letters will quite naturally be making judgments about you as a writer and about what you're trying to do even as they respond directly to your message.)

Since the readers you will be writing for in this class will most often be your teacher and your fellow students, it will help to have some idea of how your teachers and your fellow students read simultaneously as readers and overhearers. To help you, I've collected some samples:

STUDENT 1: When I read another student's paper, if the grammar (word choice and punctuation) is poor, I have to spend too much time trying to figure out what the writer is trying to say. Therefore, the majority of my time is spent reading the writer's mind and I have less time to enjoy the paper.

STUDENT 2: When reading someone's paper I can usually tell if it's going to be good by the confidence of the writer. Whether the content is interesting or boring, I can enjoy a paper whose writer has the ability to include his own style and opens with an interesting introduction. A paper that is stifled by poor grammar or is boring because of an attempt to make everything grammatically correct or to write for an audience such as teachers (using large words that are vague) is not what I consider a good paper.

STUDENT 3: When I'm reading another student's paper I know it will be a good paper if it arouses some sort of feeling or response in me (such as sympathy or anger). If a paper can get me to think about that particular subject—it's a good paper. If I have absolutely no desire to go on reading, I know something is lacking in that paper. When I get the feeling that I can't wait to find out what's going to happen but at the same time want to savor every word and never finish reading—I know that's a good paper.

TEACHER 1: I always read a paper the first time for the content only, not marking anything. I always hope to read something I didn't know, or something old said or seen in a different way. It's so disappointing when the student sticks to the obvious details, the usual arguments. It means that she only tries to be acceptable instead of challenging herself to write something alive, worth reading by someone other than the teacher.

TEACHER 2: There are papers I read with frustration and say "Oh no, not this again—I've talked about this *19* times!!" But then, others make up for it—I *do* remember what the preceding paper was like (in spite of students who call my office to say "This is Jennie. Jennie Klein. I'm in your 10:00 English 101 class. . .") and thoroughly enjoy seeing Jennie working on the details or cleaning up a particular grammar problem. And then I feel an *immense* satisfaction, a simple pleasure that something is working somewhere.

TEACHER 3: I usually read through the first paragraph quickly and if it is interesting, I continue reading. If it is not interesting, I throw it aside and tell myself I'll read it later. After reading through all the essays once (for content only), I then read through critically. Even though I try to be impartial, I cannot help responding more favorably to the ones that I enjoy.

In your one-on-one conferences with your teacher this semester, you'll see how your own teacher reads. And in draft workshops, you'll learn how your own classmates read. Think about what you learn from these encounters as you write. Anticipate your readers' needs and take care of them. Anticipate their assumptions and take them into account.

Sensing Your Reader as You Write

A genuine feeling for one's reader works surprising transformations in a writer's prose. Most poor writers are bound inside their own heads as they write. They make no imaginative leap to their reader's point of view. They see easily that their speech is a way of communicating, because they've known that most people listen when they talk. But most of their writing has been for teachers, and few students have taken the trouble to try to imagine what their teachers think as they read their papers. You know that readers come to a magazine article looking for information, for surprises, for clean, clear expressions of ideas. Well, your teacher will come to your papers looking for the same things, and she'll also make some comments to help you achieve them.

One of the first things that you'll have to learn if you want to improve your writing in this course is to overcome your *contempt* for your teacher as a reader. None of us would admit that we have contempt for our teachers, but if we stop to consider how little effort we often put into our papers and how much effort the teacher must put into reading them, we quickly realize that we really are showing contempt when we write. Keep in mind that your teacher wants to read some good material this semester. She takes no satisfaction in being a gradable-noise grader. Teachers, like any other readers, like to be informed, and they like to learn without going to too much trouble trying to figure out what you mean. See whether you can get your teacher to enjoy reading. It may be that you can if you provide some of the things that readers and teachers look for, such as:

1. Density of details
2. Challenging interpretations of details
3. Paragraphs in which every sentence is purposeful
4. Thorough research
5. Careful distinctions
6. Thoughtful introductions and conclusions

As a teacher reads, though, it's a rare paper that will delight him throughout. So at the same time that he is looking for items to praise, he'll be noting every obstacle to his comprehension of the paper. Every time he comes up against an obstacle, he'll explain to you why he found what you did an obstacle. You'll then begin to see that your punctuation, for example, and your paragraphing, and your organization are worth improving.

Of course, your teacher will not only read your essay but also grade it. Our society pays teachers (experts) to judge how well our students (future candidates for jobs) have learned the necessary skills for these jobs. The teacher must step into that role of judge for five minutes each time he gives a paper a grade. But every other minute of the semester, including the time he spends writing comments on your papers, your teacher is an ally, a skilled reader trying to help you improve, trying to help you become not only a skilled writer but a skilled reader of your own work. Many students seem to forget that this all-but-forty-five-minutes-of-the-course teacher exists.

Becoming Your Own Reader

It helps to know how your potential readers read, but to become a skilled writer, you must also gradually acquire the knack of becoming two distinct people yourself when you write. One self is a writer who types out a draft, often revising as she goes along. The second self is a reader who reads that draft as if she hadn't written it. Reading your draft aloud (advice I'm sure you'll resist) may seem childish, but it makes you acutely aware of basic needs of your readers. When you try to influence a reader through writing, you won't be there to smile, to demonstrate with your hands, to say "what I really mean is . . ." Your separation from the reader is reflected in the following diagram (Linton 27):

These gears show graphically why the actual words on the page are crucial. Only the writing, never the writer, gets to touch the reader. The writer must therefore depend on what she has transferred to the writing to do any communicating she wants to do. The first time you read one of your papers aloud in class, you'll want to change half your words, sentences, and paragraphs. It's not just a matter of hearing how your writing sounds, but of becoming really conscious of your listeners. Once you're aware of your readers, you'll have much higher standards for your writing. You'll want to reveal at least one significant thing in every paragraph. You'll develop enough respect for your readers to believe that they will be convinced not by bullying but by a complete review of the information. You will remember that a reader wants to read rapidly, but wants to be mentally challenged.

All this effort to help your readers by becoming a reader yourself is much easier to undertake if you are working with a draft on a computer screen. That screen enables you to *see* your work—to become a reader of your own writing, to develop your second self. Your second self will also grow as you write self-critiques of the papers you write in this course ("I am satisfied with this paper because . . ." or "I am not yet satisfied because . . ."). And your second self will grow as you read the drafts of papers by other students in your class. It will grow steadily in sophistication as the course proceeds.

As you develop your second self, your internal reader, you should see that you don't please an outside reader by trying to find out exactly what the reader wants. The reader often doesn't know what she wants. Editors don't know what they want until they see what a writer has delivered to them. Similarly, a teacher doesn't have a fixed form of exactly what he wants. He's looking to be surprised. He's looking for some work from you that is genuinely different, genuinely worth reading. Thinking about your readers, therefore, doesn't mean you should be pandering to their presumed tastes. It means that you should be crafting the work so well that they will have no trouble comprehending it. Our job as writers is to eliminate obstacles for readers.

Respecting Readers

What are the implications, then, of learning to respect the readers we write for? First of all, that respect helps us see the values that should guide us as we write: vitality, clarity, simplicity, and humanity (Zinsser 131). Vitality engages the reader's interest. Simplicity and clarity help the reader learn easily. Why humanity? Because we're human. Any understanding of our world is limited if we can't see the human dimensions of that understanding. Writing, like any other profession, requires both technical and human skills. Second, and very important, writing for readers we respect reinforces our respect for the craft of revision. No one can write in a first draft the kind of prose a reader would best understand. Our minds work too fast. They are too concerned during the first draft just with getting matters from brain to paper.

The transition from first to final draft is best named, I think, the transition from "writer-based" to "reader-based" prose (Flower and Hayes 449–61). The weaknesses in your first, incomplete step, your first draft—your writer-based prose—are not indications that you're a poor writer. A draft with mixed strengths and weaknesses is an essential step in the process toward excellence. This step is playful. It allows us to take risks, to try things out. It is also the best opportunity we have to think for ourselves. But a writer's first draft also usually lays out its ideas in an order in which they should seldom be presented to readers—the order in which they occurred to him. A lab notebook, for example, is writer-based: it reflects the sequence of research. A published scientific paper, however, must be reader-based: the research material must be reworked to fit into the experiences of the readers of the paper. Readers need time and space coordinates at the beginning of an essay. Readers need good transitions between paragraphs. Readers need contrasts signaled and quotations introduced. Readers are distracted by irrelevant details, unnecessary repetition, and faulty punctuation. *Readers, in short, expect the fruits of, not a record of, our research and thought.*

You have just finished a crucial chapter. Now that you're aware of a reader, that reader will keep you on your toes. Worrying about that reader will incline you to read your work aloud before you hand it in. As you read, you'll often be embarrassed, but that embarrassment is useful because it will teach you how to revise what you've already written and what to avoid the next time you write. Reading aloud will often make you wish you knew more about your subject; that's not a bad thing either. Reading aloud will also help you with your punctuation, since punctuation was once a system of breathing directions and still reflects the way we breathe as we speak. But the main value of reading aloud is in helping you to hear the voice that you project. To be a better writer, you'll have to develop that writer's voice. As you do, you will develop a sense of who you are, a sense of what tone you need for each writing assignment you're given, a sense of what words are appropriate for each writing assignment, and a sense of what effect your voice will have on your readers.

5

Systematic Patterns of Thought

I have many problems about writing essays but the biggest of which is organization.

STUDENT

The mind doesn't like chaos; ordering is its natural activity,

ANN BERTHOFF

Reviewing Your Organizational Habits

Exercise 5-1
on your own

1. Do you prefer to outline before you begin writing or after you've written out a draft?
2. Do you consider yourself generally an organized person? Why or why not?

Organization: Our Choice or Theirs?

Some of the professional writing you'll face after school will be expected to follow a predetermined order. If, for example, you plan to be a television screenwriter, you'll be asked to include in each episode:

1. Hooks (situations that viewers can identify with),
2. Laid pipe (background information on the characters),
3. Heat (tension),
4. Topspin (questions raised in the viewers' minds just before each commercial), and
5. Buttons (clever remarks made by characters leaving the scene).

If you're a personnel director, and you have to write a job description, you will be expected to include sections on:

1. Scope of responsibility,
2. Specific duties, and
3. Personal requirements.

Some of your school papers must also follow a pre-established order.

1. An introductory paragraph that concludes with a thesis statement,
2. A series of body paragraphs that all begin with topic sentences that include transitions, and
3. A conclusion in which you sum up your principal arguments.

If your paper is a biology laboratory report, you may be asked to use a structure like the following:

1. Title
2. Abstract
3. Introduction
4. Materials and methods
5. Results
6. Discussion
7. References

Most often when you write, though, you'll have to decide for yourself how to organize your material. It is you who decides how long you'll make your introduction, how many sections you'll divide your paper into, and whether you'll use a formal thesis statement.

Organization is not a simple record of your thoughts in the order that they occurred to you. Neither is it a prearranged package, a method of "filling in the blanks." Organization is making order out of chaos. It results from decisions you make from the time you first start your research to the time, just before the final revision, when you may still be tinkering with sentence and paragraph order. Organization will seldom be your first consideration when you write. The principal elements that a writer considers, and the order in which they are usually considered, in preparing a paper are:

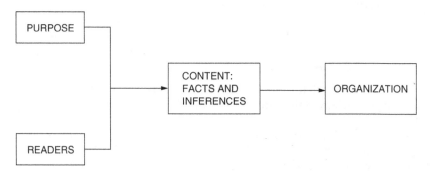

The decision to write starts in most cases in one of the two left-hand boxes. The writer starts either with a reader that wants something, or with the purpose of conveying some information, or exploring a problem, or persuading a reader, or simply showing off. She then searches for content (facts and inferences) which will serve her purpose. Perhaps the facts she finds and gathers alter her purpose. But it is usually only after purpose, readers, and content are in mind that the writer faces the task of choosing an appropriate organization for her given purpose.

Choosing a Systematic Organization

Although organization is one of our later considerations as we prepare to write, it is a consideration that rarely works itself out easily. It is seldom easy to decide where to start. It is rarely obvious how many sections or paragraphs we will need. It *is* easy to catch ourselves in mid-draft writing "as I mentioned earlier," which is a clue that your organization is still not what you want it to be. When other people complain about your organization, as they have complained about mine, they'll usually say that the piece isn't organized "logically." Although they use the word *logical*, they are only rarely talking about *induction* or *deduction*, the two forms of logic that will be examined in Chapter 6. What they mean, usually, is that the material hasn't been organized "systematically," in a pattern. Readers unconsciously expect patterns when they read, and if we can adapt our writing to the patterns they are familiar with, we can be much more easily understood. When we don't order our material in ways our readers unconsciously expect us to, we can easily bore or confuse them.

Exercise 5-2

in class

To see how unsystematic ordering can distract attention from your message by disconcerting your readers, read the following sentences. Note what is odd about the arrangement of elements in each of these sentences, and suggest an order for them that would not throw readers off:

- Cities are faced with countless problems, such as robbery, littering, gunfights, pollution, and traffic jams.
- Although the controversial speaker tried to proceed, the meeting ended because people started throwing oranges at him, people weren't paying much attention, and there was some annoying booing.
- Our spaceship brought back from the strange planet an animal that looked like a water buffalo, two small green people, and a soil sample.

The Common, Systematic Thought Patterns

My guess is that in the previous exercise you've rearranged each of these sentences so that the most important or most striking item was saved for last. This order is called *climactic* order: the items included are listed in an order that builds to a climax. Most readers find such an order systematic and satisfying. There are nine other kinds of order that are also systematic. Following is a list of the ten most common systematic thought patterns—ways of organizing material that we can put to the service of a variety of purposes in writing:

1. Chronological narration
2. Spatial description
3. Classification
4. Comparison-contrast
5. Definition
6. Cause and effect
7. Problem and solution
8. Assertion with examples
9. Assertion with reasons
10. Building to a climax

These useful thought patterns represent common ways of thinking. We find them, with equal frequency, in to-do lists, in segments of the evening news, in the lab notes of researchers. They are useful in writing because they are such common ways of thinking; no one really needs to be taught them. A reader is as likely to find a cause-effect sequence "logical" (that is, to find that he understands it) as the writer is, so it's a useful way to communicate. Since these thought patterns are common ways of thinking, they therefore become for us common *ways of*—or *strategies for*—*organizing* the facts and inferences we have selected to present. Let me explain and give some examples of each of these systematic thought patterns.

1. Chronological Narration

This method of organization is the most common, and the easiest to write. It is almost always used to organize facts rather than inferences. Skill in using chronological order lies not in arranging one's facts in the correct order but in *selecting* those facts that convey the impression we want to convey. In reading the following examples, ask yourself why the writers selected the facts they did and what their overall purpose was. The first excerpt is from an introduction to a sign language textbook:

> The first permanent school for the deaf was established in Hartford, Connecticut, in 1817. It was many years later, after Thomas Hopkins Gallaudet had seen the es-

tablishment of a number of schools for the deaf across the United States, that he also envisioned the establishment of a college. This dream was passed on to his son, Edward Miner Gallaudet, who was responsible for establishing Gallaudet College, the world's first and only college for deaf students, located in Washington, D.C. The charter for the college was signed in 1864 by President Abraham Lincoln (Riekehof 6).

From a chapter on functions in a mathematics textbook:

The Swiss mathematician Leonhard Euler (1707–1783) was the first to adopt the expression $f(x)$ for the value of a function. He systematically classified many collections of functions. Nevertheless, it was not until the middle of the nineteenth century that the division of a function into a domain and a rule occurred. This was the work of P. G. Lejeune-Dirichlet (1805–1859) (Ellis and Gulick 22).

From a student response to Exercise 1-1, "Assessing One's Current Writing Ability":

My attendance at school was no more than following my brothers and sister until the day I entered fifth grade. There I was rudely awakened by a short, compassionate, but stern teacher who demanded utter silence and total attention as she taught. My initial response to Mrs. Brewer was that she would give in, and my friends and I would rule once again, but she left no opportunity for an overthrow.

From the diary of Mary Fish, who lived in New England during the American Revolution:

In the month of May, 1770, my dear and only daughter, Mary Noyes, was taken ill of canker and worms. She was then a little more than four years old, and although so young, would take anything that was given her, if ever so bad to take. She would first taste it, and then would say, it is not good, Mama. I told her the Doctor said she must take it to make her better. She would then open her little mouth and take anything, and would foment her throat over hot steam with great discretion. She died on the 10th day of her illness . . . I closed her eyes myself; and felt in some measure resigned, knowing that God could give a good reason why he had thus afflicted me (Buel and Buel 61–62).

Chronological order is clear, and usually necessary, not only for telling a story but for explaining how to do something. A writer's purpose in explaining a process is generally to help others do the same thing or to suggest a better way to do something commonly done carelessly. Here is a brief example of using narration to describe the process of writing:

The next day, after the dishes were washed, the bed was made, and the Sunday paper was read, I began work on the first draft. I sat on the couch, pen and pad in hand, coffee and a bagel on the table, the 49ers game against the Giants on TV, surrounded by the notes I had taken. I wrote during the whole game. I then typed what I had, corrected errors, and reread it. I hated it. The quality I'd been hoping for just wasn't there. My husband read it and immediately saw that I hadn't reached what I had told him I was aiming for. I wasn't sure, though, that I wanted to change it then because I was getting tired of it. But I sat down anyway and in an hour and a half the paper had rewritten itself. I think it was rewriting while the problems were still on my mind that made the final draft work so well.

This process is carefully organized from what happened first to what happened last.

In explaining a process, the sequence of events occasionally needs to be interrupted, as this writer does in her last sentence, to give *reasons* for taking the path she is suggesting. (This is the first of many ways you'll see that these systematic thought patterns are used in concert with each other.)

2. Spatial Description

Nineteenth-century novelists, like Emily Bronte and Charles Dickens, often described the surroundings of their characters in great detail, explaining how things would look to a person starting on the left and moving to the right, or starting just in front of you and moving away. This pattern of arrangement, though it is important to be able to use it, is seldom needed any more, because we usually have the technology at our disposal, which those nineteenth-century novelists didn't have, to send pictures to supplement our writing. Though we often describe places to one another in our writing, we seldom need or want to give our readers the exact sense of standing where we're standing. Now we usually select details for their telling quality rather than for their precise arrangement in space, and then we organize those telling details in another organizational pattern such as comparison-contrast, classification, or assertion with examples. The following description, of the Bhotia river in the Himalayan Mountains by Hari Ram, an Indian surveyor and secret agent, is typical of most descriptions we would come across now (318–319):

> At one place the river ran in a gigantic chasm, the sides of which were so close to one another that a bridge of twenty-four paces was sufficient to span it. This was just below or south of the village of Choksum. Near the bridge the precipices were so impracticable that the path had of necessity to be supported on iron pegs let into the face of the rock, the path being formed by bars of iron and slabs of stone stretching from peg to peg and covered with earth. This extraordinary path is in no place more than eighteen inches and often not more than nine inches in width and is carried for more than one-third of a mile (775 paces) along the face of the cliff, at some 1500 feet above the river, which could be seen roaring below in its narrow bed.

Hari Ram describes several details of spatial arrangement here to help us picture his experience, but it's fair to say that he, like most describers of spatial arrangements, has selected his details more for the meaning they convey than in an attempt to precisely recreate the scene in space.

3. Classification

Classification is the way our minds sort out the complexity of the world that surrounds us. We classify living things into plants, animals, and humans. We classify books into fiction and nonfiction. We classify families into lower class, middle class, and upper class. Some classifications are easy (plant, animal, and human). Some are vague and quite difficult to pin down (lower, middle, and upper class). You practiced your powers of classification every time in Chapter 3 that you tried to decide how many distinct inferences you could draw from the raw material you were examining. Whenever we write a five-paragraph paper we classify our inferences into three categories in order to write our three body-paragraph topic sentences.

Here is a passage from a physics textbook in which the author has gone through essentially the same process of classifying that you've been practicing:

> There are only two methods by which energy can be transferred between two points. The first method involves the transfer of matter. A falling weight can drive a stake into the ground. Electrons moving through a wire can transfer energy from one place to another.
>
> The second method of energy transfer involves wave motion. All waves transfer energy. Sound waves transfer the energy of a vibrating string of a guitar to your ear. Light waves bring energy from the sun to the earth. Radio waves carry energy from a radio station to your home. Water waves can do tremendous amounts of damage during storms (Murphy 221).

Note that each of the two categories of energy into which energy transfer has been classified—transfer of matter and wave travel—are illustrated by a series of examples. Murphy has used assertion with examples (thought pattern 9) to help explain his classification.

This next example is from a mathematics textbook. Here the writers have used definition (thought pattern 5) to supplement their classification:

> A *function* consists of a domain and a rule. The *domain* is a set of real numbers, which are usually denoted by lower case letters a, b, c, x, t, etc. The *rule* assigns to each number in the domain one and only one number (Ellis and Gulick 16).

My final example is from a chemistry text. Here the author has also used definitions to make her classification clear. She also admits, as many classifiers do not, that the boundaries she has drawn do not always hold:

> Chemistry has traditionally been subdivided into four areas: organic, inorganic, analytical, and physical chemistry. Organic chemistry is the study of the compounds of

a single element, carbon. Inorganic chemistry is the study of compounds of all the other elements. These divisions have blurred somewhat in recent years and there are subtopics, such as organometallic chemistry, being investigated by both organic and Inorganic chemists. Analytical chemistry is the study of the methods used to determine the identity of the components of a mixture or a compound, and the relative amounts of each component. Physical chemistry is the study of the properties of matter and the development of theories that explain the observed properties (Segal 1).

Classifications are commonly used to sort out complexity, but they are most effective in persuasive papers when you may classify several alternative actions or beliefs for the purpose of helping your reader choose what you think is the best among several alternatives. If you've noted, for example, that the only three ways to give integrity to college sports programs are to pay the players and not expect them to go to school, to stop giving any special academic or financial help to athletes, or to develop an academic and personal support staff which helps athletes fill their doubly demanding responsibilities as students and athletes, you're well on your way toward persuading someone to pay for an academic and personal support staff.

4. Comparing and Contrasting

Comparing and contrasting is one of our most intuitive ways of learning, yet one that we must continually sharpen. Every day the world offers us nearly similar facts, inferences, definitions, titles, or theories that we must be alert to distinguish between. Try, offhand, for example, to explain the difference between

- an engineer and a scientist
- an Arab and a Moslem
- a politician and a civil servant
- a working mother and a working father
- racism and reverse racism
- intuition and instinct

Careful writers learn such distinctions when they're not already familiar with them, and then they make those distinctions in their writing. The following selection is from a sign language textbook:

The Congenitally Deaf are those who are born deaf. The Adventitiously Deaf are those who are born with normal hearing but in whom the sense of hearing becomes nonfunctional later through illness or accident (Riekehof 7).

From a biology textbook:

We live not on what we eat, but on what we digest (Moon 363).

From students' papers:

> The union soldiers went about their duties with such cold efficiency that one might have thought they were *hanging their flag rather than a human being.*
>
> The weekend journey across the border began for us at 16, when one of us had *secured a driver's license and, more important, a car.*
>
> The many changes in our society are moving at a pace *too rapid for the elderly to keep up with and too advanced for the young to learn.*

The inferences you make that show that you are aware of such distinctions are much more impressive to teachers than simple inferences that don't demonstrate your awareness that the issues being discussed are complex. Often you use a comparison-contrast organization, in fact, to take your readers from a simple understanding of an issue to a more sophisticated one. Precisely that strategy is used by the authors of a 1936 geography textbook who are trying to distinguish "scientific geography" from most people's casual impression of the subject:

> It is not, to be sure, in the numerous *individual* features of regions that the geographer is primarily interested. Simply a catalogue of individual plants is not botany, nor is the listing of things to be seen within a region geography. Scientific study requires grouping and classifying and the tracing of origins and connections. When it is noted, for instance, in a study of a region's landscape, that there are repeating patterns of population distribution, drainage lines, fields, or any of the other very numerous features, and when these repetitions are discovered to have definite causal relation to other features (past or present) with which they are associated, there is then the beginning of scientific geography (Finch and Trewartha 5–6).

Most comparison-contrasts you make will be relatively brief, but you will also be asked regularly during your academic and professional lives to compare two items or ideas at length. To make your comparison systematic, you need to call on your powers of classification as well as powers of comparison. Two items can be compared fairly only if you rate each by the same criteria.

One of my students recently compared the readers of the *New York Times* and those of the *Seattle Post-Intelligencer* in the areas of lifestyle, economy, and political preference. Another compared the readers of the *Seattle Post-Intelligencer* and those of the *Baltimore Sun* in the areas of interest in national and international events, business concerns, interest in sports and leisure, and political views. Each contrasted and classified but they chose different, though equally systematic, methods of organization. The first student discussed the *Times* on all issues first and then discussed the *Post-Intelligencer* on the same issues:

1. Introduction
   Specific points about readers of the *Times*
   a. Lifestyle
   b. Economy
   c. Political preference

2. Specific points about readers of the *Post-Intelligencer*
   a. Lifestyle
   b. Economy
   c. Political preference
3. Conclusion

The second student, by contrast, used his four issues as the principal structure and compared the two papers on each issue before moving on to the next:

1. Introduction
2. Interests in national and international events
   a. Readers of the *Post-Intelligencer*
   b. Readers of the *Sun*
3. Business concerns
   a. Readers of the *Post-Intelligencer*
   b. Readers of the *Sun*
4. Interests in sports and leisure
   a. Readers of the *Post-Intelligencer*
   b. Readers of the *Sun*
5. Political views
   a. Readers of the *Post-Intelligencer*
   b. Readers of the *Sun*
6. Conclusion

There is no law against the first choice, but the second pattern is generally considered more accessible to readers because it highlights the very specific contrasts by placing them right next to each other.

Why might a writer write a detailed comparison? Usually it is to understand each item compared a little better than we would if we analyzed it alone. Extended comparisons can also be used to indicate a preference, to help readers make a choice, or to help readers to understand something unfamiliar to them by comparing it to something more familiar. Most often, we don't write a whole paper contrasting, but rather introduce a contrast mid-paper to clarify what we're saying about our principal topic.

5. Definition

We are all familiar with the term *definition*. In writing, students often use dictionary definitions to jump start their writing. Whatever the topic, they begin their paper, "Webster's defines [topic] as. . . ." Then the writers start giving their own ideas. Save such definitions for when they're genuinely needed.

When are they needed? when you use a term that's unfamiliar to your readers, when you use a term that means different things to different readers, when you use a term in an unusual sense, or when you want to explain in detail what something is. A definition may be as short as a single word in parentheses. When I use the term *assertion* in this book, for example, I want you to remember that an assertion is also an inference, so I'll occasionally write:

assertion (inference)

Or a definition may take up a whole book. This textbook can be thought of, perhaps, as a 225-page extended definition of the term *thoughtful writing*.

Textbooks are usually sprinkled with definitions. Bernice Segal in her chemistry book explains why:

> You will find in the course of studying chemistry that a great many new terms will be defined. The importance of learning the definition of each new term you encounter cannot be overemphasized. If you do not know the precise definition of a quantity whose value you are asked to determine, you will have difficulty with the reasoning required to solve the problem (2).

Every word we use we use not because it is "correct" in any absolute sense but because speakers of our language have agreed to use it in certain conventional ways. Scientists and dictionary writers try to be as precise as they can about terms—to do so, they write so-called *essential* definitions, like the following:

> Fish are aquatic vertebrates, with either cartilaginous or bony skeletons. They breathe by means of gills; are usually covered with scales; and have limbs in the form of fins (Moon 239).

An essential definition places the item being defined in a broad category, then shows how it differs from others in that category. In this case *fish* are placed in the broad category *vertebrates* (animals having backbones) and then are said to differ from other vertebrates in being *aquatic* (living in the water). In this case the essential definition of the first sentence is reinforced with further contrasts, or distinctions: Fish "breathe by means of gills; are usually covered with scales; and have limbs in the form of fins."

In practice, not all definitions are so rigorous. They draw on a variety of other thought patterns as they define.

Definition through Spatial Description:

> *The cell:* In most plants and animals the protoplasm is divided into very small parts called cells. These are merely the simplest units of protoplasm of which the plant or animal is composed. A living cell usually consists of a tiny mass of protoplasm surrounded by a membrane called the cell wall. The central portion of the protoplasm, more active than the rest, is called the nucleus. The cell wall gives definite shape to the cell and the nucleus seems to regulate growth and reproduction. Cells are usually very minute, but are of innumerable shapes, varying with the special work they may have to perform (Moon 27).

Definition through Chronological Narration (from a Student Exercise):

> One day when I was babysitting, the child, Andrea, became ill and I acted like an amateur. Andrea was four years old and I had been watching her since she was an infant. She attended nursery school at the time. Her mother worked and I would meet her at the bus and take her home after school.
>
> On this one particular day she came off the bus and the bus driver told me she wasn't feeling well. I took her inside and called her mother's office. Her mother was in a meeting. By the time I got off the phone Andrea had gotten worse and was running a high temperature. I called my mother and she came over. My mother got her in bed and Andrea fell asleep. My mother told me what to do if she woke up and then left. A couple of minutes later, Andrea's mother called back and once she heard what was wrong, came home. I don't recall what happened between the time Andrea's mother left the office and the time she came home, but everything was under control by the time she got there.
>
> On the basis of what I have written, I'd say an amateur is someone who hasn't had enough experience in his field to handle all situations. In my case, I had been watching Andrea for four years but I didn't know what to do once she became sick.

Definition through Contrast with the Usual Meaning of a Term:

> Imagine that you have exerted great effort all day trying to remove a huge rock from your garden. Your muscles ache. You are very tired. In spite of all your efforts, the rock remains unmoved. You will say that you have worked hard all day. The physicist will say that you have done no work at all! According to the physicist, work is done only when a force causes an object to move some distance (Murphy 138).

Definition via Mathematical Formula:

> The role of a manager can now be defined. His goal is to be efficient, and he is most efficient when he maximizes the difference between total costs and total revenues through time (Farmer 14).

Newly Created Definition to Make Solving a Problem More Efficient (Common in Mathematics):

> Let 1 be any nonvertical line in the plane and $P(x1, y1)$ and $Q(x2, y2)$ any two distinct points on it (Ellis and Gulick 10).

When you use a term your readers are unfamiliar with or when you want your readers to see a term in a different light than they usually do, a careful definition will serve your purpose and save your reader confusion.

6. Cause and Effect

This organizational pattern is relatively easy to use. Assertion of a cause-effect relationship is usually completed in one sentence:

> Our basic argument is that the way in which managers perform determines how productive, and hence how wealthy, any country will be (Farmer 13).

Then the writer goes on to discuss both the cause and the effect in detail.

Of course the establishment of a connection between a single cause and a single effect is difficult, except in science where through experiments scientists eliminate all possible additional causes. Thus, in science we have many clear causal chains, where cause 1 causes effect 1, which in turn causes effect 2, etc. Here's an example:

> A practical application of the expansion and contraction of gases and liquids is found in systems for heating buildings. The air directly around a radiator expands as it is heated. In this way, it becomes less dense than the cool air above it. The warm air rises and the cool air moves in to take its place. This results in circulation of air (Murphy 196).

Outside the realm of science any effect we see is likely to have had multiple causes and will itself in the company of other causes influence several new effects. The process is mind-bogglingly complex, but as human beings we try to make some sense out of it. Much of your learning in many subjects will consist of sorting out cause-and-effect relationships.

An Example from Geography:

> By the time that classical antiquity drew to a close, as a result of the recorded travels of Greek scholars, such as Strabo and Herodotus, the empire building of the Romans, and the commercial enterprises of the Phoenicians, there had accumulated a considerable body of material relating to the earth's regions (Finch and Trewartha 1).

An Example from Sociology:

> If a society is to function successfully and endure through time, certain conditions must be fulfilled. What are they?
>
> First, individual psychological and biological needs must be met, and pivotal institutions (the family, religion, education, and so on) emerge to meet them. Second, new members, usually newborn babies, must be socialized, indoctrinated with the social values, and trained to occupy positions in the social structure. Third, behavior must be guided toward what is socially desirable, through norms and sanctions. Every society must have a system of control to regulate the expression of aggression, sexual behavior, and property distribution. There is no known society where people are allowed to rape, rob, or kill.

Fourth, for individuals to function in a society, interaction must be largely regular and predictable. There is always an element of uncertainty in interaction, but it is minimized insofar as the participants accept established norms or arrive at a consensus on new ones.

Fifth, the members of society must feel they belong to the group and are motivated to act according to its rules. The constellation of beliefs and values we call myth tends to meet this imperative. It sets social and individual goals, gives a sense of origin and purpose, and invests experience with meaning and value (Biesanz 12-13).

These two examples should remind you that when you write using cause-effect patterns, you should always keep in mind that there could be multiple causes of any effect you might be dealing with. If you ignore this complexity, you may sound very simple-minded.

7. Problem-Solution

The problem-solution pattern is closely related to cause and effect, though it is more restricted in time. It deals with current situations and the means that might be used to cause an improved future. Problem-solution is a pattern fundamental to education, as this example from a physics textbook will indicate:

Suppose that you need to solve an equation for an unknown. For example, you may need to find the value of a in the equation

$$F = ma$$

To do this, the equation must be solved for a. We can do this by remembering that whenever any operation is performed on one side of an equation, the same operation must also be performed on the other side of the equation. In the present example, we first divide both sides of the equation by m. This gives us the equation

$$\frac{F}{m} = a$$

It is customary to place the unknown on the left side of an equation. Thus, our equation can be rewritten

$$a = \frac{F}{m}$$

and our problem is solved (Murphy 3–4).

Since one of the most common reasons for writing is a hope for some change, problem-solution is a commonly used pattern of organization—whether in single sentences, paragraphs, papers, chapters, or whole books.

8. Assertion with Examples

"Assertion with examples" is another way of saying "inference with details." The exercises you did in Chapter 3 all enable you to write paragraphs that consist of an assertion and several examples. Assertion-with-examples is the second most common thought pattern (after chronological narration). Since this whole book emphasizes assertions with examples, one example here, this time from a physics book, should be sufficient in this chapter:

> Everything in the universe is in a state of motion. The earth itself is filled with moving things. The earth also spins on its axis. The earth and the other planets of our solar system orbit the sun. Our solar system moves through space as part of the Milky Way Galaxy. Stars and galaxies move away from one another (Murphy 31).

That explanation—an assertion with examples—should leave you spinning.

Assertion-with-examples is a pattern whose role is often to serve the other patterns. It is an easy pattern to recognize, and it should not be too difficult to use given the training you've had in this book.

9. Assertion with Reasons

Not all assertions we make need to be backed up by examples—often we substantiate assertions not with examples but with reasons.

A Brief Assertion with a Single Reason:

> We first must describe some important properties of real numbers, because real numbers, their properties, and their relationships are basic to calculus (Ellis and Gulick 1).

An Assertion with a Very Thoughtful List of Reasons:

> Biology is a required study in many schools, and we have a right to ask why it is considered so important that we are obliged to study it.
>
> In the first place there are few subjects that add so much to general culture by increasing the number of things in which we are interested and about which we should have information.
>
> Few people really see very much of the things about them—accurate observation is a very rare but valuable trait, and biology will greatly increase the powers of observation.
>
> Mere observation of facts is not enough, however, for one should be able to draw correct conclusions from what he sees. This ability to think and reason is one of the chief aims of the laboratory work in biology or any other science.

Although these reasons for the study of biology are by far the most important, others can be mentioned which may seem more practical. It is the foundation
of farming, gardening, and forestry and upon its laws are based the care and
breeding of all domestic animals and plants.

In even a more personal way, biology deals with the health and care of our
own bodies—hygiene. It also includes the study of the cause and prevention of
disease, the work of bacteria, and means of maintaining healthful surroundings—
sanitation.

One half of all human deaths are caused by germ diseases [this was written in
1921] and at least half of these could be prevented by proper knowledge and
practice of hygiene and sanitation. This in itself is sufficient reason for interest in the
study of biology (Moon 3–4).

Choosing the assertion-with-reasons organizational format means that
you are arguing deductively. Deduction will be explained in detail in the next
chapter.

10. Building to a Climax

If the nine organizational patterns above are merely servants to our purpose in writing, building to a climax is the servant of the servants. We use it to
organize narrations, descriptions, classifications, cause-effect claims, problem-
solution plans, examples, and reasons. I'll give just one example, an account in
a sociology book of the emergence of self-awareness:

As infants, we have no conception of ourselves as individuals, no notion that we
are set apart from other individuals. Only as we interact with our mothers and
others, bump up against things, find we have a name, are clothed and bathed, and
feel the boundaries of our bodies, do we begin to be aware of a separate identity.
Roughly at the age of two, we begin to use the pronouns "I," "me," and "you," indicating that we are beginning to be conscious of ourselves and of other persons
as separate individuals. This awareness grows as we acquire language and can par-
ticipate in symbolic interaction.

We next learn to perceive roles and their relationships. As we observe and
respond to others, they become meaningful objects that can bring us pleasure,
pain, security, and so on. In order to win the responses we want, we learn to anticipate their actions by putting ourselves in their places—by taking the role of the
other. In doing so we become objects to ourselves, able eventually to look at ourselves from outside ourselves, so to speak. Thus, we become aware of our moods
and wishes and ideas as objects. We can then finally act toward and guide ourselves (Biesanz and Biesanz 84–85).

The last sentence here, as in many explanations and arguments, is the
most important. This is very satisfying to readers, and it helps them remember
what you most want them to remember.

Writing and Recognizing the Common Thought Patterns

Exercise 5-3
homework, then in class

To become more familiar with the systematic thought patterns available to you and to help you realize that those patterns are not infinite in number or complexity, try the following. Choose one subject from among the first three below:

First Class	**Second Class**	**Third Class**
Procrastination	Money	Confidence
The Elderly	Guilt	The Best Movie I've Seen Lately
High School Education	Marriage	Working Mothers

Write a brief (approximately one page) analysis of your chosen subject organized according to any one of the ten thought patterns:

1. Chronological narration
2. Spatial description
3. Classification
4. Comparison-contrast
5. Definition
6. Cause and effect
7. Problem and solution
8. Assertion with examples
9. Assertion with reasons
10. Building to a climax

When you've finished, write a *second analysis of the same subject*, using a second pattern of your choice. For example, if you wrote first an analysis of procrastination using a problem-and-solution organization, then write a second analysis, this time organizing, perhaps, according to assertion with examples.

During a class session, then, read, in turn, some of your papers aloud. After each reading by another student in the class, jot down (1) the method of organization you think the writer used and (2) a sentence or two explaining your decision. As soon as you've written down your estimates, compare them with those of other members of the class, and finally, ask the author what his or her intention was. You'll begin to see the variety of possibilities for organizing and the ways organizational patterns can be mixed with each other.

To reinforce your organizational sense, repeat the exercise a second and third time, each time choosing a new subject from a new column and writing about your chosen subject twice, using two different thought patterns. By the end of three classes, you will have used six patterns of organization, and you will have heard—from the rest of the class—the other patterns, and other ways of using the same patterns. You are building up your intuitive resources for organization.

All the thought patterns used in the exercise above are aids to readers. A definition makes clear a term that your reader may be unfamiliar with. Classification helps a reader sort a product or an issue into its important parts. A contrasting example helps a reader to see the subject you're focusing on more clearly. A cause-effect explanation helps a reader see *why* a certain event occurred. A narrative helps a reader see how certain issues might affect his or her life.

After this week of practice, you should be able to explain, better than a textbook can, what uses each pattern serves. You will also see that the patterns are not too complicated, and that they often overlap—we almost always use more than one pattern in any extended piece of writing. As you listen to the sketches written by others, you'll probably also be reminded of how important details and examples are in backing up any assertions that are made.

Recognizing Patterns in Everyday Messages

Exercise 5-4
in class

Any message, no matter what its length and no matter where it's posted, will, if it wishes to be clear and persuasive, be grounded in an organizational pattern. The messages on cereal box panels and matchbook covers, in junk-mail circulars, on traffic signs, in department memos and political ads, and on medicine bottles were all written by someone, and each writer, often more intuitively than consciously, used some thought pattern to organize the message. In the examples below, try to determine the author's principle of organization.

From a Side Panel of a Box of Post Grape-Nuts:

HERE'S HOW TO
GO GRAPE-NUTS®
cereal
OVER DANNON.®

1/2 container (1/2 cup) plain or vanilla-flavored DANNON® Yogurt
1/4 cup POST GRAPE-NUTS® Brand Cereal
1/4 cup (about) fresh, frozen or canned fruit*

Or use 1/2 container DANNON® Yogurt, any fruit flavor, and omit the fruit.

Spoon yogurt into dish. Top with cereal, then add fruit and serve at once. Makes 1 serving.

Sign on a Bathroom Door:

MEN'S ROOM

Sign on a Staircase Door:

FIRE DOOR
KEEP CLOSED AT ALL
TIMES TO PREVENT
FIRE FROM SPREADING

From the Side Label on a Bottle of Pepto-Bismol:

Caution: This product contains salicylates. If taken with aspirin and ringing of the ears occurs, discontinue use. If taking medicine for anticoagulation (thinning the blood), diabetes, or gout, consult physician before taking this product. If diarrhea is accompanied by high fever or continues more than 2 days, consult a physician.

From the Inside Cover of *National Geographic*:

The National Geographic Society is chartered in Washington. D.C., in accordance with the laws of the United States, as a nonprofit scientific and educational organization. Since 1890 the Society has supported more than 2,350 explorations and research projects, adding immeasurably to man's knowledge of earth, sea, and sky.

The Lyrics for a Harry Chapin Song, "Cat's in the Cradle"

My child arrived just the other day.
He came to the world in the usual way.
But there were planes to catch and bills to pay.
He learned to walk while I was away.
And as he was talkin' 'fore I knew it, and as he grew
He'd say "I'm gonna be like you, dad.
You know I'm gonna be like you."

Refrain:

And the cat's in the cradle and the silver spoon
Little boy blue and the man on the moon
"When you comin' home dad?"
"I don't know when, but we'll get together then.
You know we'll have a good time then."
My son turned ten just the other day.
He said "Thanks for the ball dad, come on let's play."
"Can you teach me how to throw?" I said. "Not today."
"I got a lot to do." He said, "That's OK."
And he walked away, but his smile never dimmed.
And he said "I'm gonna be like him, yeah.
You know I'm gonna be like him."

Refrain

Well he came home from college just the other day
So much like a man I had to say
"Son I'm proud of you can you sit for a while?"
He shook his head and he said with a smile
"What I'd really like Dad is to borrow the car keys.
See you later, can I have them please?"

Refrain

I've long since retired. My son's moved away.
I called him up just the other day.
I said "I'd really like to see you if you don't mind."
He said "I'd love to dad if I can find the time.
You see my new job's a hassle and the kids have the flu
But it's sure nice talking to you."
And as I hung up the phone it occurred to me
He'd grown up just like me.
My boy was just like me.

Each of the messages above was organized according to some principle. And the longer the message was, the greater the chances that its organization could get out of hand. You'll begin to see, I hope, that even the brief papers you write for this class are complex documents, much in need of careful organization.

I don't claim that the thought patterns listed in this chapter comprise a complete list, or a closed system. Every textbook writer's list of organizational strategies differs, and many of these strategies overlap. But our inability to say "these are the only possibilities" should not lead us to despair of the strategies' usefulness. Keep your eyes open to whatever organizational strategies you find most common and most useful. If you find more useful strategies, add them to the list. In the meantime, this list is a valuable resource that you can turn to for any paper that you write.

Writing Patterned Answers to Essay Questions

Not being aware of these ten strategies for being systematic sets us back when we're writing a paper, but it sets us back most when we're trying to write an effective answer to an essay test question. When we're writing such an answer, the clarity with which we can present what we know becomes almost as important as what we know. Our instructors expect us not only to remember the course material but to be able to control it. But excitement or nervousness often leads us to write down all we remember at the moment, instead of setting time aside to try to organize an appropriate answer. A too-little-recognized part of our job in answering a test question is discovering what thought pattern the teacher is suggesting that we use.

Exercise 5-5
in class

With the practice you gained in writing your six short organizational essays, look at the following questions—see if you can become expert at pattern spotting. For each question, decide on the principal organizational pattern that the teacher in each case would expect, and mention any secondary patterns that might be useful as well.

1. *History:* Compare and contrast the founding and development of the colonies of Massachusetts and Virginia. Be sure to discuss political, economic, social, and religious issues.
2. *Business:* Discuss three elements of risk that you discern in the business conduct of a public utility. Which is most serious?
3. *Biochemistry:* What are ketone bodies? Explain why and how they are formed in instances of starvation.
4. *Sociology:* How would you explain the differential earnings of men and women?

5. *History:* How did the concept of equality change in the period from 1607 to 1865? Be sure to trace the change through time.
6. *History:* What were the five most critical events leading to the Civil War? Be sure to explain thoroughly what each event was and why it led to the Civil War.

You should quickly become impressed with your ability to tackle the organization of a question even when you know nothing about the subject matter being questioned.

If you become an expert pattern spotter, half your work in answering essay questions is already done. Once you recognize a pattern, you can make a quick outline. Here, for example, is an outline for question 4, which I think calls for an assertion-with-reasons response:

Men earned 40 percent more than women in the United States in 1983

- Because pregnancy takes many women out of the job market during crucial years of advancement
- Because many women are in a dependent role where duties are expected of them at home
- Because young boys are brought up to expect careers, while many girls are not brought up to expect them
- Because job discrimination and job segregation conditions still exist

Each of these reasons will need details or examples to back it up, but now we are ready to start writing, *trying* to keep our minds thinking—and not just filling in the blanks—as we do.

We can use this three-step method—choosing a pattern, then building an outline, and finally supporting the outline statements with examples—in writing any paper. The method short-circuits much of the work and time usually involved in writing. But it also short-circuits some of the thinking. On a test, when we've done most of our thinking before we begin to write, and where we have (we hope) the examples readily at our disposal, this three-step method can be effective. A paper not done on the spot, though, at school or on the job, will require much more research and thinking, and the longer but more thorough writing method detailed in Chapter 13, "The Writing Process," will serve us much better when we wish to present not just our current knowledge but a helpful and thoughtful piece of work.

6

Persuasion: Writing with Authority

The persuasion paper was the hardest because you couldn't just do research and write down a lot of facts. You really had to convince the reader that you were right.

STUDENT

Newspapers, television, movies, advertisements, parents, and friends, all, at one time or another, attempt to persuade you to accept a particular point of view. Theirs. If you are aware of the basic argumentative techniques, you may either use them to persuade others, or analyze how someone else has used them in an attempt to persuade you.

JOYCE MIDDLETON, WRITING TEACHER

Unless you settle first the questions that are on your readers' minds, they won't listen to a thing you want to say.

HUBERT MILLER, NUCLEAR REGULATORY COMMISSION

Writing . . . is an act of aggression disguised as an act of charity.

DAVID BARTHOLOMAE

Earning, and Then Using, Authority

Most of us have very little faith that we are capable of changing another person's opinion or affecting another person's action. We have very little faith because we have no strategies in mind for influencing people. As a result, when we are asked to argue, we talk or write without thinking, and we produce something as muddled as this excerpt from a lab report of an eighth-grade student trying to persuade her teacher that the melting point and the freezing point of a substance will be two different temperatures:

> Personally I think that, when a substance has a freezing point and/or a melting point in its graph measurements, that they don't equal each other. In other words, the heating points and melting points do not equal each other (their answers are different). The reason I think this is because when something freezes it pretty much always has air bubbles and when a substance melts it is a solid. So when weighing the substance the freezing point is heavier plus the freezing point is colder and the melting point is hot and they both can't be heated and melted at the same time, plus there is no movement in the frozen substance, but there is movement in a melted substance, so there is no way a freezing point and a melting point can equal each other.

(In fact, the melting point and the freezing point of a substance are identical—for water, for example, both are 32°F).

This student is floundering, partly because she is ill-informed, but partly because she is intimidated by the great knowledge gulf she sees as separating herself from her teacher. In order to persuade people, we must overcome that feeling of intimidation: we do so by becoming well-informed, not only about our subject, but about methods of persuading. It's up to you to become well-informed about your subject by doing research—observing, interviewing, reading. In this chapter I'll help you become better informed about the chief methods of persuading, first explained to us by Aristotle. They are *ethos* (appealing to readers or listeners through one's "character"), *logos* (appealing to readers or listeners through logic, usually with facts), and *pathos* (appealing to readers or listeners through their emotions).

Persuasive writing is a form of selling. We in school sometimes pretend that we are above selling things, but just as Skippy peanut butter would be off the shelf in five years if Best Foods stopped advertising it, so, too, would our ideas be lost if we stopped speaking and writing on their behalf. So let's take a few pages out of the advertiser's book of strategies.

Discriminating among *Ethos*, *Logos*, and *Pathos*

Exercise 6-1
in class

How do the ads on the following pages, the first two from the 1930s and the last five from 1904, try to get us to buy the products or ideas advertised? Take a few notes about the strategies you notice, and compare them with those noted by your classmates. Can you classify the strategies as employing *ethos*, *logos*, and *pathos*?

LION HATS
The Right Hat for Real Men

YOU find Lion Hats on the heads of men who do things. Men who are leaders. The kind of men who demand the best. But whose time is too valuable to be wasted in endless shopping, picking and choosing.

Perhaps one reason why they like Lion Hats is because all they need to do is to go to a good hat shop, ask for the size they wear and look for the Lion Seal on the inner band.

You will be quickly pleased—and have the satisfaction of knowing that there is nothing better.

LANGENBERG HAT CO.
St. Louis, Mo. U.S.A.
ESTABLISHED 1860

Manufacturers of Lion Hats, Caps and Gloves

[handwritten note:] Ethos - they're claiming their product is superior to others.

Logos –
Statistics

A Bushel of Food

In a Package of Quaker Oats
And At One-Tenth the Cost

A 35-cent package of Quaker Oats contains 6221 calories—the energy measure of food value.

You would buy a bushel of ordinary mixed foods to equal that calory value. And that bushel would cost you ten times 35 cents.

Here is what it would take of certain good foods to furnish you 6221 calories:

To Supply 6221 Calories			
In Quaker Oats . .	1 Pkg.	In Potatoes	21 Lbs.
In Round Steak . .	7 Lbs.	In Hubbard Squash .	65 Lbs.
In Hens' Eggs . . .	7 Doz.	In Young Chicken	20 Lbs.
In Cabbage	55 Lbs.	In String Beans . .	36 Lbs.

And here is what those calories would cost at this writing in some necessary foods:

Cost of 6221 Calories			
In Quaker Oats . . .	35c	In Hens' Eggs . . .	$3.12
In Round Steak . . .	$2.06	In Fish about . . .	2.25
In Veal or Lamb . . .	3.12	In Potatoes	65c

Consider these facts in your breakfasts. The oat is the greatest food that grows. It is almost a complete food—nearly the ideal food. It supplies essentials which most foods lack.

At least once a day use this supreme food to cut down your table cost.

57 Cents	**5½ Cents**	**50 Cents**
Per 1000 Calories	*Per 1000 Calories*	*Per 1000 Calories*

Quaker Oats

Only 10 Pounds From a Bushel

Get Quaker Oats for exquisite flavor. They are flaked from queen grains only—just the rich, plump, flavory oats. We get but ten pounds from a bushel.

When such an oat dish costs no extra price it is due to yourself that you get it.

15c and 35c per Package
Except in the Far West and South
Packed in Sealed Round Packages with Removable Cover

3191

Casa Grande

Hotel. . .

Lately refitted.   Everything about the house new and clean.   Most conveniently located hotel in town.   Directly opposite S. P. Depot.   First-class dining-room.   Mattie Shamp has charge of the kitchen – no better cook in the valley.

**William Gould
Proprietor**

Ethos – playing themselves up

What a Horse Thinks

when hitched to a plow so poorly shaped and tempered that it pulls hard, we may never exactly know. He ought to, and probably does, think it mighty hard work, and so does his owner. It would be lighter, yea, the **lightest**, were he drawing a

BRADLEY X RAYS.

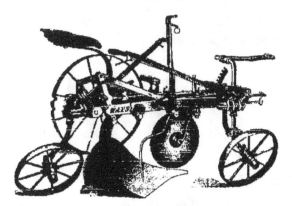

**New
Principles,**

**New
Features,**

**New
Ideas,**

Ethos

which has never been equaled. They draw light, they scour, they work well, they please.

For the above or anything in FARM MACHINERY call on

MACK BROS.

Pathos - mentions horse's feelings

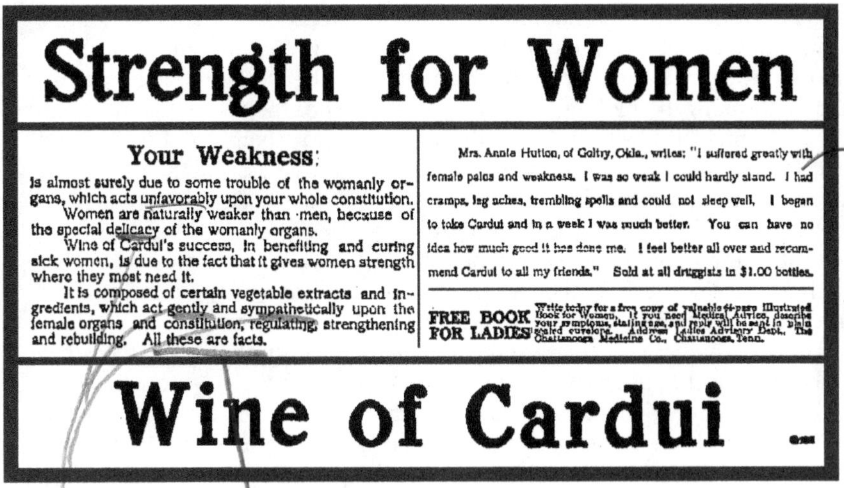

Strength for Women

Your Weakness:

Is almost surely due to some trouble of the womanly organs, which acts unfavorably upon your whole constitution.

Women are naturally weaker than ·men, because of the special delicacy of the womanly organs.

Wine of Cardui's success, in benefiting and curing sick women, is due to the fact that it gives women strength where they most need it.

It is composed of certain vegetable extracts and ingredients, which act gently and sympathetically upon the female organs and constitution, regulating, strengthening and rebuilding. All these are facts.

Mrs. Annie Hutton, of Goltry, Okla., writes: "I suffered greatly with female pains and weakness. I was so weak I could hardly stand. I had cramps, leg aches, trembling spells and could not sleep well, I began to take Cardui and in a week I was much better. You can have no idea how much good it has done me. I feel better all over and recommend Cardui to all my friends." Sold at all druggists in $1.00 bottles.

FREE BOOK FOR LADIES Write today for a free copy of valuable 64-page Illustrated Book for Women. If you need Medical Advice, describe your symptoms, stating age, and reply will be sent in plain sealed envelope. Address Ladies Advisory Dept., The Chattanooga Medicine Co., Chattanooga, Tenn.

Wine of Cardui

[handwritten annotations: "Ethos outside credibility validates", "pathos", "poor attempt at Ethos, no sense"]

The strategies employed by writers fall into precisely the same categories as do the strategies employed by these advertisers. Every writer who succeeds does so by using *ethos, logos,* and *pathos*—by presenting a trust-worthy character (ethos), by substantiating all claims (logos), and by influencing the reader's emotions (pathos).

Logos

Perhaps we should talk first about *logos,* or logic, since most people are afraid that they aren't competent in this area. The term *logic* includes a wide variety of systematic ways of thinking, specifically the ten common thought patterns discussed in Chapter 5. But the two most fundamental logical patterns are induction and deduction, referred to in Chapter 5 as "assertion with examples" (induction) and "assertion with reasons" (deduction). Induction and deduction are in fact never wholly independent of each other, but it is easier to understand them if we first assume that they can stand alone.

You have been practicing induction ever since Chapter 3—induction is the drawing of a reliable inference from a set of examples. If, for example, I were a Laplander who arrived in St. Louis and watched, for a few weeks, the way people worked and the way they were paid, I might notice the following: that doctors work hard and that they are paid handsomely; that judges work hard and that they are paid handsomely; that construction workers work hard and that they are paid handsomely. I'd surely draw the inference that Missourians who work hard are paid handsomely. I might check my inference, my inductive thinking, by looking at trash collectors. Since they work hard and are paid handsomely, I'd begin to think that my logic was foolproof. But if I then turned to shoe repairers, or mothers, or administrative assistants, who work hard but are not paid handsomely, I'd be very confused. Or if I were a well-schooled Laplander, I'd be aware that induction is never foolproof. Induction is our most common method of reasoning. And several examples are often enough to convince. But neither writers nor readers can ever be certain that a counterexample, or even many counterexamples, won't turn up.

I doubt whether you've heard the term *induction* very often, even though it describes the most frequent way we think. If I said "deduction," though, you'd probably think immediately of detectives, perhaps of Sherlock Holmes or of the characters on CSI who often speak of making "simple deductions" from facts. These so-called deductions are, just to make things confusing, inferences, the products of inductive thinking. Genuine deduction is quite a different matter.

Both writers and readers are less conscious of deduction than of induction, but deduction can be very helpful. It is based on a logical device called the *syllogism*. A syllogism has three parts: a general principle (or common assumption), a specific example of that principle, and finally a conclusion.

> *General principle:* All human beings die.
> *Specific application:* My father is a human being.
> *Conclusion:* Therefore, my father will someday die.

If you use this method of reasoning and your general principle is fool-proof, then your conclusion is foolproof. Deduction thus seems to be a very powerful tool. But there's a catch. Very few general principles are as certain as the one—"All human beings die"—that I began my sample syllogism with. There aren't many principles (assumptions) that you can be *sure* your audience will share. Most statements that concern human issues are at best probable rather than certain.

When I try to think of general principles with which no one could disagree, I fail again and again:

> All people have a right to respect. (*Even criminals?*)
> A human being, to be ethical, must regard people as intrinsically more valuable than animals. (*Does this mean that we can kill and eat animals without qualms?*)

Any such statement that I make *I* will call a general principle. *You* are more likely to call the same statement my assumption. If you make such a statement, *you'll* consider it a principle, while *I'll* call it your assumption. Deduction begins to look a little shaky as a means of convincing people.

Let's look at a few more examples. Suppose I wanted to argue that women should be drafted. The syllogistic structure of my argument might look like this:

General principle: Men and women are equal.
Specific application: Men are subject to the U.S. draft.
Conclusion: Therefore, women should be subject to the U.S. draft.

This argument, like most attempts at deductive argument, becomes complicated when you look into it carefully. A reader might at first agree with my general principle, but once he saw my conclusion, he might go back, fairly, and ask me to define *equal*. Another reader might not want to listen because she feels that not even men should be subject to a draft. I'm stopped in my tracks because my readers will not accept my assumptions. Deduction is therefore fraught with risks. Readers can ignore your whole train of thought if they disagree with your assumptions. Still, deduction is useful for writers in fields like engineering or the law, where fixed codes exist, that is, where decisions are often based on "first principles."

General principle: Those guilty of second-degree murder should serve eight to ten years in prison.
Specific application: Derek Smith has been found guilty of second-degree murder.
Conclusion: Therefore, Derek Smith should serve eight to ten years in prison.

Deduction is also helpful when you can find some assumption that is shared by the person you want to persuade. If I, for example, wanted the principal of my daughter's junior high school to require three years of language study, and the principal was opposed to language study because he had never "used" the French he had learned but was also worried because the students in his school were having difficulty with English grammar and vocabulary, I might argue as follows:

General principle: Any study which improves students' grammar and vocabulary ought to be encouraged.
Specific application: The study of other languages improves students' mastery of English grammar and vocabulary.
Conclusion: Therefore, the study of languages other than English ought to be encouraged.

Since I had found for the basis of my deductive argument a general principle on which we both agreed, the principal would have to think twice before throwing out my suggestion.

Following are two responses to a court case in which the federal government attempted to force the parents of a child born with severe birth defects and brain damage to agree to have partially corrective surgery attempted. One writer emphasizes deduction in making his case, the other writer induction:

Deduction

Conclusion Backed by General Principles (Assertion with Reasons)

The decision of the U.S. surgeon general to intervene in the case of severely retarded Baby Jane Doe must be condemned quickly and completely.

By what right does the surgeon general presume to involve himself in the tragedy of this family? Is he a close friend or relative? Has he volunteered to pay the cost of the child's care? Does he share the parents' heartbreak?

No! Yet, he comes into their lives unasked, to challenge a decision that they have made with the help of their doctors, their family, and their God. I pray that the courts will not allow the surgeon general's unjustified, self-serving interference to continue.

Induction

Conclusion Backed by Facts (Assertion with Examples)

The government lawyer says "what the family wants is not the issue here." Why? Will he take over Baby Doe's care? Who does he expect to care for and love this poor suffering girl? Will society in its callous way take the place of caring parents?

I had a sister—born two years before me. She was made brain damaged by blood poisoning (before 5 years of age) when the scab of her smallpox vaccination was pulled off by a rusted suit button of a loving uncle who was playing with her. She was confined to the Memorial State Hospital in Elkhart, Indiana, for 35 years.

She knew little family love after that.

At first we had no transportation, and with seven others to care for, little time to visit her. Did she know? We will never know. The state cared for her through the many convulsions—keeping her a prisoner in her room (for her own sake). She never roamed the beautiful grounds. Her care was protective and skillful. But she was not a contributor to society—just sick and alone and jailed. She mercifully died at the age of 40.

Baby Doe will have 100 times the agony my sister survived.

As I write this I am listening for the telephone to ring—announcing the birth of our second grandchild. I would *hate* for a lawyer to intrude in this child's life.

Though induction and deduction can be explained separately, all thinking, all arriving at conclusions, contains elements of both. As you saw in Chapter 3, the inferences we draw from facts are never just a simple response to those facts. They are colored by assumptions (sex-role assumptions, assumptions about what certain categories of people are attracted to, assumptions about why photographers take photographs), that is, by deductive reasoning. And here in this chapter, when I gave a reason as the foundation of my deductive argument—"Any study which improves students' grammar and vocabulary ought to be encouraged"—that reason might be more persuasive if I added a few examples, that is, used inductive reasoning, to back up my deductive reasoning.

Perhaps a diagram can clarify this point better than words can. Stephen Toulmin, in *The Uses of Argument* (1958), includes a diagram which helps us visualize the interconnectedness of induction and deduction (97–107). Two slightly adapted versions of that diagram follow:

The Simpler Version:

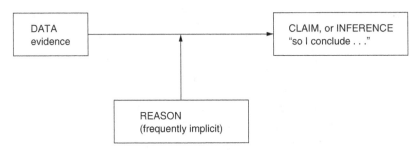

To take an example from the Sister Rebecca exercise (3-5) in Chapter 3:

My data is: Her name appears in all capital letters six times.
My claim, or inference, is: She is egotistical.
My reason for making the inference is: Only 2-year-olds, kings, queens, and people of great ego refer to themselves as if they were a separate person.

The More Complex Version:

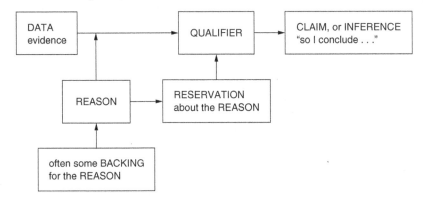

My data and *reason* are the same as in the simpler version.

My backing for the *reason* is contained in the following two examples: Queen Elizabeth is known to say, "The Queen is ready to dine." Evil Knievel once said in an interview, "Evil Knievel can jump that canyon—no problem."

My reservation is: But perhaps Sister Rebecca just wants readers to think she's a great person.

My qualifier, therefore, is: Sister Rebecca might in fact be humble, but so poor that she feels she needs to make herself seem great to attract customers.

So my modified claim now is: Sister Rebecca is egotistical, but perhaps she has to be egotistical to succeed in her line of work.

When you write with the care necessary to fill in all the boxes in this complex version of the Toulmin diagram, you are writing as responsibly as possible, using logos as convincingly as a writer can use it.

Whether we emphasize induction (using examples) or deduction (starting from a common assumption), or consciously employ both as above, we hope of course to influence our listeners, but we must remember that our conclusions are never going to be certain. "Proofs" are not possible in writing. We all know the vulnerability of inductive arguments. No matter how many examples we include, a counterexample can embarrass our argument. With deductive arguments, our assumptions are vulnerable. Advertisers can't prove that their products are best; similarly, we can't prove that our ideas or our proposals are best. Since *logos*, then, is always vulnerable, since it can't prove anything beyond a doubt, we see why there's plenty of room for the two other means of persuasion, *ethos* and *pathos*, to play significant roles when we try to persuade people.

Ethos

Ethos (the Greek word for "character") is our most powerful tool in writing. Every writer must employ logic, *logos*, before we'll trust him. But much of our trust comes not from a writer's logic but from other, less tangible qualities. Just as a musician wins a competition not only by playing the correct notes but by giving the musical phrasing "character," just as a salesclerk who is both knowledgeable and friendly earns more substantial commissions than one who is merely knowledgeable, so a writer with both a command of the material and a clear enjoyment of writing succeeds when a plodding writer doesn't.

A strong *ethos* does not come easily; you cannot fake an *ethos*. Every experience you seek out, everything you read, everything you write, every conversation you have, enriches the *ethos*, the voice, the character that is available to you when you write. You may do these things to enjoy yourself or perhaps to increase your ability to make friends and to find someone who'll want to spend a lifetime with you. But at the same time, through your experience, you are also building your writing *ethos*. If your *ethos* building succeeds, some letter you write when you are 24 may get you the job you want; some memo you write when you are 34 will get you a promotion; some report you write when you're 44 will make you a well-respected leader. But thousands of hours of curiosity, and learning, and conversation will go into building the phrase, the sentence, the tone that will later come naturally at a time when you'll need it. If you can come through in your writing as a person of intelligence, integrity, confidence, goodwill, and maybe even good humor, you have done everything that *ethos* is capable of.

Whenever we write, we reveal ourselves—our intelligence or lack of it, our care or lack of it, our honesty or lack of it. When we revise and look at the "character" that emerges in an early draft, we can make adjustments in the way we wish to present ourselves. But we can't, once we hand in a finished copy, avoid responsibility for the character that comes through. Building up a trustworthy *ethos*, a trustworthy writer's character, is the biggest challenge we face as writers.

Pathos

Pathos (often thought of simply as an appeal to the emotions) does not have a great reputation. We're glad to acknowledge that we respect writers who are logical and writers whom we can trust. But we don't like to admit that writers succeed by making emotional appeals to us. *Pathos*, though, is not simply the raising of violent emotions in a reader. A writer can make an emotional appeal to the audience's sense of integrity, as John Kennedy did with his famous sentence, "Ask not what your country can do for you; ask what you can do for your country." But a writer needn't even be that dramatic to make good use of *pathos*. If we can, through our writing, reduce our reader's irritation and increase our reader's pleasure, we have employed *pathos* effectively. By not writing down to a reader, we make the reader more comfortable. By acknowledging the reader's point of view, we make the reader more ready to listen to ours. By using standard grammar and punctuation, we allow the reader to enjoy reading the substance of what we have to say.

Self-Checklist: Ethos, Logos, Pathos

When you're looking over a draft, before you print it and turn it in, look back over the checklist that follows to make sure you've employed ethos, logos, and pathos as effectively as you can.

Self-Checklist: Ethos, Logos, Pathos

Ethos	Logos	Pathos
1. Do I sound intelligent?	1. Are the facts I've used well-chosen?	1. Have I made a skilled use of emotional appeal?
2. Interested in my subject?	2. Are my inferences justified by my facts?	2. Have I shown a concern for the needs of my reader?
3. Well-informed?	3. Are my assumptions justifiable?	3. Have I done as little as possible to distract or irritate my readers?
4. Fair-minded?	4. Is my paper well-organized?	
5. Trustworthy?	5. Is my purpose clear?	
6. Confident?		

Fallacies

While you try to use *ethos, logos,* and *pathos* in your own writing to make it effective, you should also become aware of the ways in which others, or you in your early drafts, misuse them. Misuses of *ethos, logos,* or *pathos* are called *fallacies* or *attempts to deceive,* although we usually commit fallacies without intending to do so. Some of the more common writers' fallacies are the following:

1. *Hasty generalization* (weak induction: not enough facts considered). *Example:* "I can't write. I got D's on my first two papers."
2. *The citing of illegitimate authorities* (devious induction: use of an authority's opinion as a fact to reinforce an inference you want to make, when that authority's qualifications for offering the opinion are suspect). *Example:* "Eli and Peyton Manning think this beer tastes great."
3. *Unstated assumptions* (devious deduction: not stating the first principles of your arguments). *Example:* "He'll never graduate. He's an athlete."
4. *Undefined key terms* (weak or devious deduction: carelessness about whether the audience really knows what you mean). *Example:* "He's more qualified than she is. We'll hire him."
5. *Inappropriate comparisons or analogies* (weak or devious deduction: unstated general principle is that the two items compared are essentially alike). *Example:* "Since Napoleon made France strong again by attacking Austria and Italy, we should make the United States strong again by attacking Canada."
6. *Unsubstantiated cause-effect claims* (weak or devious deduction: unstated general principle is that your cause caused your effect). *Example:* "The English are a morose people because their weather is so cloudy."
7. *A claim that there are only two choices* (weak or devious deduction: unstated general principle is that there are only two possibilities). *Example:* "Either fight terrorism wherever it rears its head, or live always in fear of a terrorist attack."

8. *Ignoring the point at issue* (absence of *logos:* not constructing arguments that are to the point). *Example* from a paper on nuclear power plant safety: "A hydrogen bomb could destroy half of Connecticut."
9. *The hurling of insults* (misuse of *pathos:* trying to get readers emotional about irrelevant matters). *Example:* "You can't trust a politician."
10. *Appeal to irrelevant emotions* (misuse of *pathos:* this one is often very difficult to decide). *Example:* "No one who loves children can fail to put $25 in an envelope and send it to P.O. Box 47, New York, New York."
11. *Exaggeration* (abuse of *ethos:* readers won't trust a writer who overstates). *Example:* " 'You can't judge a book by its cover' is probably the best statement ever."

These eleven fallacies are the most frequent of the many ways that you can annoy your reader or lose your reader's trust. Each fallacy can be attributed to a weakness in *ethos, logos,* or *pathos,* but ultimately, all weaken *ethos.* They all weaken the reader's trust in the writer, and thus they weaken also the reader's willingness to take the action that the writer was hoping for in writing.

Detecting Fallacies in Argument

Exercise 6-2
in class

Referring to the list of fallacies above if you need to, note what makes you uncomfortable about each of the following attempts to persuade.

1. I feel I can honestly say that motorcycles, in some instances, are safer than cars. How many motorcycle accidents have you heard of in which the driver went through the windshield or was speared by the steering column? In some motorcycle accidents the driver flies clear of the object he hit, as I did when I struck that woman's car.
2. Fidel Castro says that communism is the best form of government.
3. Birth control clinics are the cause of increased teenage sex.
4. If a thing can be produced without art or preparation, much more can it be produced with the help of art and care. (Aristotle)
5. If a thing is possible for inferior, weaker, less intelligent people, it is more so for people who are superior, stronger, and more intelligent. (Aristotle)
6. Buy Giant Panda hot dogs.
7. The virtues and corresponding works of a man are nobler than those of a woman. (Aristotle)
8. Those things are good which are one's own, possessed by no one else, and exceptional. (Aristotle)
9. It's time we take notice. The trend is now unmistakable. You need to understand *what it means!* Suddenly the United States no longer enjoys the highest per capita

income of any nation. Sweden has now risen above us. The United States' world's \|\
highest living standard has *started on the way down.*

10. Most of the advanced nations of the free world—many of which are critical of
America as supreme leader of the West—are suffering from faltering and divided \|
leadership, lack of purpose, and lack of will to act unitedly against onrushing crises.

Exercise 6-3
on your own

In order to ensure that you understand the ways in which you can easily offend,
try to write a brief letter of complaint about some aspect of your school services using
as many fallacies as possible. Your letter will be given to other members of the class and
rated according to how outrageous you've been able to make it.

All Writing Needs Effective Ethos, Logos, and Pathos

Ethos, logos, and *pathos* will be useful to you not just in overtly persuasive
writing. You can judge the quality of any piece of writing—whether a formal
speech by Barack Obama or a quick email from your mother—by evaluating
its *ethos, logos,* and *pathos.* But *ethos, logos,* and *pathos* are most useful as tools,
of course, when they are most necessary—that is, when your expected audience is indifferent or hostile, when you must fully employ all your writing resources.

Planning to use *ethos, logos,* and *pathos* impressively may seem, at this
point, to be a hopelessly complex task. But as you plan a persuasive paper,
you can generally reduce your concerns to three: (1) to collect all the information you can about the subject (the key aspect of *logos*); (2) to try to understand
as well as possible how your readers will respond emotionally to what you're
writing (the key aspect of *pathos*); and (3) to screw up the courage to write
with confidence (the key aspect of *ethos*).

First, information, not cleverness, is your best ally when you're writing.
(Information, you remember, includes not only facts, statistics, and examples
but the writer's own experience and the recorded opinions of authorities.) As
psychologist Carl Rogers has noted, readers have a natural tendency to judge
rather than to listen (284–89). We give our readers much less opportunity to
judge if we refrain from throwing about our own judgments while we stay for
a while with the facts. John McPhee, one of the most admired current writers
of nonfiction, has successfully argued for the preservation of several wilderness areas, including New Jersey's Pine Barrens, by writing articles that simply describe life as it is lived in those areas. When we fail to be specific,

readers with views opposite to ours usually stop listening, as when we assert, for example, that Bush had a better foreign policy than Obama, or that Obama has a better foreign policy than Bush. Specificity reduces the readers' opportunities to rush to judgment, thus allowing for some real communication, even if differences of opinion do continue to exist.

Second, to quote one of my students, "one cannot tell his reader that he is totally right and doesn't care how the reader feels." A reader whose beliefs or values are being threatened won't listen. *Learning to write is (far more than we might expect) learning to understand other people.* As John Stuart Mill paraphrases Aristotle, "He who knows only his side of the case, knows little of that" (36). Before you begin any argument of your own, try to write out a one-page argument from your reader's point of view. Then think in terms of values you might agree on. See whether you can find an assumption you share, as in the example of the uses of foreign language instruction a few pages back. What values make you most committed to your position? What values does your reader hold most strongly? Even if your reader agrees with you about the facts, he still needs nudging in your direction, usually because you are asking for some of his valuable money, or work, or time.

Third, most of us are timid about making judgments, and therefore we don't write much in the margins of our books, or say much in class, or spell out our views to our elected representatives in government or even to our friends. It takes some courage to speak out rather than to just acquiesce to the opinions and actions of others. In order to have courage to make judgments, we first need plenty of information. But then we also need the courage to risk displaying our judgments—in discriminating between good work and bad, the correct and the incorrect, the moral and the immoral. We're all very careful (and we should be) to substantiate our assertions, but we should also encourage ourselves to be willing to stick our necks out, to make assertions. One of your goals for this semester should be to become more assertive—not in the sense that you aggressively state opinions without any facts, but in the sense that when you've found enough facts, you feel confident in expressing your well-founded opinions.

7

Paragraphing, Introductions, and Conclusions

I don't like to stop to break things up into paragraphs unless I have to.

STUDENT

No one ever told me before that I could write the introduction last.

STUDENT

Paragraphing

A four-page paper, as you may well know from counting yourself, contains roughly 1000 words. A thousand words of chaos? Sometimes it seems so. We begin, of course, with an introduction and end with a conclusion, but what happens in between? The writer has given some organization to the 1000 words by ordering them into perhaps seventy-five or eighty sentences. But no writer could recall the seventy-five ordering decisions that went into arranging those sentences. Neither could a reader. However, if the piece is well organized, both writer and reader can spell out the ordering principles linking the paper's seven or eight paragraphs. Paragraphs are the clearest, most memorable means a writer has to show a reader the steps in his or her thinking.

Paragraphing is, in the long view of history, a fairly recent convention of written communication. Until the seventeenth century, paper was too expensive to allow for such waste of space. But since that time, periodic indenting has become a conventional way to avoid tiring the reader. Paragraphing is like punctuation in that it makes reading easier, though writers are freer to choose how they paragraph than how they punctuate. When we paragraph, we ask our readers to pause, take a half-second break, and think about all that's been said since we last indented before moving on. Paragraphing is much like picture taking. It's a way of selecting, focusing, emphasizing. Like a photograph, a paragraph can be comprehended at a glance. Like a photograph, it allows the artist to highlight. Like a photograph, it shouldn't be shown to anyone but a family member until it contains something worth thinking about.

The conventional definition of a paragraph is that it is a group of sentences expressing a single idea. But a single idea is open to considerable interpretation (many paragraphs can comfortably contain three or four ideas as long as their arrangement is systematic). The paragraphs that writing teachers like most, and that readers of all kinds find easy to follow, consist of an inference or two (the topic sentence or sentences) followed by several examples and occasional commentary from the writer. Here are two excellent examples from Paul Fussell's book on World War I, *The Great War and Modern Memory*. The first follows an assertion-with-examples pattern, describing a practice that would be unbelievable if Fussell didn't have the examples to back it up (27):

> One way [that the British had] of showing the sporting spirit was to kick a football toward the enemy lines while attacking. The feat was first performed by the 1st Battalion of the 18th London Regiment at Loos in 1915. It soon achieved the status of a conventional act of bravado and was ultimately exported far beyond the Western Front. Arthur ("Bosky") Borton, who took part in an attack on the Turkish lines near Beersheeba in November, 1917, proudly reported home: "One of the men had a football. How it came there goodness knows. Anyway we kicked off and rushed the first [Turkish] guns, dribbling the ball with us" (Slater 137). But the most famous football episode was Captain W. P. Nevill's achievement at the Somme attack. Captain Nevill, a company commander in the 8th East Surreys, bought four footballs, one for each platoon, during his last London leave before the attack. He offered a prize to the platoon which, at the jump-off, first kicked its football up to the German front line. Although J. R. Ackerley remembered Nevill as "the battalion buffoon" (57), he may have been shrewder than he looked; his little sporting contest did have the effect of persuading his men that the attack was going to be, as the staff had been insisting, a walkover. A survivor observing from a short distance away recalls zero hour: "As the gun-fire died away I saw an infantryman climb onto the parapet into No Man's Land, beckoning others to follow. As he did so he kicked off a football. A good kick. The ball rose and travelled well towards the German line. That seemed to be the signal to advance" (Middlebrook 124). Captain Nevill was killed instantly. Two of the footballs are preserved today in English museums.

You will have noticed that while Fussell was using an assertion-with-examples organization, he also built—painfully—to a climax.

Excerpts from pp. 27 & 43 from *Great War and Modern Memory* by Fussell P (1975). By permission of Oxford University Press, Inc.

The next example follows a comparison-contrast (with examples) pattern in order to contrast model trenches in a London park with the real World War I trenches in France and Belgium (Fussell 43):

> The trenches I have described are more or less ideal, although not so ideal as the famous exhibition trenches dug in Kensington Gardens for the edification of the home front. These were clean, dry, and well furnished, with straight sides and sandbags neatly aligned. R. E. Vernede writes his wife from the real trenches that a friend of his has just returned from viewing the set of ideal ones. He "found he had never seen anything at all like it before" (112). And Wilfred Owen calls the Kensington Gardens trenches "the laughing stock of the army" (429). Explaining military routines to civilian readers, Ian Hay labors to give the impression that the real trenches are identical to the exhibition ones and that they are properly described in the language of normal domesticity a bit archly deployed: "The firing-trench is our place of business—our office in the city, so to speak. The supporting trench is our suburban residence, whither the weary toiler may betake himself periodically (or, more correctly, in relays) for purposes of refreshment and repose" (97).
>
> The reality was different. The British trenches were wet, cold, smelly, and thoroughly squalid.

Note that neither of these two paragraphs stands on its own. Though each is internally well ordered, they beg to be linked with the paragraphs before and after them. Good paragraphs never stand alone comfortably. They are meant to lean on each other.

In my experience with student papers, the most common weaknesses in paragraphing are: (1) using a paragraph as a series of unsupported assertions, or (2) using paragraphs that are far too long or far too short. Long-paragraphers, by not making any decisions about linking, force their readers to organize the material themselves. Short-paragraphers are even harder on readers. Short paragraphs don't force a writer to do *any* linking, and thus that entire chore is left to the reader.

Over the years your teachers have probably asked you several questions about your paragraphs when they've commented on your papers. Their questions may have looked like the following:

1. What is the American Congress doing in the middle of a paragraph about France?
2. This seems to be a new idea. Why don't you begin a new paragraph?
3. Franklin's age certainly does not deserve a paragraph to itself.
4. One sentence doesn't make a paragraph. Doesn't this idea fit with the ideas above?
5. Does all this information belong together in the same paragraph?
6. This paragraph is very short. Can this information be combined with the information in some other paragraph?

We all know what to do, with a little thought, with comments like these. Most paragraphing errors stem from carelessness rather than ignorance. There are other basic guidelines about paragraphs, however, that you may not be aware of. What are those paragraphing basics?

1. If you write often enough, paragraphing will become intuitive for you. Until that time comes, most writers decide on their paragraphs in their outline or as they write their first draft. But it is not wrong, and it can often be fruitful, to "discover" paragraphs during revision rather than to compose them while drafting.

2. Your reader, in pausing briefly after each paragraph, naturally focuses most on the first and last sentences of paragraphs. These sentences (during revision) should not be wasted. They represent the writer's best opportunities for emphasis, and for clear transitions.

3. The first sentence of a paragraph, unless you're writing a narrative, should usually consist of a subthesis, a more accurate name than our usual "topic sentence," that suggests the direction of argument in your paragraph.

4. At least as important as the paragraphs themselves are the bridges between paragraphs, the transitions that link what we've just read to what the writer would like us to read next. A transition—often only a single word or a phrase—should be built into the first sentence of every paragraph. When not given a clear link, a reader will often quit rather than continue with any interest. That link is often made with a simple word or phrase—"more important," for example, or "equally helpful."

5. When most of your evidence consists of quotations, the usual pattern for a paragraph will be (a) begin with a subthesis with a transition, (b) offer background if that would be helpful, (c) introduce the first quotation you'll use as evidence, (d) quote, (e) cite correctly, (f) explain and analyze the significance of what you've quoted, (g) introduce another quotation you'll use as evidence, (h) quote, (i) cite correctly, (j) explain and analyze the significance of your second quotation, (k) repeat this pattern for a third quotation if you're using one, and (l) make any final comment you might have about the subject of this paragraph before moving on.

6. The best way, late in your drafting process, to see whether your work makes sense is to try to write a one-sentence-for-each-paragraph summary of what you've written. Your attempt to write such a summary will quickly expose any irregularities in organization.

With these six guidelines in mind, you shouldn't need any paragraph "rules." Your future supervisors or printers or editors, or even the size of the paper you use, will tell you how frequently you'll be expected to paragraph.

Because we can't write paragraphs following set forms, it helps to practice paragraphing techniques until we become confident that we can control their flexibility.

Writing a Paragraph Outline

Exercise 7-1
in class

Write a one-sentence-for-each-paragraph summary of "What Every Girl Should Know," by Robertson Davies, on p. 201. For each paragraph, state how that paragraph serves the writer's purpose in writing the essay. Your finished summary should tell you whether the piece makes sense, and so of course you can use this technique with your own work to see whether your own writing makes sense.

After completing your sentence-per-paragraph summary, you can take this technique for checking on the purposes of the parts of our writing to another level by choosing one of the paragraphs in Robertson Davies' essay and explaining, sentence by sentence, how each sentence relates to the summarizing idea you've given for the paragraph. This task may seem complex at first, but if you force yourself to think, and if you compare your answers with those of other class members, you'll learn a great deal about how sentences serve our paragraphs and how paragraphs help us structure our thinking.

Choosing, and Giving Reasons for, Paragraph Breaks

Exercise 7-2
in class

Newspapers and magazines are often more flexible than academic writing about paragraphing so you can see a greater variety of reasons for paragraphing by looking at newspaper articles. In order to test your assumptions about how paragraphs are formed, read through the following newspaper essay by Fred Reed and decide where you would begin paragraphs if you were the writer of this essay. The sentences have been numbered to make class discussion about your choices easier. The paragraph choices made by Mr. Reed are identified at the beginning of Chapter 14.

Lean, Healthy, and Forty-Five

Fred Reed

(1) The anti-jogging column threatens to become a mainstay of such literature as we have, perhaps replacing Watergate memoirs. (2) As I imagine it, the anti-jogging writer packs his slanderous tendencies into a briefcase and goes to a place where jogging is committed—a trail along the Potomac, say. (3) He waits. (4) A jogger thunders by in $65 waffle rubber shoes, $68 jogging suit of

parachute fabric crafted to reduce wind resistance, and Navajo jogger's sweatband. (5) He carries organic dextrose pellets and several pounds of electronics—an integrated-circuit wrist pedometer, a digital blood-pressure indicator and a solar-powered pulse-counter with built-in coronary alarm. (6) The well-equipped jogger has the circuitry of a small fighter plane. (7) He also has a certain amount of philosophical baggage. (8) He is jogging to find out Who He Is, information that he might have gotten from his wife or his driver's license. (9) He is Probing the Limits of Self. (10) The writer tries to make this sound ridiculous. (11) This is to misunderstand the jogger. (12) He is usually over 30, and has noticed that stairs are getting perceptibly steeper. (13) He is a bit disturbed by it, suspicious that something new has been slipped into the contract. (14) The moment of truth usually comes when he realizes they aren't really letting girls into college at age 14. (15) He looks uneasily around the office at men 10 years older. (16) They have smoker's cough, liver conditions, and look as though they are smuggling medicine balls. (17) In all important senses they are sessile. (18) At this point he acquires a deep desire to go white-water canoeing, to try rock-climbing or to go on a commando mission into Botswana. (19) By the end of the afternoon he is persuaded that he has only a few hours to live. (20) That evening he wheezes around the block while his wife shadows him in a rented ambulance. (21) There is something noble, tragic and silly in it. (22) The jogger lives for 30 years on a diet of lard and French fries, plugging up his arteries and taking years from his life. (23) Then he jogs to expand the arteries around the lard, getting the time back. (24) The anti-jogging writer sniggers at this inconsistency, as well as at the mystical hooha that surrounds jogging—the confusion of crumbling cartilage with enlightenment, the Oneness with Nature, and the High, which is in fact indistinguishable from the onset of flu. (25) The jogger tends to be a fiercely competitive fellow who is not about to be intimidated by God, metabolism, time and destiny. (26) He persists, that being what the fiercely competitive do best, and, lo, soon he is running five miles a day. (27) The American male believes that if a thing is worth doing, it is worth overdoing. (28) The children slowly forget him ("Ma, who *is* that guy . . . ?"). (29) His knees fill with bone fragments and his kidneys begin to loosen, so he buys shoes. (30) By now he has noticed that running is work. (31) The jogger tries to conceal this behind a fraudulent jauntiness—"Yes, ran 40 miles today, just didn't have time for a good workout. (32) Usually do it on one leg." (33) Yet it is most dreadful work. (34) Worse, it is boring. (35) The body really can be brutalized into condition, after which it will go on forever. (36) To have a reasonable expectation of cardiac arrest, one must run for hours. (37) The nirvana promised after Mile 5 doesn't materialize. (38) Stir-craziness comes. (39) He still doesn't know Who He Is. (40) Nobody but a thorough-going damned fool would suffer so much without an analgesic and a reward. (41) The analgesic is toys. (42) It is fun to get a new piece of running instrumentation—preferably with LEDs, the *sine qua non* of spiritual experience. (43) He may not go faster in his new, absurdly expensive, helium-filled shoes, but it is nice to unwrap them, like having an extra birthday. (44) The reward is showing off.┃(45) Face it: people get very little recognition in this anthill society. (46) It's a kick to be lean, healthy and 45, to be 11 miles into a run of 20, to be bounding along at an easy lope and sticking his chest out at the high school girls. (47) They never notice—they figure a fellow of 45 belongs in the Smithsonian—but there's hope that their mothers will come along. (48) And he feels so pleasantly superior to the majority, who would collapse at anything more arduous than relaxed breathing—among whom one inevitably finds, *hey hey*, the authors of anti-jogging columns.

Once you've made your decisions, defend them—first in a small group, then with the whole class. There will probably be much disagreement. The important thing, though, is that you can explain *why* you thought each paragraph division should be made. Your reasons for paragraphing, taken together with the reasons given by the rest of the class, should give you a good idea of how paragraphs are formed. People choose to paragraph for reasons as various as content, length, emphasis, and tone. At least one new reason comes up each time a class tries this exercise.

You may want to repeat this same exercise using papers from other students in your class. Be sure, whenever you do this kind of exercise, to specify *why* you would begin a new paragraph in each place you have chosen, for it is in deciding *why* that you train yourself as a paragrapher of your own essays.

Coherence

Many of us are afraid that our writing within paragraphs isn't smooth enough, but we're not quite sure what *smooth* means. Clear signposts help, as in the following example (Kolb 16):

The attorneys state that the defendant acquired additional property after the divorce hearing, and that he left a will. They further state that the court's ruling on the present motion will have a substantial effect upon the property rights of the plaintiff and the defendant's heirs. If the divorce decree is not entered, the plaintiff would take the real property as tenant by the entirety, would have widow's rights in the after acquired property, and could dissent from the will. *On the other hand,* if the divorce decree is entered nunc pro tunc, the plaintiff could have a one-half undivided interest in the real property as a tenant in common, would have no interest in the after acquired property, and could not affect the will.

Two questions are involved. First, can a successor judge enter a nunc pro tunc decree involving the action of a predecessor judge? Second, is this a proper case for the entry of a nunc pro tunc decree? The answer to both questions is yes.

From *A Writer's Guide* by Harold Kolb.

The writer above used signposts ("Two questions . . . First . . . Second . . ."), clear contrasts ("If . . . *On the other hand*, if . . ."), and parallel structure ("would take . . . would have . . . could dissent . . .") to make his work smooth. These subtle signposts do wonders for your clarity.

To see in greater detail how we most naturally connect our work, try the following exercise.

Exercise 7-3

in class

Here is a set of data based on an article in the business section of a newspaper (Ross 5). The data, though raw, is complete and is in about the right order. Shape it into a piece of efficient prose, using whatever connecting words you need and paragraphing wherever you wish. Later we will compare your result with the results of others in the class and with the original, which you'll find at the beginning of Chapter 14.

past decade—supermarket chains deserting inner cities in alarming numbers—residents with no cars few or no alternatives to expensive convenience stores—number in Boston, Washington, and Chicago urban areas declined 28–50% in past five years—Community Nutrition Institute—new manual—how inner cities can maintain or bring back food markets—six case studies—including Santoni's Market in southeast Baltimore—offers practical guide—establishing food co-ops, farmers' markets—independently operated supermarkets—hints—limiting food assortment to 1000 or so staple items—selling products that cater to neighborhood needs—Do food-stamp users need appliance and camera equipment counters?—Sunday hours—wine and beer sales—minibus transportation—child-care centers—urge community to lobby local government—get a low-cost lease on adjacent city-owned property—use as parking lot—resurface sidewalks—high-powered street lights—available Community Nutrition Institute—Washington, D.C.

When you finish your smooth version, circle *every* word that you've added or altered. A comparison of the choices you've made could take an entire class period. You have hundreds of options to choose from as you link, but my guess is that you'll find that:

1. Your most effective link is repetition of a term or the use of a pronoun to replace that term.
2. When you do use connective words, your best choices are simple words like *and, but, or,* and *so.*
3. Parallel structure (*"limiting* food assortment . . . ," *"selling* products . . . ," *"avoiding* appliance counters . . . ," *"providing* minibus transportation") is one of your most useful linking devices.
4. Only occasionally do you need blockbuster connectors like *moreover* or *nevertheless.*

Having completed the exercises in this portion of the chapter, you should now be more conscious of the writer's techniques—paragraph choices, choices of linking words, and choices of tone of voice—that hold writing together and make it sound "smooth and coherent." Since it is during revising that we make most of our decisions about how to ease our readers' passage through our writing, Chapter 8, "Revision," will include further advice about those decisions.

Introductions

Just as you guide the reader throughout the body of your paper using paragraphs, coherence, and transitions, you guide the reader at the beginning and at the end of your work with your introduction and your conclusion.

Exercise 7-4   Review

on your own

Before you read what I have to say about your introductions and conclusions, write in your notebook your current thinking about them:

1. What do you try to do in an introduction?
2. What do you try to do in a conclusion?

Students often like to begin a paper by leaning on the dictionary:

Webster's defines "health" as "the general condition of the body and mind with reference to soundness and vigor."

Another often favored opening is to introduce your credentials:

This 500-word essay which I am about to start is based on my knowledge of and experience in high school and college.

Is that too obvious? Too dull? Perhaps you're tempted to begin by philosophizing:

For everything in life we all have two choices. As we have two sides to every coin, we have two sides like positive or negative, win or lose, profit or waste. Ohio State has made my life different than I had thought it would.

Is your reader following your reverie? Perhaps not. A fourth alternative is just to "sort of start writing," as the student who wrote the following did:

On July 23, 2006, I was dropped off on a desert island. I was permitted to take three things along with me. The first thing I took was a knapsack full of government books. This would enable me to keep up with my studies in school. The next product I took along. . . .

There are better ways to begin than any of these four. In writing an introduction, the bottom line is that you'll come up with something appropriate to say if you ask yourself two questions:

1. What do my readers need to know to understand what I want to say?
2. How can I interest my readers in what I want to say?

Something will click. Most students are instinctively skilled at getting a paper rolling. Because we've read so many introductions, we develop an intuitive sense of what might work. Whatever you decide to write after thinking about these two questions, link that material to a thesis sentence or sentences that will conclude your introductory paragraph. If you can manage that, your paper will be off to an excellent start.

Critical Reading of Introductions and Conclusions

Exercise 7-5

You can learn to write better introductions and conclusions by collecting some from various media to see how professionals go about that part of their business. Bring to class on a given day three or four of the following:

1. a textbook from another class
2. a newspaper
3. a popular magazine
4. a work of fiction
5. a how-to manual
6. a cookbook
7. a piece of junk mail

Your teacher might add to this collection a scholarly journal and a nonfiction film.

Take all or part of class to view and read to each other the introductions and conclusions from these various media. Comment on the means used by each to hook readers in, and to let them go thoughtfully.

Conclusions

Students usually write intriguing and effective introductions. Conclusions are another matter. Writer after writer resorts to a summary of exactly what he's said in the paper (as if the reader couldn't remember) or perhaps to a grand comment about how understanding the issue treated in this paper may save the world. There is plenty of fertile ground between those two extremes, though too rarely does anyone occupy it.

When you reach the point in your essay where you're ready to conclude, lift your hands from the keyboard. Ask yourself, *so what?* Why have I bothered to write this paper? Before plunging right back in with an answer, write out some notes. Answer the *so what* question in several different ways. Then *select* the answer that is most promising and draft your conclusion. Simply because you've taken time to select the best at this point where most writers have allowed themselves to stop thinking and sail to the end, you'll impress your teacher and your other readers with your results.

Final Thoughts

Your own practice with introductions and conclusions will help you most in learning to write them, of course. So take advantage, during this class, of your opportunities to have your introductions and conclusions read by others and to learn from reading theirs.

Introductions and conclusions, far more than any other aspects of a paper, test the writer's skill in understanding others. In an introduction you must bridge the gap between yourself and your readers. Because "shared context builds up between writer and reader as the piece proceeds, . . . the chances of losing, confusing, misleading, or frustrating a reader are at their greatest in the opening sentences" (Britton 21). Whether you raise an issue in your introduction, or provide background information, or both, before stating your thesis, your reader should know by the end of your first paragraph *why* you took the trouble to write this paper. An introduction has done its work if it shows that you respect your reader and that you know what you want to talk about. A conclusion has done its work if it shows that you know—and care about—the significance of what you've written.

8

Revision

Editing—which can be described very simply as the assembling and joining of selected pieces of film—is regarded by many directors as the creative peak of the entire film-making process, the preliminary shooting being largely a matter of collecting together the necessary materials to be assembled into a coherent whole.

IVAN BUTLER

Writing is committed speech—speech we are willing to polish, fix, and vouch for.

DENNIS DRABELLE

The rate at which one recognizes his own badness is the rate at which he grows as a writer.

JOHN CIARDI

Now I see for the first time that discarded writing is not wasted effort.

STUDENT

Giving Yourself the Power of Two

Reviewing and revising what we've written, when we already have enough words on paper to fulfill an assignment, requires more effort and more patience than most of us are willing to give unless we're forced to. Yet this book attempts to force you to do just that—to make reviewing and revising your work a routine—because the practice you get in revising while you're in school will save you countless hours and serious frustration when you've left school and revision becomes necessary for your success and your livelihood.

Exercise 8-1   Review of Your Current Practice
on your own

How much revising do you do when you write papers or lab reports for school? What kinds of changes do you make?

Any piece of writing that you write in one session at your desk or computer is the product of one person. A piece that you write—and then consciously revise—becomes the work of two people, and it's often twice as good. During a first draft, a "discovery" draft, we are most curious to find out how much we have to say on the issue we've chosen to work with. We revise a bit during this draft as we change major ideas to minor ones, reorder our paragraphs, and occasionally change sentences, phrases, and words if they don't sound the way we want to sound or don't say what we want to say. But most successful writers take special pains during their first draft to ignore back-of-their-mind questions about words or sentences or even whole sections, special pains to suppress the reviser in them so that they can concentrate on finding the most interesting and appropriate facts and on interpreting those facts thoughtfully. But then as a deadline approaches, because they want to get their message across as clearly as possible and because they want to avoid embarrassment, they get very careful (even ruthless) not only about their facts, their inferences, and their introductions and conclusions, but about their sentences and even their words.

It has become common recently among politicians to try to take their words back by saying that they "misspoke." But I haven't yet heard any writers excuse themselves by saying that they "miswrote." We can't take our writing back. Filmmakers, who know they can't take their films back ("I misfilmed"?), routinely spend six months editing until they have revised a film into the precise form that they want it to take. Of course, the filmmaker is hoping to make $20 million on a film, and you're only trying to please yourself, some of your classmates, and your teacher, so you may (understandably) decide to give less than six months to the task.

Revising, like the other aspects of writing, is a skill that improves with practice. At first, you'll probably feel awkward and unworthy of making judgments. If you're like most of us, you'll start by criticizing surface problems, like short, choppy sentences:

> This is a real story. It happened six years ago. I had a very close circle of friends. One day somebody proposed to climb a mountain. Actually a volcano. I was sure I was going to get lost. It was a terrible day and night for me.

Or an awkward repetition of words:

> When junior high school *started*, I *started* getting my first taste of real discipline.

Or poor grammar, word choice, or spelling:

Santity depends mainly on the way one *discipline* himself.
I could *dare* his bet.

These things do matter, but it takes practice to break away from judging words, which is comparatively easy, and to start to judge the thought that went into your paper. Revision is not just changing a few words and fixing some punctuation, but looking back (*re-vision*) and making substantial changes in what we've thought or written. Learning to see the whole picture of what you are trying to say is one of the most difficult habits that you'll try to acquire during this course.

Student writers have a history of revising very little. Our habit of starting our papers just before they're due often leaves too little time for revision. But even when we have the time, we often change very little: (1) because it's too much trouble to make changes, since a substantial change in one part of

precise form that they want it to take.

Of course, the filmmaker is hoping to make $20 million on a film, and you're only trying to please yourself, some of your classmates, and your teacher, so you may (understandably) decide to give less than six months to the task.

draft stage and is ready for full-time

Add the section I now have later in the chapter on "revising improves with practice."

has reached the clean-
By the time a paper ~~is ready for~~ revision, the writer is not always the

critical reading necessary to decide
best person to do the ~~pruning. An opinion~~ *what should stay, what should go, and what should*
~~of a potential reader—class-mate—~~ *or* teacher, *be added.*

Also add the two paragraphs I wrote up for the department handout on the Garrison method of drawing a line down the middle of the page.

or friend—is fresher and will often help *The reading of a classmate,* more because that reader has not become fond of ideas or phrases, as the writer has. In this chapter, I will call this collaborator, this reader, your reviewer.

Explain this in practical detail. What kinds of people serve as "reviewers"? What do they do?

the paper often requires changes elsewhere, (2) because it's hard to see both our draft and our ideas for changes at the same time, and (3) because even when we read over our work and are puzzled by a sentence or a paragraph, rather than change it, we complacently decide that we must have had a reason for writing it that way the first time.

These excuses must be attacked head on. First, it's not difficult to allow time for revision. If we believe in its value, we will make time for it. Second, we're fools if we wholly trust the self that wrote our first draft, figuring "we must have had a reason." At this point we need some help from a person who is less uncritically fond of our work than we are. Third, we need a visual strategy for making legible revisions. To become good revisers most people need to print out their drafts, hand write changes and ideas for changes (see the example on the previous page), and then return to the draft on the computer.

By the time a paper has reached the clean-draft stage and is ready for full-time revision, the writer is not the best person to do the critical reading necessary to decide what should stay, what should go, and what should be added. The reading of a classmate, teacher, or friend is fresher and will often help more because that reader has not become fond of ideas or phrases, as the writer has. These reviewers are trying not just to "fix" your work, but to help you say best what you are trying to say. Some of their comments hurt when you first read them, but all the comments, particularly those that hurt, help you to improve the final draft.

In this class, you will probably be given the opportunity to review the work of your classmates, in the process not only helping them see those particular papers more clearly, but training you both in the skills of revising. Following is a list of the broad questions that should be asked of any paper:

Draft Review Checklist

1. Is there enough fresh information here to make you glad you read this paper? What kinds of facts do you feel are missing? What further research do you think the writer should do?
2. Does the writer seem to have a genuine interest in the subject and a good grasp of the information connected with it?
3. What are the most important assertions, or inferences, that the writer has made about the subject of this paper? Which inferences need to be made clearer or more specific?
4. What does the writer attempt to do in the introduction to the paper? Does the introduction provide the background you need to understand the analysis that follows?
5. Describe the writer's organizational strategy paragraph by paragraph. Which paragraphs don't proceed smoothly from the paragraph they follow? Note every point in the paper where you were temporarily confused.

6. Read over the concluding paragraph. What emotion does the writer try to leave you with? Can you make any suggestions for improving the conclusion?
7. What are two possible objections, or alternatives to the writer's point of view, that you think the writer has naively neglected so far?
8. What thoughts or questions occurred to you as you read through this paper?
9. After reading this paper, what would you, as a thoughtful reader, now want to say about this subject? How has reading this paper affected your attitude toward the subject discussed?

Of course, the author of a paper is not bound to take all the advice that you give in answering these questions, nor are you bound to take all the advice that you get from others. *You* are responsible for your final decisions, and you may have reasons for disagreeing with some of the advice that you get. But even if you disagree, the comments from your reviewers will aid you in rethinking your paper, which is the purpose of revision. And ultimately, the goal of all this reading and rereading is not only to give you sources of advice but to make you a better reviewer of your own work—now, later in college, and as you write in your profession. Having become someone else's reviewer, someone else's reader, you should now be more fully ready to become your own.

Self-Critique

Exercise 8-2
in class

You may have thought when you printed your paper last night that you were printing a "final draft." But no draft is ever final. A draft that we hand in is only a "deadline draft." We can't keep our work forever; a deadline forces us to quit. But that doesn't mean we could not have done better.

This time you're going to get one more chance not only to proofread but also to revise so that we can compare notes on what late-in-the-process revisions people make.

First, take ten minutes just to proofread your paper, that is, to check for typing errors, spelling errors, and obvious errors in punctuation. When you finish, compare notes with the class on what you've changed. Check whether your habits are similar to those of your classmates. Which of you has the best strategy?

Next, take ten minutes to revise any parts of your paper you can without making major rearrangements (if a major rearrangement might be desirable, you can make a note to that effect at the end of your paper). Again, when you've finished, discuss with the class the kinds of changes you've made, and listen carefully to the kinds your classmates made.

Finally (even if there has not been enough time to complete the steps above), answer briefly in writing the following questions:

1. What have you learned about research from writing this paper?
2. What have you learned about writing from writing this paper?

3. If you were to start work over on this paper, what would you do differently? And finally,
4. I am satisfied/dissatisfied with this paper because . . .

Revision Checklist

When we revise, we attend not only to the major issues—adequacy of facts, thoughtfulness of inferences, clarity of organization, helpfulness of the introduction and conclusion—mentioned in the checklist above, but also to many "smaller" points that help us cleanse and clarify our work, often improving it from satisfactory to solid or from solid to excellent. The fifteen items listed below (roughly in order of importance) are items that you'll want to check each time you revise. You needn't consciously think about them every time, but many of them should become part of your intuitive revising process.

1. **Make reading as easy as possible for your reader by organizing your work clearly.**
   - Check that your introduction makes clear your sense of direction and that your conclusion answers the question "So what?"
   - Check your organization by doing a one-sentence-per-paragraph outline of your paper to see whether it reads systematically.
   - Check the opening sentences in your paragraphs. Not all paragraphs need topic (subthesis) sentences, but the first sentence should at least suggest the paragraph's direction of movement.

The movement of ideas (inferences) in any essay should be roughly clear from the way the paragraphs begin. Here are the extremely uninformative, and undisciplined, opening words of the paragraphs in an essay I received recently:

> The first item in . . . that struck me was . . .
> The following ad read as follows . . .
> I also enjoyed . . .
> I found it quite interesting how . . .
> The most interesting content in . . . to me was . . .
> The last items I have chosen to deal with are . . .
> I would like to say that viewing these newspapers was a good experience for me.

But was it a good experience for the reader?

   - Give your reader the *results* of your research, *not a record* of it. Take out references to what you are doing. Just do it. Skip words like those italicized below:

> There is a distinct difference between "professional" and "amateur." *First of all, I will give you my definitions for "professional" and "amateur."* A professional is a person who . . .

I'm reporting on a movie that real movie hawks will enjoy the technical effects of.

The best inference I can think of is that Baton Rouge parents care about their children.

▪ Check that you've used all your inferences to make worthwhile comments. Don't waste your reader's time or lose your reader's respect with inferences like that italicized below:

Forty-five percent of the voters polled felt that the worst possible punishment for a crime is the death penalty. Fifty-five percent felt that a life sentence without parole is an even worse punishment than death. *These opinions vary to some extent.*

▪ Read through your draft to make sure that it reads "smoothly."

Confused	**Clear**
The Red Army then looted bicycles, telephones, washbasins, light switches, door locks, in an attempt to bankrupt the Germans.	The Red Army then looted bicycles, telephones, washbasins, *and even* light switches and door locks in an attempt to bankrupt the Germans.
After the end of the war the Soviets printed marks by the billion, creating an economic nightmare.	After the end of the war the Soviets printed marks by the billion, creating an economic nightmare *in Germany.*

▪ Parallel structure makes any similar set of ideas easier for a reader to comprehend.

Confused	**Clear**
Keith, my nephew, was only 13, skied like he was born on the slopes, fast, fluid, and he never fell.	Keith, my 13-year-old nephew, skied as if he was born on the slopes—*he* was fast, *he* was fluid, *and he* never fell.
The happiest moments in my life were getting married and having two kids, then see my two kids graduate from high school and college.	The happiest moments in my life were getting married, having two kids, and seeing my two kids graduate from high school and college.

▪ Make sure you've made your transitions in thought clear to your reader—often a simple "but" or "though" can help signal a contrast and make reading your work easier.

Confused	**Clear**
Before the strike had started, many industries had begun stockpiling steel. By the end of October 1959, those stockpiles had been almost completely used up.	Before the strike had started, many industries had begun stockpiling steel. By the end of October 1959, *though,* those stockpiles had been almost completely used up.

2. **Identify for your reader the people, terms, and times that you want to talk about.**

■ Don't leave your reader stranded in time or space. Specify, near the beginning of your work, where and when the events you are talking about took place.

Confused	**Clear**
John Llewellen Lewis dominated the United Mine Workers for half the union's life.	John L. Lewis, *an Iowa and Illinois miner,* dominated the United Mine Workers *from 1933 to 1960,* more than half the union's life.

■ Identify any wars or speeches or documents or organizations you refer to.

Confused	**Clear**
Chiang Kai-shek led the Kuomintang.	Chiang Kai-shek led the Kuomintang, *a party founded by Dr. Sun Yat-sen in 1911 and challenged by the Communist party only after 1930.*

■ Define terms that the reader may be unfamiliar with.

Confused	**Clear**
Dr. Sun's party didn't appeal to Chinese peasants because most of his lieutenants were from Canton.	Dr. Sun's party didn't appeal to Chinese peasants because most of his lieutenants were from Canton, *a rich coastal province with several large cities.*

■ Don't define terms that readers can be expected to understand. There is no need, for example, in an article for adults about birth control practices, to stop and define *conception.*

■ Use a person's name the first time you refer to him or her in any paragraph. After that, you can switch to a short form of the name or to *he* or *she.*

Confused	**Clear**
In 1966, *he* gained new popularity in *his* party, and *he* entered the bid for the 1968 presidential nomination. To alter *his* reputation as a political loser, *Nixon* countered with a strategy aimed at settling the nomination in a series of presidential primaries. *He* won the first victory in New Hampshire easily. After *Nixon* had won most of the primaries, Governors Nelson Rockefeller of	In 1966, *Nixon* gained new popularity in *his* party, and *he* entered the bid for the 1968 presidential nomination. To alter *his* reputation as a political loser, *he* countered with a strategy aimed at settling the nomination in a series of presidential primaries. *He* won the first victory in New Hampshire easily. After *he* had won most of the primaries, Governors Nelson Rockefeller of New York

New York and Ronald Reagan of   and Ronald Reagan of California
California entered the contest,   entered the contest, but it was
but it was too late.   too late.

3. **Be as specific as you can whenever you can.**

■ Don't leave details to the readers' imaginations.

When stopped at the light at the intersection of Quesada and Dodge Streets, a driver could see *all kinds of interesting things going on* through the open windows of the hotel.

Often in revision you'll see that you need more details. You may have written an error-free paper, but you may not have given us a clear picture of your subject.

■ Even when you're generalizing, make sure your statements are specific enough to be comprehensible.

It's funny how many different kinds of things there are of one thing.
Keats achieves *this* by *organizing the subject matter in a certain order* and *comparing it with something else.*
Working at the Jersey City Medical Center *was certainly an experience in itself.*

More thought is all that's necessary to make these phrases more specific. Many writers, for example, have a fondness for unfocused words like the pronoun *this* or the noun *thing*:

The thing of it is, if you're onto a thing, it becomes a priority.

When you're tempted to use the word *thing*, remember the following advice:

The Thing was a movie made in the 1950s, starring James Arness as a monster with the cellular structure of a giant carrot. Only use the word *thing* to refer to the carrot or to the movie (in which case it is capitalized and italicized). If you use the word *thing* in your papers, your teacher will substitute the word *carrot*. If the sentence then makes sense, you are correct (King).

■ Make your verbs as specific as you can. There are quite a few "easy" verbs in English—*go, make, have, do*, for example—that don't tax the writer's mind when they're used and that don't, therefore, engage the reader's mind. When you search for a stronger verb, you're in fact searching for a more specific verb.

books we *did* in class
books we *read* in class (*more specific*)
books we *studied* in class (*still more specific*)

■ Learn the names for items you want to talk about. If you start talking to me about "the object blocking the tube when the tube was shaken" and you're really talking about a *cork*, I'm going to lose interest in the way you write. We all should be working constantly to expand our vocabularies, not so much to SAT words like *ineffable* and *callow* as to the names of everyday objects. Do you know what a mullion is, or a sill, a baseboard, a wainscot, or a socket? Do you know that a leather hat with a "thing sticking out" is a leather hat with a *visor*? Do you know the difference between asphalt tile and cedar shingles? between macadam and an oiled road? between elms and oaks and hickories?

■ Not all specifics are interesting. Details from which no useful or appropriate inferences can be drawn lie heavy on the page if they appear in too much abundance.

> The scoreboard can also be seen from any part of the field and keeps the time, the score, the down, the quarter, timeouts, the number of yards to go, and what yard the ball is on.

These are boring, not telling, facts. The reader asks, "So what?" But because our tendency to generalize is so strong, it is rare that we make the mistake of offering too many details rather than too few.

4. **"Tighten" your writing until only the important words, phrases, and sentences remain.**

Loose	**Tight**
There is a certain unfairness in that.	That's unfair.
A waiter can tell by the customers' actions and body language that they are impatient.	A waiter can tell by the customers' body language that they are impatient.

Every word, phrase, and sentence must earn its place, usually with the meaning it adds, but sometimes also by how it helps emphasis, rhythm, or grace. One way to get yourself to be more careful when you revise is to force yourself to reduce your draft by 10%, or 20%, or some other arbitrary figure (*this doesn't mean cutting out telling details*). Often your boss or your editor will do this cutting for you. It's excellent discipline, and it will lead you to making many qualitative, not just quantitative, decisions.

The following is an excellent exercise in tightening, adapted from Ken Macrorie's *Telling Writing* (60).

Tightening

Exercise 8-3
In class

Strengthen the following paragraph by cutting it in half. You may rearrange the ideas if you wish. Think about what might make a good beginning and what might provide a sense of closure for the conclusion.

~~Hands, did you ever notice how many different kinds of hands there are? I first began to notice hands when I found that~~ all men's hands were not as large as my Dad's ~~hands.~~ They were large, strong, and forceful, yet ~~always~~ gentle like ~~the man.~~ *h.'ω* ~~His hand encompasses mine even now when he takes it gently yet firmly,~~ as ~~though providing it with a cover of protection against the outside world.~~ But he has always been like that, ~~strong and protective, yet gentle.~~ When those hands hold a baby, the baby stops crying ~~and is quiet as though calmed by their strength and gentleness.~~ When those hands take a pencil and draw an idea, the lines are firm and confident. Other men ~~seem to~~ respond when they shake his hand to the friendliness and strength behind the handshake.

You see when you attempt this exercise that you've been forced not only to omit words but to rethink organization, to consider using parallel structure, and to decide what you most want to say. Tightening shows respect for the meaning of words and respect for our readers' time. It also helps us to specify, without unnecessary noise, the essence of what we want to say. Tightening teaches us one of the most useful writing skills: being selective—giving the reader not our all, but our best.

5. **Don't let yourself be satisfied with words that are only *close* to the meaning you want.**

   ▪ Check the meanings of words you're not quite sure of.

   > Ms. Winston is not sparing in the use of *acrimonious vituperations* against certain mental health practitioners; and in her case, this is *justifiably understandable*.

The writer here, in an attempt to impress the reader with multisyllabic words, has achieved the reverse. How are *vituperations* different when they are *acrimonious*? Not at all. What does *understandable* gain by being modified by *justifiably*? Nothing. The writer isn't trusting the meaning of her words. Losing *acrimonious* and *justifiably* improves the strength of the words that remain.

   One of the most common carelessly used words is *revolve*, which must sound impressive to us, because it doesn't mean much and yet it is used frequently:

   > This essay will *revolve around* answering the question of whether studying at the University of Texas has been a positive or negative experience for me.

   > The world *revolves around* the word *survival*.

What are these writers trying to say? What do the words say? If you catch yourself using larger words than you want, you can use a thesaurus to find simpler words. You could change, for example, *approximately* to *roughly*. If you do use simpler words, your writing may achieve the same virtue that the Canon 35-mm camera claims to have: "it's so advanced, it's simple."

- Remember that words have not only their strict meaning (called the *denotative* meaning) but also emotional colorations (called their *connotative* meanings). Even the names of cities—Paris, New York, Montreal, Liverpool, Las Vegas—call up emotions at the same time that they specify a place. We rarely make mistakes in connotation. We all know the difference in connotation, for example, between *cheap* and *inexpensive*. We all know the difference between *crafty* and *intelligent*. What we need to pay attention to during revision, though, is whether a word for which we have one connotation might have another connotation for our reader. I might think that *intellectual* has positive connotations, but some people don't, so I may well, in revision, when talking about my reader's favorite president, substitute *intelligent* for *intellectual*.

  Making such a change is attending carefully to the *pathos* I'm using to persuade my reader.

- Finally, look for differences between spoken English and written English as you review your final draft. *Really* should always be replaced. *Got* is often suspect. Even *this* must sometimes be questioned. When we're telling a story orally, we frequently use the expression, "We went down *this* road for miles." *This* is pointing to a specific road in the speaker's mind, but to a reader *this road* is only *a* road. The correct form in writing, unless the road has already been identified, is *a road*.

6. **Check your punctuation.**

   The most common punctuation error is to use a comma rather than a period between two complete sentences.

   Wrong: I have learnt English for more than six years, it seems like a long time.

   Wrong: Speaking and listening is so easy for me, I am still wondering why I cannot do writing as well as speaking and listening.

   - Review the rules for using commas and semicolons with dependent and independent clauses - IC;IC ~ DC,IC ~ and IC$_o$DC - in Chapter 9.

   Check that you have followed them in your paper.

   The second most common punctuation error is to punctuate a partial sentence, or sentence fragment, as if it were a complete sentence.

   Wrong: After one semester in high school.
   Wrong: Chu Zhang not being with me.

   - If you have trouble writing complete sentences, read through your paper backward, sentence by sentence. When you read backward, you're less likely to miss fragments that don't sound too bad when they follow a good sentence in normal order.

7. **Make revisions on the basis of your understanding of how English grammar can best serve your meaning.**

   ▓ Check whether you've accidentally switched back and forth in your verb tenses (between present and past, for example) without any desire to change the time that you are referring to.

   ▓ Strike out adjectives and adverbs that steal impact from your nouns and verbs.

   Many questions ~~still~~ remain unanswered.

   ▓ Often you can strengthen your prose by making the subject you're writing about the grammatical subject of your sentence.

Foggy	**Clear**
To relieve academic pressures and personal problems one may encounter was another purpose of the Nyumburu Center being formulated.	*The Nyumburu Center* was established to help students relieve academic pressures and talk through personal problems.

   ▓ Likewise, it often helps to make your verb active when you're describing an action.

Foggy	**Clear**
The pleasures of canoeing *were described* by John McPhee.	John McPhee *described* the pleasures of canoeing.

   ▓ Check that your verbs match the number (singular or plural) of their subjects, even when a prepositional phrase has intervened.

   The *success* of my plans *depends* on you.

   ▓ Check that each pronoun you use refers directly to some noun that appears before it (a writer often doesn't notice whether pronouns agree with their antecedents until looking back over her paper).

Foggy	**Clear**
He may use whatever *methods* he wants as long as *it* is effective.	He may use whatever *methods* he wants as long as *they* are effective.

8. **Listen to the sounds of our language.**

   ▓ Note the meaningless repetition of sounds.

   His *marks* improved *markedly.*

Many people are bothered by the repetition of sounds when they read through their own writing. Are there good reasons to avoid repeating a word or a sound? There are. A similar sound makes it seem to readers, if only for a moment, that they have come across a similar meaning. Then, as in the example above, if the meaning is not similar, they have to sort out both meanings, and this takes time, if only a moment. But repetition of sounds is not necessarily an evil. Often, not only is it not awkward, but it serves your purpose.

The best guide to repetition is the end of Lincoln's Gettysburg Address (Macrorie 27):

> government of the *people*
>   by the *people*
>   and for the *people*
>   shall not perish from the earth

Lincoln chose to repeat *people*, his main idea. We'd think he was too much concerned with his own role as President if he had said:

> *government* of
> *government* by
> and *government* for
>   the people shall not perish from the earth

If repetition is justified by your ideas, by all means use it. If it is only confusing, rethink your expression. Above all, don't make matters worse by going to a thesaurus for synonyms. Don't, in a paper about the actor Errol Flynn, call him Don Juan, then Casanova, then Romeo, then "the deceiver," then "Mr. Insatiable." Such "elegant variation" doesn't fool anybody. In fact, it calls more attention to the fact that you're uncomfortable about repeating. Instead of looking for an alternative term, what we should do is examine our thinking that has led to so much repetition. If we're repeating a reference to a person and that person is the subject of our paper, we should expect to be making repeated references to that person. If we're repeating an idea and the idea is worth repeating, it should stay in. If it is not worth repeating, perhaps some large-scale revision is needed.

9. **Check to see that you've placed your emphasis where you want it.**

   ■ The principal place of emphasis is the end—the end of a sentence, the end of a paragraph, the end of a paper. When we read a poor ending, we have a strong sense of anticlimax:

   > The audience of the eighteenth-century *Gentleman's Magazine* was intelligent gentry and merchants, although there were some exceptions.

The reason why a thesis seems to fit so well at the end of the first paragraph of a paper is that the end of a paragraph is an obvious point of emphasis. If you'd written the following introductory paragraph, you'd probably want to revise it because it ends on a quite unimportant note.

> *Vietnam Tien-Phong*, a very popular magazine back in my country, has continued its progress after 1975 in America and it has become the most sought-after bi-

weekly magazine in the Viet community everywhere in the world. The reporters and editors serve the Vietnamese well with serious political views as well as with entertainment like novels, anecdotes, and jokes. The reporters work very hard. The magazine starts with a full-page resume of the world's events.

Sentences have the same emphasis pattern as paragraphs. Linguists have recently—and tentatively—suggested that the easiest sentence pattern for a reader to follow is this one: given information first, new information last. Thus a skilled writer begins a sentence with a word or a phrase already familiar to the reader and then continues by adding something new about the subject:

> When Ted Taylor was growing up, in Mexico City in the nineteen-thirties, he had three particular interests, and they were music, chemistry, and billiards. His father had been a widower with three sons who married a widow with a son of her own, so Ted had four older half brothers—so much older, though, that he was essentially raised an only child, in a home that was as quiet as it was religious. His maternal grandparents were Congregational missionaries in Guadalajara. His father, born on a farm in Kansas, was general secretary of the Y.M.C.A. in Mexico. His mother was the first American woman who ever earned a Ph.D. at the National University of Mexico. Her field was Mexican literature (McPhee, Curve 8–9).

The circled words start the reader on familiar terrain, while the rest of each sentence moves on to new information. This pattern is by no means always necessary. But it *does* make the reader comfortable at the beginning of the sentence, and it leaves the reader free to *notice* what comes at the end, in the emphatic position.

■ Emphasis also falls on the verb.

> She *spends* her days sewing patchwork quilts and blankets.

This sentence puts the emphasis on *spends*, not on the *sewing*. Thus, it deliberately makes her work seem like drudgery. An alternative—"She *sews* patchwork quilts and blankets"—calls more attention to her artistry.

10. **Check over your paper to see what it looks like.** Then revise with an eye to emptiness and fullness. If you have a brief paragraph, you may want to add details to it, combine it with another paragraph, or remove it entirely. If you have a paragraph that fills a whole page, you may want to eliminate weak sections of it or find places to divide it into two or three paragraphs of more readable length.

11. **Check the spelling of any words you're not sure of.** Don't trust spell check fully. It recognizes all the correct words in English but of course it can't know what you really meant.

12. **Proofread carefully to ensure that you haven't left in any words you meant to take out, and that you haven't omitted words that you meant to use.**

13. **Check that the "style" that comes through in your work is the one that you'd like to come through.** Efforts to inject some style by adding words or phrases usually backfire, but we should be concerned, as we revise, about the tone of voice that comes through. One alteration in tone that many inexperienced writers ought to consider is making their writing slightly stronger, slightly more confident than they're actually feeling. In a few cases this will lead to unintentional cockiness, but in most cases the alteration will reflect the confidence that the writer deserves but doesn't yet have. Inexperienced writers often find themselves hedging at every opportunity:

> An amateur *is thought of* as not knowing as much as a professional *to an extent.*

The qualifying phrases here suck the life out of the writer's point. When we write something, we should legitimately think of ourselves as challenging our readers. A reader of the sentence above is left with nothing to think about. Most readers like to meet strength with strength. Unless they meet a strong writer, they don't want to give a paper a strong reading.

14. **Give your work a title that it deserves.**
Let me quote an expert on this matter (and many others), Harry Crosby, who sees a "high correlation between the quality of a written composition and its title" (387–91):

> I have long believed that the shuttlecock process of finding an appropriate title stimulates creativity, unity, and significance. The writer starts out with a working title, writes a few pages, and then pauses to tinker with the title to make it fit what he has written. This helps him go back to writing with a sharper focus on what he is really trying to say. This back-and-forth process continues. If a good title emerges, the writer has evidence that he or she is developing a significant message expressed in a unified manner. If no title is possible, something is wrong.

Crosby notes several kinds of titles, among them:

> *Clever titles:*
> "Two Cheers for Democracy"—E. M. Forster
> "The Scrutable Japanese"—Craig Spence
> *Titles that announce the thesis:*
> "We Scientists Have the Right to Play God"—Edmund F. Leech
> "This Thing Called Love Is Pathological"—Lawrence Cusler
> *Titles that indicate the controlling question:*
> "What is a Classic?"—Charles Augustin Sainte-Beuve
> "What Does a Tune-Up Include?"—Charlotte Slater
> *Titles that indicate a specific topic:*
> "Desegregating Sexist Sports"—Harry Edwards
> "Substitutes for Violence"—John Fisher

Titles that announce the general subject:
"On the Middle Class"—Steve Slade
"Historical Lessons About Great Leaders"—Arnold Toynbee

The first three types are admirable, and the fourth and fifth types get gradually weaker, but many titles on the papers students hand in wouldn't even reach the bottom of this list. No thinking is necessary if you use as your title the title of the assignment, such as "Description of a Curious Place," or "Persuading a Classmate." Another good number of students use no title at all. Think before you write a title; give your work a title that it deserves.

15. **Review your work to eliminate the following frequently made word and phrase mistakes, often referred to as mistakes in *usage*.**
accept, except: Accept is a verb meaning *receive willingly, except* is a preposition meaning *other than.*

> I'd be pleased to *accept* the award in her honor.
> The whole family will be there *except* Uncle Gus.

advice, advise: Advice is a noun, *advise* is a verb.

> I appreciate your *advice.*
> I *advise* you to take a long trip.

affect, effect: In normal use of these terms, both have the same meaning: *influence.* As a verb the word is spelled *affect,* and as a noun it is spelled *effect.*

> Flower pollens don't *affect* me very much.
> Grass pollens have a strong *effect* on me.

all ready, already: These are two different words. *All ready* means *prepared, already* means *before in time.*

> The family was *all ready.*
> Her father was *already* waiting.

all right: This is the correct spelling. *Alright* is not a word.

> Fortunately, the people in the back seat are *all right.*

a lot: You haven't seen this phrase in print very often (because professionals and teachers have discouraged its use), so you may guess that it's spelled *alot.* It's not. *A lot* is two words, like *all right.*
among: See *between.*
amount, number. Amount is a measure of some mass that can't be divided into parts, *number* the measure of several items in a large group of items. (The difference between *less* and *fewer* explained later is based on the same distinction.)

> The computer thief stole a staggering *amount* of money.
> The bank robber stole an undisclosed *number* of twenty dollar bills.

as: See *like.*

assure, ensure, insure: All three words mean "to make certain, to make safe." Use *assure* with persons, *ensure* with things, and *insure* when talking about money.

I *assure* you I sent the check yesterday.
You can *ensure* quality if you treat your employees with respect.
You may *insure* the package if you wish.

between, among: Use *between* when dealing with two things, *among* when dealing with three or more.

The playoff race was *between* the Tigers and the Twins.
The playoff money was divided *among* the Dodgers, Giants, and Astros.

can, may: Can means you are able to do something, *may* asks permission.

Can she climb that 10-foot wall?
May I offer an explanation?

capital, capitol: A state or country's *capital* is spelled with an *-al.* That same state or country's *capitol* building is spelled with an *-ol.*

cloths, clothes: Occasionally we might refer to more than one cloth as *cloths.* More often we are writing about what people wear every day and that is *clothes.*

He picked out several colorful *cloths* from the bazaar table.
He put his *clothes* on right after taking a shower.

conscience, conscious: Our *conscience* is the part of us that decides between right and wrong. To be *conscious* of something is to be aware of it.

My *conscience* bothered me after I refused to help.
I was never *conscious* that I had offended her.

contractions: There are many common contractions in English—*I'm, I'll, we'll, we're, you're, it's, can't, don't,* to name a few. Until ten or fifteen years ago, writers were discouraged from using them. In recent years, though, they are regarded increasingly as a more natural way to write. Be conscious, therefore, as you write, of the level of formality you create as you choose, for example, between *I'll* and *I will.*

could have, would have, should have: These three phrases are often abbreviated to *could've, would've,* and *should've* when we speak. And then we sometimes assume that the spelling should be *could of, would of,* and *should of.* But all these pairs are helping verbs and therefore *have* is the correct form. *Of,* a preposition, doesn't belong in the middle of a verb.

With two more computers, we *could have* finished on time.
Sharon *would have* brought the ice if she had known that we needed it.
We *should have* come before the dinner was served.

criterion, criteria: Criterion is a Greek word which has become an English word. It is one of very few words in English that still form their plurals in the original language rather than in English. Thus, we don't write several *criterions* but rather several *criteria*.

The most important *criterion* for a good play is that it entertain the audience. I've based my overall judgment, though, on at least three other *criteria*.

dessert, desert: This distinction at first seems easy. *Dessert* (accent on the second syllable) is the sweet we eat after a meal, a *desert* (accent on the first syllable) is a waterless land. But *desert* (pronounced just like *dessert* just to make things confusing) is also a verb meaning *leave*.

disinterested, uninterested: A *disinterested* person is uninfluenced by bias, an *uninterested* person would rather be doing something else.

We expect Olympic judges to be *disinterested* observers.
He was totally *uninterested* in the Olympics.

effect: See *affect*.
ensure: See *assure*.
except: See *accept*.
fewer: See *less*.
good, well: These two words mean the same thing, but *good* is used when the word serves as an adjective, and *well* is used when it is an adverb.
hear, here: *Here* is a place, *hear* is what we do when people speak to us.
insure: See *assure*.
its, it's: *It's* always stands for "it is." *Its* is possessive (like the other pronouns *her*, *his*, and *our*) even though it doesn't contain the apostrophe that we often associate with the possessive. Nouns have apostrophes when they become possessive, pronouns don't.
judgment: For no particular reason, *judgment* is the preferred spelling in the United States for the word that you might think should be spelled *judgement*.
know, no: These words sound the same but look so different that they should be easy to distinguish. *No* means *none, know* refers to knowledge.

I expect *no* nonsense during this week at camp.
I *know* you'll be good boys.

lay, lie: Lay/laid/laid means *to put or place*. It takes a direct object.

Please *lay* the dress on the bed.
I already *laid* it on the dining room table.

Lie/lay/lain means to rest or recline. It never takes a direct object. A common source of confusion is that the past tense of lie is *lay*.

She *lies* down for a nap every afternoon these days.
She *lay* down yesterday before 2:00.

lead, lead, led: Lead is a present tense verb, *led* is its form in the past tense, and *lead*—when pronounced like *led*—is the metal.

Today I'll *lead* you through the new computer manual.
Yesterday she *led* me through it.

less, fewer: Less refers to a portion of some general quantity, *fewer* to actual numbers.

There is *less* water in this lake than there should be to sustain large fish.
There are *fewer* students in this class than I expected.

like, as: Like and *as* have the same meaning. *Like* is expected when the word is a preposition, *as* when it is a subordinating conjunction.

He acted *like* a hero.
He acted *as* a hero might have acted.

loose, lose: Loose is an adjective with what you might think of as a *hard* "s," *lose* is a verb with an "s" that is *softer* and sounds like "z."

He always wears his tie *loose*.
Please don't *lose* the book I lent you.

may: See *can*.
number: See *amount*.
numbers: No one seems quite sure what the rule is about spelling out numbers. Any number from 1 to 10 can be spelled out and readers can follow with no trouble. But generally it is easier to read a number larger than 10 in its numerical form. The numerical form is only awkward at the beginning of sentences where a number can't be capitalized and therefore the spelled out form is preferred, no matter how large the number is.

past, passed: Most commonly this word is spelled *past*. It can be a *noun* meaning a time before now, an *adjective* referring to time before now, or a *preposition* meaning moving next to something. *Passed* is used, though, when the word is a *verb* indicating movement next to something.

My grandmother lives, more than I would like her to, in the *past*.
That rocker is a remnant from *past* times.
The grocery store is just *past* the movie theatre.
I *passed* the movie theatre on the way to the grocery store.

principal, principal, principle: The noun *principal* means the chief officer. The adjective *principal* means the most important. *Principle* is a noun which means either a general truth (the *principles* of the law) or moral ideas (she lives by her admirable *principles*).

The *principal* worked every weekend this month.
His *principal* reason for leaving was his fight with Jerry.
His behavior doesn't give me much confidence in his religious *principles*.

proceed, precede: These two words are never mixed up, but their spellings often are. *Proceed* means *continue* and has its two e's linked. *Precede* means *come* (or *go) before* and separates its e's.

proof, evidence: Be modest about claiming that you've proven something. In most cases the matter you are discussing will never be resolved with certainty. What you've done is offer not proof but evidence.

quiet, quite: These words have *et* and *te* reversed, but they have very different meanings. *Quiet* is an adjective meaning *not loud, quite* is an adverb that can substitute for *very*.

raise, rise: We *raise* an object, we and objects *rise* without help.

They all helped *raise* the side of the barn.
The children wanted to watch the bread *rise*.

set, sit: We *set* an object somewhere, we and objects *sit* without help.

He *set* his book on the teaching table.
The flowers *sit* on the windowsill.

should have: See *could have*.

stationary, stationery: Stationary is an adjective referring to something that is not moving. *Stationery* is the paper we write letters on.

supposed to, suppose to: It's difficult to say these two words carefully because the last sound of *supposed* is the same as the first sound of *to*. So inexperienced writers often think there is no *d* on *supposed*. The *d* is necessary, though, because *supposed* is a passive voice form of the verb *suppose*. Memorize this spelling. *Used to* is often misspelled for precisely the same reason.

She's *supposed to* be here before 6:00.

than, then: These words are pronounced somewhat similarly, but they are quite different in spelling, meaning, and grammatical function. *Then* refers to time, and *than* makes a comparison.

Then he swept into the room after keeping them waiting 45 minutes.
He's less prompt *than* he used to be.

there, their, they're: They're, like all contractions, can be spelled out as *they are*. *There* refers to a place. *Their* is a possessive pronoun similar to *his* or *her*.

They're expected tomorrow from Milwaukee.
My wife keeps her keys *there* whenever she's out of town.
They sold *their* children's bikes last week.

till, until: Both these words are respectable, but note their spellings. *Til*, which you might regard as a third choice, isn't a word.

too, to, two: These words sound alike. *Two*, the number, is rarely confused with the others. But *too*, meaning *too much*, and *to*, a preposition (*to* the store) or part of an infinitive (*to* arrive), need to be carefully distinguished.

try to, try and: When we speak, we frequently use phrases like *try and ac-complish, try and get, try and find.* There is no real *and* intended. In writing, the more precise forms of *try to accomplish, try to get, try to find* are expected.

used to, use to: It's difficult to say these two words carefully because the last sound of *used* is the same as the first sound of *to.* So inexperienced writers often think there is no *d* on *used.* The *d* is necessary, though, because *used* is a passive voice form of the verb *use.* Memorize this spelling. *Supposed to* is often misspelled for precisely the same reason.

He's less prompt than he *used to* be.

utilize, use: Both these words mean the same thing. There's nothing wrong with the shorter word *use* so it is usually a better choice.

where, were: Wh has a harsh sound, *w* alone a softer sound. *Where* refers to an (unknown) place, *were* is a verb referring to past time.

Where are our friends living since they left?

They *were* living in a very dirty apartment until last week.

whether, weather: As in the above example, *wh* has a harsh sound, *w* alone a softer sound. *Whether* refers to a choice we have, *weather* to the raininess or sunniness of the day.

I can't decide *whether* to get married.

The *weather* is bound to get worse before it gets better.

who, whom: Who and *whom* mean the same thing, but are correct or incorrect choices depending on whether they are used in a subjective or objective case slot in a sentence. If you don't know the grammatical rules for determining the case of a noun, choose *who* or *whom* by comparing them with the more familiar *he* and *him.* Where you would use *he*, use *who.* Where you would use *him*, use *whom.*

who's, whose: Who's means who is. *Whose* doesn't.

Who's home?

Whose watch is this behind the couch?

woman, women: Woman refers to one adult female, *women* to more than one.

would have: See *could have.*

your, you're: You're means you are. *Your* doesn't.

You're the best friend I have left.

I like *your* brother.

9

Sentence Sense: Making Grammar Your Ally

My grammar is not that hot, in fact it's not even warm.

STUDENT

I had grammar viciously driven into my head for eight years.

STUDENT

I find training in grammar to be quite a bore, especially with all the emphasis placed on subjects like dangling modifiers, etc., which really don't play a major role in my life in my opinion.

STUDENT

I am a good writer. Writing usually comes easy to me. I have a quality of sensitivity so the papers I write usually represent that quality. Although writing comes easily to me, grammar does not.

STUDENT

My high school training in English consisted of several poorly taught classes and one that was well taught. The teacher for my junior year was the head of the school's English department. She was a very strict lady who preached nothing but grammar. For most of the semester we were bombarded with pronouns, clauses, participles and more. I admit that I hated every minute of it. But now I realize she was the only teacher who took the time to concentrate on grammar. Other teachers, most likely bored by the subject, skimmed over grammar in order to do more interesting things. Even though I hated her and the course, I learned more than I did in my other high school classes. Today I am more at ease when writing because of that class.

STUDENT

133

The easiest and most enduring way to learn grammar and punctuation is to invent sentences in a group and then to compare notes on what, grammatically, you have invented. Much of this chapter consists of such exercises.

Self-Assessment: Common Punctuation Errors

Exercise 9-1
in class

The following sentences are punctuated improperly. Revise each and explain in each case why your revision is correct.

- I hope to become an accountant when I graduate, sometimes I look in the classified ads to see what qualifications most companies want their accountants to have and all of the ads I read wanted a college degree.
- The reason for this is simple, they do not have large brains.
- College offers a variety of topics to learn from, for instance people who are interested in rocks and have been collecting them all their lives, can major in geology.
- The listing didn't include; however, the schedules for services in any other religious faiths.
- "Several hundred persons turned out Sunday at Marlboro College," several hundred is a lot for Rutland.
- The *Rutland Herald* and the *New York Daily News* have different types of readers, however, they both serve their readers in the same manner.
- It was our first chance to break open the game and put a few runs on the scoreboard; against the first-place team.
- People begin to congregate at the Rendezvous early in the evening it is mostly a light crowd.
- He heard me looked over smiled and started walking to the car.
- In a world that is constantly changing, and more and more is being discovered. There will always be something new to learn.

While you're in a correction frame of mind, look at the plumbing preface in Chapter 12 on p. 189 and decide what changes should be made in that writer's grammar and punctuation. I think you'll find it entertaining to try to fix his punctuational and grammatical woes.

If you can correct the punctuation in all the sentences above and in the plumbing preface with little trouble, you probably don't need the rest of this chapter. If you have had some difficulty, though, with these corrections, this chapter will help fill in the gaps in your knowledge of grammar and punctuation, and by doing so improve both your confidence and your performance.

Self-Assessment: Grammar and Punctuation Terms

Exercise 9-2
on your own

Before beginning the review of English grammar and punctuation in this chapter, test yourself to see what you already know. What rules do you remember for using:

1. A comma?
2. A semicolon?
3. A colon?

How would you define:

1. A sentence?
2. A clause?
3. A phrase?

Compare your answers here with what you learn as you continue reading this chapter.

In most college courses, a substantial part of our study time is spent learning the vocabulary of the field—*norms, sanctions, stratification,* and *diffusion,* for example, in sociology; *genus, species, in vitro,* and *in vivo* in biology. If it weren't for grammar, the number of terms you would need to master for a writing course would be very few: *fact, inference, thesis, ethos, logos, pathos, paragraph, introduction, conclusion.* But even dreaded grammar increases the list of essential terms to learn in a writing course only to roughly twenty-five. The grammatical terms that *all* students should know are listed below.

Table 9-1 Terms Essential to the Study of Grammar

Basic parts of speech	Sentence elements
Nouns	Subjects
Verbs	Verbs, or predicates
Adjectives	Objects
Adverbs	Phrases
Conjunctions	Noun phrases
	Verb phrases
	Prepositional phrases
	Verbal phrases
	Clauses
	Independent clauses
	Dependent clauses

Conjunctions	Verbals (Demoted Verbs)
Coordinating conjunctions	Gerunds
Subordinating conjunctions	Participles
Conjunctive adverbs	Infinitives
Relative pronouns	

You've reviewed subjects and verbs so many times by this point in school that I'll assume you can pick them out of any sentence. Most of the other terms should at least sound familiar, though you might be hard-pressed to explain them. The two items in the list on the previous page that most people refuse to learn are *gerunds* and *participles*, yet we use gerunds and participles almost every time we talk or write. It's time to learn what they, and the other basic elements of sentences, are.

What Is a Sentence?

The most important knowledge that you as a speaker and writer of English should have is a sense of what a sentence is. In English, as in most other languages, the basis of a sentence is a relation between a noun and a verb, a relation between matter and energy. Einstein's theory of relativity, $E = mc^2$, tells us that all life consists of mass m and energy E. Very conveniently, sentences, too, consist of matter (a subject, or noun) and energy (a predicate, or verb). Readers don't want to hear about matter without energy, or energy without matter. They'll accept:

My baby	sleeps.
[matter]	[energy]

or

The nuclear reactor	is leaking.
[matter]	[energy]

But they won't accept:

My baby.	
[matter only]	

or

	Is leaking.
	[energy only]

Intuitively, we realize that to say something meaningful, we have to include some matter, and we must give that matter some energy. Nevertheless, students (and others) often enclose collections of words between a capital letter and a period that are *not* sentences:

1. Knowing what you can do and cannot do.
2. A person of always good intentions.
3. Which I liked a lot, because it gives you the feeling of being in college.

The writers of these collections of words are having difficulty getting their ideas across either (1) because they don't know what a *subject* is, or (2) because they don't know what a *verb* is, or, most likely, (3) because they don't know that *a sentence must contain an unsubordinated subject and verb.* Perhaps you are able to see the errors in the above sentences, but still you don't know what I mean by that last phrase, "unsubordinated subject and verb." You probably wrote, in answer to the questions that open this chapter, that a sentence is a "complete thought." Well, what makes a thought "complete" (in English, and also in Swedish, Swahili, or Sanskrit) is an unsubordinated subject and verb.

Destroying a Sentence by Adding to It

Exercise 9-3
in class

Write out, on a sheet of paper, the following sentence:

Ieshia majored in political science.

We all know that we could destroy this sentence by taking away either the subject or the verb. But can you *add* a word in front of this sentence that will destroy it as a sentence? Try.

How many examples did the class come up with? If none, then look at the following partial list of words that would work:

after	before	when
although	if	where
because	since	while

I like to call these words *sentence destroyers.* Grammarians call them *subordinating conjunctions.* All conjunctions provide links between more important words than themselves; a subordinating conjunction not only provides that link, but makes the group of words, the clause, that follows it *subordinate,* or less than a sentence.

Read your new less-than-sentences aloud to each other and try to hear that they don't sound like a complete sentence or a complete thought. Then be careful in the future not to leave such strings on their own in your writing, punctuated as if they were a sentence.

Repairing a Sentence Fragment by Adding to It

Exercise 9-4
in class

Use a subordinating conjunction at the beginning of the sentence "Ieshia majored in political science," and then add as many words as you like either before or after this sentence fragment to finish the thought in some way that satisfies you.

Read your new sentences aloud in turn. Now you should be able to see more clearly why these sentence destroyers have the name *subordinating conjunctions*. They are *conjunctions* because they *connect* things, in this case the two ideas in your sentence. You should also be able to hear that your new sentence is complete; it makes a satisfying point.

Discovering an Independent Clause

Exercise 9-5
in class

From the sentence you most recently created, take away your sentence destroyer and "Ieshia majored in political science," and note what's left. Is what's left a sentence? Yes. Its subject and verb don't have a subordinating conjunction in front of them. They are an *unsubordinated subject and verb*, the definition I gave you earlier for a sentence. Compare your sentence with those of the rest of the class. All of them will read as solid sentences.

Clauses

You now should be able to understand easily one of the most useful terms in English sentence structure: a *clause. Because Ieshia majored in political science* is a clause. And *she wants to get an internship next year with a member of the Congressional Black Caucus* is also a clause. What makes a group of words a clause? *A clause is a group of words that contains a subject and a verb.* But clauses come in two types that are punctuated very differently. The two types are dependent (or subordinate) clauses and independent (or main) clauses. An independent clause is a complete sentence. It can stand on its own, as *She wants to get an internship next year with a member of the Congressional Black Caucus* does. Dependent clauses have subjects and verbs, but they also have a subordinating conjunction, so they can exist only as parasites, attached to an independent clause.

One last point about dependent clauses. Dependent, or subordinate, clauses are not necessarily subordinate in the importance of the ideas they convey. The idea in a dependent clause can be as important as, or even more important than, the idea in the independent part of the sentence—for example: "I'll stop by to see you Friday *if I finish my paper*." *If I finish my paper* is the dependent clause in this sentence, but it is, I think, the more important idea. Subordinate clauses are subordinate, or dependent, only in grammatical terms, not in terms of meaning.

Adjectives and Adverbs

I'm sure you noticed that you use words other than nouns, pronouns, verbs, and conjunctions in the sentences you've written. Almost all of those additional words, and groups of words, can be classified as either adjectives or adverbs. For the moment, let us say simply that adjectives help us understand nouns, and adverbs help us understand verbs (adverbs, in fact, do more than this, but helping us understand verbs is their principal function).

Exercise 9-6
in class

To see what adjectives and adverbs are, let's take advantage (as we will throughout this chapter) of those among your classmates who have learned these grammatical terms before and who remember pretty well how to use them.

Take a basic sentence. I suggest:

The coach traveled.

First, tell us *which* coach traveled by adding a word or a group of words to this sentence. Compare your suggestions. All your additions—whether single words, or prepositional phrases (soon to be explained), or clauses—will be serving as adjectives.

Now return to the base sentence:

The coach traveled.

Can you tell us something about *how, when, where,* or *why* the coach traveled by adding a word or a group of words? Again, compare your suggestions. All your suggestions this time—words, prepositional phrases, or clauses—will be adverbs.

Those of you who added single-word adverbs to "The coach traveled" may have noticed that most of them end in -*ly*. Charles Dickens spoofs writers who rely too much on adverbs in a passage from *A Tale of Two Cities* when he describes an indictment against his character Charles Darnay, who is said to have "wickedly, falsely, traitorously, and otherwise evil-adverbiously" revealed English secrets to the French (93).

The main reason for learning the difference between adjectives and adverbs is to know whether to write *She rode smooth* or *She rode smoothly*, or *He wrote good* or *He wrote well*. In most cases, an adjective has a plain ending, while the adverb with a similar meaning ends in -*ly*.

Adjective	**Adverb**
happy	happily
sure	surely

But in one very common case, that of the adjective *good*, the form changes entirely as a word shifts from being an adjective to being an adverb:

Adjective	**Adverb**
good	well

Because so many people don't know the difference between adjectives and adverbs, we often hear on television, "He pitches good in relief" or "She skates good under pressure," when the correct adverb in both cases should be *well*.

In adding adjectives and adverbs to our base sentence, one or two of you, instead of adding single words or phrases, probably added whole clauses, such as *when the season ended* or *because she needed a left-handed pitcher*, or *who needed a shave*.

Enriching Sentences with Clauses

Exercise 9-7
in class

There is a special class of dependent clauses called relative clauses that begin with one of the very small set of words—*who, whom, whose, which,* and *that*—that are called relative pronouns. We use these relative clauses—"who serves fish every Friday," "whose mother is Japanese," "whom I admired for being able to work with difficult kids"—frequently in English, usually as adjectives to modify nouns.

Now I'd like you to practice adding two clauses to *The coach traveled* sentence, one to enrich our sense of the coach (a relative clause) and one to tell us *how, when, where,* or *why* the coach traveled (an adverb clause beginning with a subordinating conjunction).

The coach [   ] traveled [   ].

Compare your answers. What, again, is the definition of a clause?

Enriching Sentences with Prepositional Phrases

Exercise 9-8
in class

   Some of the adjectives and adverbs you came up with in Exercise 9-6 were not single words nor clauses with a subject and a verb, but prepositional phrases, like "in the bus" or "of the track team" or "after the game." Prepositional phrases are for most people the easiest part of English grammar to remember. But to make sure that you *all* know how to use prepositional phrases, add any prepositional phrase you please (a new one if you used one last time) to our base sentence:

   The coach traveled ...
   _____

How many different prepositions did the class come up with? There are forty or so in all. A good list, with sample objects attached, follows:

about the winner	*concerning* your father	*over* the hedge
above the garage	*down* the sewer	*past* the sign
across the pond	*during* the heat wave	*since* the war
after breakfast	*except* vegetables	*through* the woods
against the brick	*for* your uncle	*to* Arkansas
along the street	*from* your aunt	*toward* the clock
among the players	*in* a box	tower
around the corner	*inside* the chest	*under* the sink
at the game	*into* the pool	*until* Saturday
before dinner	*like* her husband	*up* the hill
behind the house	*near* the cliffs	*upon* demand
below the high-water mark	*of* the plumber	*with* my friend
beneath the window	*off* the chimney	*within* an hour
beyond hope	*on* the plate	*without* any worry
by the farmer	*outside* the tavern	

You may have noted that a few prepositions (*after, before, since,* and *until*—marked with an asterisk above) can also be used as sentence destroyers (that is, subordinating conjunctions). How can you tell, in a given sentence, whether a word like *before* or *after* is a preposition or a subordinating conjunction?

   Subordinating conjunctions introduce clauses, i.e. subject-verb combinations—"since he visited Cambodia" or "before she took her first job." Prepositional phrases introduce nouns only (no verbs), are usually briefer, and have a nice rhythm to them: *under the table, without regret, during the play.* Prepositional phrases are not clauses because they have no verb—just a preposition, an object, and often an adjective or two modifying the object. Prepositional phrases play a peripheral role in a sentence; they help explain nouns and verbs; they don't act themselves.

   The purpose   of the rule   is to protect the committee's members.

   subject   prepositional phrase   verb

The <u>success</u>   <u>of my plans</u>   <u>depends</u> on you.
  subject   *prepositional phrase*   *verb*

Also, prepositions desperately need their objects. Prepositions and their objects are so closely connected that it wasn't until the thirteenth century that prepositions were separated from their objects when people wrote. A twelfth-century writer, if he used modern spelling, would have written "inthetree" or "behindthebush."

Phrases

Prepositional phrases are the most common of several kinds of *phrases* in English sentence structure. A phrase is a group of words not easily separated that includes either a noun or a verb, but *not both a subject and a verb*: i.e. a phrase is less than a clause.

A noun with its modifiers is sometimes called a *noun phrase*:

The old school will be torn down.
A good leader could solve our problems.

A verb with its helping verbs is often called a *verb phrase*:

Refugees *have been helped.*
Victory *might be achieved.*
John *can be bribed.*

These helping verbs (and combinations of them) can be used along with the main verb of a sentence to form a *verb phrase*:

am	has	could
is	have	will
are	had	would
was	should	shall
were	may	do
be	might	does
being	must	did
been	can	

Participles, gerunds, and infinitives also introduce phrases, but we need to review them before we look at their phrases. Steel yourself while we look at these common but strangely named grammatical animals, participles and gerunds. There are two bizarre paradoxes in sentence structure. One, you've already seen, is that you can add a word to a complete sentence and by doing so make the sentence incomplete. The second paradox is that you can take a verb's "verbness" away from it by adding -*ing*. Watch.

Participles

Exercise 9-9
in class

Fill in the blank below with any word you choose. You may add words within the brackets, too, if you wish.

_____ing [   ], Gary left for the park.

When you compare your suggestions, you'll find that every word you suggested for the opening blank is a verb, but that each new word you created—*running* or *laughing* or *coughing*, for example—is clearly not the verb in the sentence. *Left* is the verb for the sentence. Your newly created word is an adjective modifying *Gary*. Thus a *participle* is a verb plus -*ing* which acts as an adjective, and is thus demoted—because of its -ing— from the lofty status that verbs maintain in a sentence.

If you added words within the brackets above, you created not just a participle but a participial phrase.

Past Participles

Exercise 9-10
in class

Fill in the blank below with any word you choose.
The _____ ed long distance runner stumbled toward the medical services station.
Again, comparing suggestions, you'll find that you filled in the blank with a verb but that your newly created -*ed* word is an adjective (a past participle) modifying *runner*.

Omitted -*ed* Endings

I read an article call "Trouble for Dads."

Your ear probably tells you that *call* above should be *called*. But your ear may not help you in a case like this. And you probably don't know why it should be *called*. *Called* is not the subject of the sentence; *I* is. It's not the verb; *read* is. It's not the direct object; *an article* is. *Called* is a participle, one of those verbs demoted to adjectives. It is easy to recognize *-ing* participles, *present* participles, like *driving* in the phrase *a driving rain*. But equally important, though a little harder to recognize, are *past* participles.

> a *crumbled* brick
> a *renewed* contract
> a *broken* twig

We talk about a *washing* machine, a machine in the act of washing, but we also speak of *washed* clothes, where the washing is already completed.

Most past participles end in *-ed*. But some end in *-en*, and a few are very irregular. (Common past participles which don't end in *-en* or *-ed* are *bent, bet, hit, held, hurt, lost, made, rung, sung, strung, struck*, and *taught*.) All have the same form of the verb (called the "third principal part") that you use when you say "I have *fixed*," or "I have *broken*," or "I have *run*," or "I have *helped*." Past participles are frequently used in English:

> Ruth bought 60 acres of *cultivated* land.
> The stone structures in London, *blackened* by coal soot in the nineteenth century, are now being cleaned.

Here are a few common errors related to the use of the past participle (or its identical twin, the verb form that follows the helping verb *have*):

> *Wrong:* The college buildings were in the *old-fashion* design.
> *Wrong:* Here in college I have been *force* to study more.
> *Wrong:* I've *notice* some changes in myself.

If you make similar errors, try to check over your writing, after you have everything else straight, to see whether some of your participles, and verbs following *have*, are missing their *-ed*.

Gerunds

Gerunds, unfortunately, look just like present participles. They also are made up of a basic verb plus *–ing*.

Exercise 9-11
in class

Fill in the blank in the following sentence with any word you like. You may add words within the brackets, too, if you wish.

> _____ing [   ] pays off in the long run.

Compare your answers. You all filled in a verb, but you wound up with a subject for your sentence, a gerund. If you added words in the brackets, you created not just a gerund but a gerund phrase.

Gerunds are frequently used as subjects of sentences.

Swimming exercises every muscle in the body.
Writing is less difficult when you write regularly.

You might remember the difference between participles and gerunds by remembering that a gerund is a verbal noun and that a participle is a verbal adjective. "Gerund" and "noun" share a "u." "Participle" and "adjective" share an "a."

You've just seen in action a very important grammatical principle: once a verb has *-ing* added to it, it is no longer a verb. It's been demoted to a mere *verbal*—a participle or a gerund (or an infinitive, which you'll meet soon). Many sentence fragments that we write are fragments because we've included only a verbal, not a verb, in what we thought was a sentence:

Wrong: Sophie *having* the best earned run average of all our pitchers.

The only way a verb with *-ing* added to it can regain the status of a verb is with the aid of a helping verb from the *is* family—*is, are, be, been, was were, am*:

Correct: Sophie *is having* her best year as a pitcher.

Converting Verbs into Participles and Gerunds

Exercise 9-12
in class

To give you some idea of how versatile these *-ing* forms are, try returning to your base sentence:

The coach traveled.

Now, convert the verb, *travel,* into a participle modifying the coach and add a new verb to the sentence. Compare your sentence with those of your classmates: e.g. *The traveling coach reached for his coat.* Next, convert the verb into a gerund and make a statement about the coach: e.g., *Traveling is a coach's curse.*

Just to make sure that you can recognize when a verb plus *-ing* is still a verb, take our base sentence and alter the verb so that it contains an *-ing* form that is still a verb: e.g. *The coach will be traveling next week.*

Infinitives: The Third Verbal

Participles and gerunds are both called *verbals*—not verbs but *verbals*. A verbal is a sort of verb that has been demoted to noun or adjective status. There is one other kind of verbal, the *infinitive*. Compared to participles and gerunds, infinitives are easy. They're marked with an extra word, *to: to knit, to see, to travel*. Like the other verbals, infinitives cannot serve as *the* verb in a sentence.

I   want   to study.
   verb   *infinitive object*
To breathe freely is a sign of health.
infinitive subject   *verb*

Converting Verbs into Infinitives

Exercise 9-13
in class

To practice just for a moment, take our original sentence, convert *traveled* into an infinitive, and add a new verb; e.g. *The coach liked to travel.* Note how the verb ending changes. Try another example:

The mayor of Phoenix attends many dinners.

Now alter this sentence to indicate that the mayor only *plans* to be at these dinners. Again, note how the verb ending on *attends* changes. Also note the ending on *plans*. The practice of adding an -s ending to a verb attached to a third-person-singular subject doesn't apply to an infinitive because an infinitive is not the verb in the sentence.

While the verbals—participles, gerunds, and infinitives—have been demoted from main-verb status in the sentence, they still retain some of the characteristics of verbs: they are often accompanied by direct objects or modified by adverbs or adverb phrases:

At Lodi, near Medea, fifteen rebels attacked workers repairing   the railway.
   participle   and its object

A conference of specialists in cultivating   rice will be held Tuesday in Calcutta.
   gerund   and its object

Decisively   defeated   in the New Hampshire primary,
its adverb   *participle*   *another adverb, this one a prepositional phrase*

Henri LaComte was forced   to offer   his resignation
   infinitive   *its object*

when he was caught taking bribes.
an adverb, this one a dependent clause

A verbal with its adverbs or objects is called a *verbal phrase*.

Parallel Structure

The exercises that you've just completed will help you write with more variety in your sentence structure. You should now be able to see many, many options that you have when you write your sentences. But sentence variety is not as important as it is sometimes said to be in writing. In fact, sentence similarity, or similarity of sentence patterns, is an often neglected virtue. Repetitive, or parallel, structure within and among sentences is one of the writer's principal tools for achieving coherence, clarity, and a pleasing rhythm. Few of the devices available to the writer are as helpful, as frequently applicable, and as strengthening to style as parallel structure. The ease with which the English language doubles and triples its subjects, its verbs, or its phrases or clauses makes parallel structure a fluid way to write.

Exercise 9-14
in class

If you practice imitating parallel structure in the writing of others, the rhythm of parallel writing will soon come naturally to you.

Model: The town stopped noticing National Suicide Day because they had absorbed it into their thoughts, into their language, into their lives. (Toni Morrison)
Sample imitation: The boys stopped practicing basketball because they had pushed sports out of their afternoons, out of their summers, out of their concerns.
Your imitation: _____
_____
_____

Model: Her blindness has limited her to puttering in the garden, walking to the mailbox, and listening to the radio.
Your imitation: _____
_____
_____
_____

Model: Without the mitochondria in our cells, we would be unable to move a muscle, to drum a finger, to think a thought. (Lewis Thomas)
Your imitation: _____
_____
_____

Punctuation

With a knowledge of the basic elements of grammar reviewed above, you can easily learn all the important rules for punctuation. Punctuation is your readers' best friend. It helps words on a page sound as much as possible like the human voice. So you owe it to your readers to punctuate as clearly as possible. Erratic punctuation distracts a reader the same way that backstage stage-crew voices distract an audience at a play. In both cases the "noise" is clearly unprofessional, and it prevents the listener from concentrating on the main event.

Punctuation Review

Exercise 9-15
in class

To review your abilities and preferences in punctuation, try to reintroduce the punctuation into the following passage, from which all punctuation has been removed (McPhee, *The Pine Barrens*, 11–12):

I asked Fred what all those cars were doing in his yard and he said that one of them was in running condition and that the rest were its predecessors the working vehicle was a 1956 Mercury each of the seven others had at one time or another been his best car and each in turn had lain down like a sick animal and had died right there in the yard unless it had been towed home after a mishap elsewhere in the pines Fred recited with affection the history of each car of one old Ford for example he said I upset that up to Speedwell in the creek and of an even older car a station wagon he said I busted that one up in the snow I met a car on a little hill and hit the brake and hit a tree one of the cars had met its end at a narrow bridge about four miles from Hog Wallow where Fred had hit a state trooper head-on

Fred apologized for not having a phone after I asked where I would have to go to make a call later on he said I don't have no phone because I don't have no electric if I had electric I would have had a phone in here a long time ago he uses a kerosene lamp a propane lamp and two flashlights

You may be able to punctuate the above passage correctly even if you don't know many rules of punctuation. Your ear will help you punctuate if you are a frequent reader. But if you do make some mistakes, or if you find your ear unreliable, you can only learn punctuation if you learn the rules. So whether you need them or whether you just want a quick review, here are the rules for punctuation in English, each introduced in connection with a common writing problem.

Common Problems in Punctuation

1. Comma Splices and Fused Sentences

The most common grammatical fault in our writing is the so-called *comma splice*. One reason we have trouble with it is that we don't know what *splice* means. *Splice* is a word used regularly only by sailors and boy scouts. To splice is to join, usually to join two pieces of rope. Here's a rope splice:

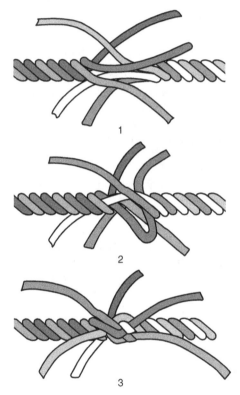

Sequence of steps in making a short splice

A comma splice is the use of a comma rather than a semicolon or a period to join two complete sentences. The following three sentences are all incorrectly punctuated because the writer has not used a period (or a semicolon) to separate the two sentences:

I haven't decided how many kids to have, there are a lot of factors to consider when we decide to have kids.

She is capable of doing the work, that is what is so puzzling.

In New York, Philadelphia, and Baltimore, the sugar refineries ran out of raw sugar; this led to the layoff of 15,000 workers.

Sentences, of course, shouldn't be joined by a comma. If there's a complete sentence on both sides of a comma, the comma should be replaced by a semicolon:

She is capable of doing the work; that is what is so puzzling.

Or the comma should be replaced by a period and a capital letter:

She is capable of doing the work. That is what is so puzzling.

A comma is only useful in sorting things out within a sentence. It has no use between sentences.

Occasionally, writers join two sentences without using even a comma.

I am glad I chose this school it is now my home.

Such a sentence is called a *fused sentence*. *Fused*, like *splice*, is a technical term. When two wires from separate electrical circuits come too close to each other, the heat generated can melt the wires and join them together so that the circuits are no longer distinct and useful. Similarly, in a fused sentence, the two distinct sentences are damaged because they are brought so close together that readers can't tell them apart.

Comma splices and fused sentences are both often called *run-on sentences*. But *run-on sentence* is a much misunderstood—and unnecessarily feared—term. When you write a long sentence and worry about whether it's a "run-on," you're usually worrying needlessly. *Run-on* is a technical term for the error of joining two complete sentences with no punctuation, or with a mere comma. There's nothing wrong with a long sentence as long as it's punctuated correctly.

In New York, Philadelphia, and Baltimore, the sugar refineries ran out of raw sugar; this led to the layoff of 15,000 workers.

When a sentence is finished, shut it up with a period or with a semicolon. Don't leave its gates wide open (with no punctuation) or even half open (with a comma).

2. Sentence Fragments

You may not feel quite confident yet about your ability to locate and avoid comma splices and fused sentences, but I want to mention one more common problem—the sentence fragment—before trying to clear up all three. *Fragment* is a more familiar term than either *splice* or *fused*. A fragment is a broken part of something—part of a vase, part of a hammer, part of a sentence. Here are some common types of sentence fragments:

Because each person's definition of success is different.

Something I could be proud of.

All of which was prepared by the infamous hospitality crew.

Comma splices and sentence fragments are related errors. A comma splice is too much of a good thing (two sentences between a capital letter and a period); a fragment is too little of a good thing (not even one sentence between a capital letter and a period). In both cases, inexperienced writers usually go wrong because they don't know which connectors—sometimes conjunctions but often pronouns—make a sentence or clause grammatically dependent, and which allow a sentence or clause to remain grammatically independent.

3. Punctuation with Connectors

To clarify in your mind the distinction between independent and dependent clauses, you need to know the following lists of common connectors.

1. *Personal pronouns—he, she, it, they*, etc.—do not make a sentence dependent.

   Darian practices hour after hour. He wants to play college basketball.

   The sense of the second sentence here does depend on the first sentence having been there, but the second sentence is grammatically independent. It is not wholly independent in meaning, but it's a rare sentence in any piece of writing whose meaning is *wholly* independent of what comes before and after. *Punctuation decisions must be based not on meaning independence but on grammatical independence.*

2. So-called *demonstrative pronouns*, pronouns that point out (*this, that, these, those*), are like personal pronouns (he, she, it, they) in that they do not make a sentence dependent.

   Jameille chose to play at Alabama. *This* made his parents very happy.

3. *There* and *here*, in the constructions *there are* and *here are*, do not make a sentence dependent.

   Gugii in the first half had eight rebounds. *There* were three other players who had five.

4. *Conjunctive adverbs—a list follows—do not make a sentence dependent.*

also	likewise	then
besides	immediately	therefore
consequently	moreover	similarly
finally	instead	thus
first	nevertheless	still
otherwise	now	on the other hand
on the contrary	meanwhile	in fact
furthermore	sometimes	
however	indeed	

   Phoebe threw out their fastest runner. *Now* she feels more confident at shortstop.

   Business is booming. *Still* Beimnet worries about our loans.

For all but the shortest conjunctive adverbs, like *now* and *still* above, a comma is normally used to separate the conjunctive adverb from the body of the sentence:

Finally, our rosebush is blooming. The peonies, *however*, won't bloom for another week.

Conjunctive adverbs get their name because they act as adverbs—they tell *how, when, where,* or *why*—while at the same time they serve as conjunctions, making connections clear.

5. *There are two kinds of connectors, subordinating conjunctions and relative pronouns, that do make a clause dependent.* They really must be memorized so you can distinguish them from conjunctive adverbs.

Subordinating conjunctions		**Relative pronouns**
after	though	that
although	even though	who
because	whereas	whose
before	as	whom
if	whenever	which
since	till, until	
when	unless	
where	as if	
while	as though	
so that	as much as	
wherever	as long as	
how	in order that	
whether		

Elizabeth is home *because there was a fire at the library*.
I know a lawyer *who works every Saturday in a Boulder legal aid clinic*.

To see what these sentence destroyers can do, compare the following examples:

When caffeine ($C_8H_{10}N_4O_2$) is burned in a limited supply of O_2, the products are CO, H_2O, and NO; all are gases.
When caffeine ($C_8H_{10}N_4O_2$) is burned in a limited supply of O_2, the products are CO, H_2O, and NO, all *of which* are gases.

Which, being a relative pronoun, is a sentence destroyer. Even *of which* will do the trick, and so "all of which are gases" can't stand alone. It must be connected to a whole sentence with a comma.

These conjunctions are often given little respect. We have studied nouns, verbs, adjectives, and adverbs a hundred times. But the connectors, the conjunctions, are the keys to clear punctuation, for they give us the keys to knowing whether our subjects and verbs are subordinated or not.

The common definition of a sentence as a "complete thought" doesn't help us much in punctuating. But when we keep in mind that a sentence is an "unsubordinated subject and verb," we realize that recognizing clauses, independent and dependent, is the key to punctuation. When clauses are linked, and most sentences link clauses, they are linked by punctuation in very predictable ways:

Independent clause	;	Independent clause
Dependent clause	,	Independent clause
Independent clause	o	Dependent clause

Let me give several examples of each of these three basic punctuation rules:

■ IC ; IC

I like pizza; Kathy likes hot dogs.
I wonder where our neighbors found the money; perhaps they've been robbing banks.

Of course, you can always use a period and a capital letter in the place of a semicolon.

■ DC , IC

When Errol paints his house, we'll celebrate.
Unless he loses, Jack will still be arrogant.

In sentences of this type, the comma serves as a sort of warning that now the independent (or main) clause is coming.

■ IC $_0$ DC

We'll celebrate when Errol paints his house.
Jack will still be arrogant unless he loses.

In these sentences no comma should intrude because the independent clause is not intended to be understood without the dependent clause that follows it.

The IC ; IC and the DC , IC are absolute. The third rule does have exceptions. When the concluding dependent clause is not essential to understanding the meaning of the independent clause, a comma should precede the dependent clause.

Stefanie is one of the better players on the team when her competitive spirit is engaged, as she demonstrated against Paul VI and other tough teams.

There is properly no comma before the dependent clause *when her competitive spirit is engaged* because the independent clause is not intended to be understood without it. But there is a comma before the dependent clause *as she demonstrated against Paul VI and other tough teams* because that clause is not essential, though it adds a nice detail. Your ear is a more reliable judge of punctuation on this issue than it is on most.

4. Punctuation with *And*

If you now have the punctuation of independent and dependent clauses straight, you've learned the most important part of this chapter. I'd like, then, to introduce a less frequent but still common punctuation problem: punctuation with *and*.

I've said that IC ; IC is correct. And, of course, IC . IC is correct. But there is a third way of connecting independent clauses—that is, with a comma and a so-called *coordinating conjunction* (this is the last conjunction that you'll meet). The coordinating conjunctions are *and, but, or, nor, for, yet*, and *so*, but the most common by far are *and* and *but*. These conjunctions (connecting words) are called *coordinating* rather than *subordinating* conjunctions because they do not subordinate. They leave the two things they connect grammatically equal.

> John loves Abby, *and* Abby loves John.
> The government gives, *and* the government takes away.
> I like pizza, *but* it doesn't like me.

Exercise 9-16
in class

And, of course, can be used to connect many things other than independent clauses. To give you some idea of the variety possible, finish, with the rest of your class, the following sentence:

> George bought a hammer and . . .

When you've finished completing the sentence, decide whether you should put a comma after *hammer*. When you compare your answer with your classmates' answers, you'll see how easily any of the grammatical parts of our sentences can be doubled. Some of you doubled the object (*George bought a hammer and some nails*), some the verb plus the object (*George bought a hammer and returned the lumber*), and some the subject, verb, and object (*George bought a hammer, and Maria bought firewood*). Only in the last case do you need a comma before the *and*. Only when *and* is connecting two entire independent clauses do you need to put a comma before it.

So, our earlier rule is revised:

IC ⓧ IC is correct, and IC⟨, and⟩IC is also correct.

Here's another way to look at it:

Verb	⟨and⟩	verb
phrase	⟨and⟩	phrase
object	⟨and⟩	object

$$\text{IC} \qquad \overset{\textit{but}}{\underset{}{\boxed{,\text{and}}}} \qquad \text{IC}$$

5. Interrupting Words, Phrases, and Clauses

How many times have teachers or editors told you that you must use a comma both *before* and *after* a certain word, or phrase, or clause. Do you know why? The principal use of commas (e.g., DC , IC) is to highlight the independent clause in a sentence. And that's the same reason why you use a comma before and after any *interrupter* of the independent clause.

Independent(*Interrupter*)Clause
Peter, *however*, is the one you can depend on.
Jessica, *you may remember*, was our first choice.

The rule might be stated as follows: "Use a pair of commas to set off material that adds information without affecting the meaning of the rest of the sentence" (Raymond and Goldfarb 49). Using one comma but not both is a common mistake:

Wrong: The prison system, he believes attempts to be fair.
Wrong: Barbara soon made friends, or at least acquaintances of her own age.

Deciding where to put the second comma depends on our being able to pick out the sentence's independent clause. The second comma follows the interrupter; it comes just before the flow of the independent clause resumes.

Correct: The prison system, he believes, attempts to be fair.
Correct: Barbara soon made friends, or at least acquaintances, of her own age.

There are a number of *types of interrupters*:

■ Single-word comments, including conjunctive adverbs:

The Kangfu Textile Company in Shanghai will, *incidentally*, start production in November of medical elastic stockings.

■ Nouns, with their modifiers, giving further information (called *appositives*):

El Arish, *the main depot for Egyptian forces in the Sinai peninsula*, was the last bastion to be attacked.

■ Participial phrases:

Raiders of the Lost Ark, written and produced by George Lucas and Stephen Spielberg, offered the same style of appealing adventure as Paul Newman and Robert Redford's *The Sting*.

■ Adjective clauses:

The Jordanian fighter plane, *which was built in Seattle*, was intercepted while flying in international air space.

■ Words that express an alternative:

A new scarf is an extra, *if minor*, responsibility.

■ Long prepositional phrases:

Will the Russians now try, *under cover of the world's preoccupation with Middle East-ern events*, to reassert their sway over former territories of the Soviet Union?

A problem that many writers take to their graves is being unsure of which phrases and clauses are interrupters and which are not. For example, consider this common maxim:

People who live in glass houses shouldn't throw stones.

The clause *who live in glass houses* is not set off by commas. Why? Because the independent clause, the main part of the sentence, doesn't have the same meaning if that clause is eliminated:

People shouldn't throw stones.

We need the clause *who live in glass houses* to know what people the writer is talking about. Note the contrast in the following sentence:

Bill, who spent last year in Thailand, plans to begin study at the University of Wyoming in the fall.

This sentence makes sense without the interrupting clause. The clause is not necessary to our knowing who Bill is. Therefore, it is a genuine interrupter and merits two commas. The difference between non-interrupting and inter-rupting clauses goes by several names—*restrictive* versus *nonrestrictive*, for example, and *defining* versus *commenting*—but the easiest vocabulary to re-member is, I think, the distinction *identifying* versus *supplementary*. *Identifying* clauses make it possible for us to know exactly who or what the noun preced-ing them is. *Identifying* phrases and clauses should *not* be separated from their main clauses with any punctuation. *Supplementary* clauses give interesting in-formation, but not information necessary for identifying the noun that they follow. *Supplementary* words, phrases, and clauses need two commas to show that they are supplementary, to acknowledge that they are interrupters. To see how the two are commonly used and to make yourself confident of the way they are punctuated, try the following exercise.

Phrases and Clauses: Identifying or Supplementary

Exercise 9-17

in class

Make the following statements more specific by adding an appropriate phrase or clause in each of the blanks. Decide whether your additions should be separated from the main clause by commas.

Women _____ have power _____.
The Exxon station _____ ordered a sign _____.
The veteran _____ raised a flag _____.
An earthquake _____ killed 700 people _____.

When your clauses are *supplementary*, when they *interrupt* the main flow, they'll have been set off by two commas. When your clauses *identify* the nouns they follow, they'll fit right in without any punctuation.

If you've understood the IC; IC and DC, IC and IC$_0$ DC rules, and if you've understood the "interrupter" rules, you should from now on be able to punctuate that troublesome word *however*.

> The list, *however*, didn't include the rest of the family: Mary, Louis, Carol, Ralph, and Theresa.

> I ran out of gas; *however*, soon afterward a passing motorist gave me a ride.

However is the most commonly used conjunctive adverb. It is surrounded by commas when it interrupts a single independent clause. But when it introduces a second independent clause, it will have a semicolon before it, dividing the two independent clauses, and a comma after it, separating the *however* from its own independent clause.

6. Introducing a Quotation

The key to deciding what punctuation is appropriate when introducing a quotation is, once again, understanding where the independent and dependent clauses begin and end.

When punctuating a lead-in to a quotation, you have three choices: a comma, a colon, or no punctuation at all.

> Professor Sniegowski summarized his views on revision: "A writer's principal work is rewriting."

> Professor Sniegowski summarized his views on revision by saying "A writer's principal work is rewriting."

> Professor Sniegowski said, "A writer's principal work is rewriting."

What is the difference between these three lead-ins? Why the need for different punctuation? Sentence structure. In the first example, the grammatical sentence is complete before the quotation begins. The colon says, "Wait, there's more, even though the grammatical sentence is complete." In the second example, the structure of the sentence before the quotation is not complete. We must add an object for *saying*. *Saying* what? Since the gerund *saying* needs an object to be completed, we can't pause, so we use no punctuation. The quotation serves as the object of the gerund *saying*. (A quotation always serves grammatically as a noun in a sentence.)

What about the third example? The use of the comma in the third sentence is a matter of convention. *She said* or *he said* are so common in English that they get their own rules. To be precise, we should say:

Professor Sniegowski said that "The writer's principal work is rewriting."

That the writer's principal work is rewriting is a noun clause, a clause which is acting as a noun, the object in the sentence. But the expression is so common that we save ourselves trouble and skip the *that*. When we do, we replace it with a comma. To summarize, then:

Special Punctuation Rules for Quotations

1. When the sentence structure is complete before the quotation, use a colon to introduce it.
2. When the sentence is continuing, particularly when the quotation is the object of a preposition, or a participle, or a gerund, no punctuation is needed.
3. When you introduce a quotation with "says" or "said," or with equivalent words like "commented" or "stated," use a comma to introduce the quotation.
4. Place all citations *inside* the final punctuation of your sentence; in most cases this means that your sentence will end like this: "quotation" (citation).

Note: The same rule that governs the use of colons in quotations governs their use elsewhere too. We all "know" that a colon introduces a list, but not every list needs a colon. What about the following?

The Rossborough Inn is used by faculty, staff, and alumni for: conferences, luncheons, banquets, cocktail parties, and wedding receptions.

The colon here is intrusive. It blocks the path from a preposition (*for*) to its objects (*conferences*, etc.). The structure of the sentence is not complete at *for*. A colon would be appropriate if *for* were given the object *the following*.

The Rossborough Inn is used by faculty, staff, and alumni for the following: conferences, luncheons, banquets, cocktail parties, and wedding receptions.

Punctuation Rules and Guidelines: A Final Review

1. The key to punctuation is locating the sentence's independent clause.
2. IC;IC.
3. DC,IC.
4. IC_0DC (except when the dependent clause takes a surprising turn of thought or sounds like an afterthought, in which case a comma should be used).
5. I, interrupter, C.
6. IC, and IC.

7. A colon builds anticipation. Use a colon to introduce a quotation or a list *if* the structure of the sentence is already complete.
8. The purpose of most commas is to highlight the main clause of a sentence: to signal the end of introductory phrases or clauses, to separate out interrupters, or to signal the beginning of afterthought phrases or clauses. A comma is also used to separate in lists of three or more items (e.g., "apples, oranges, and bananas"). And commas can be used at our discretion to indicate pauses for emphasis.

Four Lists of Conjunctions You Need to Memorize

1. Coordinating Conjunctions: **and, but, or, nor, for, yet, so.** These conjunctions connect independent clauses and need a comma before them.
2. Conjunctive Adverbs: **also, besides, consequently, finally, first, otherwise, on the contrary, furthermore, however, likewise, immediately, moreover, instead, nevertheless, now, meanwhile, sometimes, indeed, then, therefore, similarly, thus, still, on the other hand, in fact.** These conjunctions also connect independent clauses; a semicolon should separate those independent clauses, and if the conjunctive adverb is not a single syllable, it needs a comma after it.
3. Subordinating Conjunctions: **after, although, because, before, if, since, when, where, while, so that, wherever, how, whether, though, even though, whereas, as, whenever, till (until), unless, as if, as though, as much as, as long as, in order that.** These conjunctions introduce a dependent clause. A comma follows that clause if it comes first in a sentence. No punctuation is necessary before the clause if it comes after the independent clause.
4. Relative Pronouns: **that, who, whose, whom, and which.** In most cases, no punctuation is necessary before these relative pronouns.

Punctuation conventions have shifted many times in history as writers and publishers have tried to find the most flexible system for making their meanings clear. When Thomas More wrote in the early sixteenth century, he simply used a virgule (/) anytime he wanted his reader to pause:

> First yf he have cause to fere / yet fereth he more than he nedeth / For their is no devil so diligent to destry him / as god is to preserve hym / nor no devill so nere hym to do hym harme / as god is to do hym good / nor all the divelles in hell so strong to invade & assawte hym / as god is to defend hym / yf he distrust hym not but faythfully put his trust in hym / (153)

Within a hundred years, though, the virgule was replaced by a four-part breathing system: a comma (,) meant a short breath, a semicolon (;) a slightly longer breath, a colon (:) an even longer breath, and a period (.) a full stop. Our current uses of these four marks are partly related to this sixteenth-century breathing standard, but in the eighteenth century, their uses were firmly tied to sentence structure. The eighteenth century has bequeathed us the rules we've worked through above, such as IC; IC and DC, IC. But the virgule, or a new form of it, the dash, is coming back. Even in the eighteenth century it could be found in the novel *Tristram Shandy* by Lawrence Sterne:

> —My mother, who was sitting by, looked up,—but she knew no more than her backside what my father meant,—but my uncle, Mr. Toby Shandy, who had been often informed of the affair,—understood him very well (3).

Sterne used the dash to reinforce commas, which we no longer do. The wonderful thing about the modern dash is that it is so flexible. We can use it to substitute for a period:

> You may say that this business of marking books is getting in the way of your reading. It probably will—that's one of the reasons for doing it.

For a colon:

> Consider some of the things the blues are about—work, love, death, floods, lynchings.

For a semicolon:

> One day I absentmindedly started crossing the street without looking up or down—the street was empty.

For commas:

> In order to communicate with the dying, we must ourselves understand—and try to feel—the process of dying.

And for opening and closing parentheses:

> So I walked on and on—horses were too expensive—until I had wandered beyond railways, beyond stage lines, to a land of "varmints" and rattlesnakes.

When you're not sure how to punctuate, try a dash. It may not win you any prizes, but it won't get you into any trouble either. Then head back to this chapter for a quick review of the more sophisticated comma, semicolon, colon, and period.

7. The Apostrophe

The apostrophe is often confusing to people who write infrequently because we don't need it when we talk, so we are careless about learning it for when we write. One of the apostrophe's uses is simple. It fills in for missing letters in contractions:

it's for *it is*
you're for *you are*
let's for *let us*

The second use is equally simple. When a noun is converted to an adjective (as *Tom* is in the phrase *Tom's pipe*), *'s* is added to the noun. If the word already ends in *s* (*boys, gloves*), a simple apostrophe is added to make the word possessive (i.e., to make it an adjective): *boys', gloves'*.

One of the most frequently made errors is using *'s* to indicate the plural when a simple *s* will do.

Wrong: I was at San Francisco State for two year's.
Wrong: There were 300 student's in my first college class.

The other case where writers tend to use an unnecessary apostrophe is in the possessive pronoun *its*. This word has no apostrophe. But because it indicates possession, we just itch to stick one in: we want to write *it's* or even *its'*. Resist the urge. You don't have the urge to put an apostrophe in *his* or *her* or *our* or *their*, do you? Well, *its* is in the same family of possessive pronouns:

her house	our house	its house
his house	their house	

Its needs an apostrophe no more than *his* or *her* or *their* or *our* does. *Its* is a good clean word without any little squiggles above the line. Save your apostrophes for converted nouns that need them.

The survey of grammar in this chapter is not complete. Nor is it 100 percent reliable (the very mention of the word *grammar* triggers the association *exceptions*). But the exercises and checklists here are a solid foundation and are intended to be practical: they cover the grammar you need to know to punctuate correctly, and they are brief enough that you shouldn't be afraid to come back to them anytime your confidence needs a boost.

10

Research on the Internet and in the Library

The assignments were interesting, but involved a very lot of work and research for some of them.

STUDENT

I learned the most from my research assignment because (1) it taught me how to use databases, (2) it helped me with my organization problems, and (3) it helped me to take advantage of the libraries.

STUDENT

Before now, my teachers wanted research papers but didn't tell us how to approach the job mentally. . . . I never heard until now that actually developing the thesis or the purpose and approach of the paper was such a lengthy, active process. I thought that I must be dumb. . . . So, I'd pile up the facts and try to organize them into paragraphs and hope the teacher would think I had said something new or meaningful.

STUDENT

Exercise 10-1   Review
on your own, then in class

Before you begin this chapter, write a bit about your research experiences in the past and what you found valuable or frustrating about them. Then compare those experiences with those of your classmates.

You may already have written research papers that you've learned from and been proud of. If so, you know that an invitation to write another research paper is an opportunity to learn yet another subject well. On the other hand, you may never have written a research paper, or you may have written several that you didn't much care for. If you are in this "other hand," let's start fresh this time and make the most of our opportunity.

Research: The Way We Find Raw Material for Our Papers

Research is *not* looking up a few Wikipedia entries and copying out some information appropriate to your topic. It is *not* looking into the first five items that come up on a Google search and pasting together paragraphs from those items. It is *not* taking ten books out of the library and picking out pieces of each of them to pull together into a term paper. It is *not* "changing" the words of your sources into your own words so that you can hand in a paper. Research *is* bringing the knowledge of the past to bear on problems of the present. It is delving into internet archives, libraries, and other storehouses of information to find facts from which *you* draw inferences. If and when you become a professional researcher, it will be very important that you find *all* the important facts and *all* the important sources of information on a subject before you begin to write. The purpose of professional research is to arrive at the soundest possible judgments based on the best information available.

But until you're in graduate school, or have started your profession, you will be assigned research papers not because your teachers expect you to know everything about your topic, but because your teachers value curiosity, reflection, and creativity, and they know that you can increase those skills only if you practice them. Thus when you research a subject in this class, it's important for you to dig for telling facts, but by no means will you be expected to find all of them. Your teachers will be most interested not in your total command of the subject you've studied, but in the creativity with which you draw inferences from the facts you do find. The facts you'll find are of several kinds:

1. The "fact" that something happened:

    In February 1965, President Lyndon Johnson ordered the first bombing raids into North Vietnam (Kearns 261).

2. The "fact" that someone said something:

    Sir Thomas Browne, a seventeenth-century father of eleven: "I could be content that we might procreate like trees, without conjunction, or that there were any way to perpetuate the world without this trivial vulgar way of union: it is the foolishest act a wise man commits in all his life" (Browne 79).

3. Statistical "facts":

    Of the 389 Africans who guided Henry Morton Stanley through the Congo in 1887, more than 200 died during the expedition (Hochschild 99).

4. The "fact" that some authority interpreted a given fact in a given way (*their* inference, *your* fact):

    Eleanor Roosevelt thought early in 1952 that Adlai Stevenson would make a good president, but she doubted whether he could get the Democratic nomination (Lash 206).

You must tell your reader where you found any of these four kinds of facts, as I've done above with my citations in parentheses. What can't be cited, because they can't be borrowed, are the inferences you draw from these facts. Your paper will be shaped by these inferences. When you're writing a research paper, *you* are the thinker (and the selector) at work in the history of information and ideas. When you finish a research paper, you will understand a subject much better than you did when you began, partly because you've found so much more information, but primarily because you've been forced to draw so many inferences, to make so many judgments, about the facts that you've found. If you're afraid to draw inferences (because you're underinformed), that will come through in the hesitant or dependent voice you project in your paper. Or if you avoid thinking by plagiarizing, your teacher will quickly notice the absence of your voice in your writing. On the other hand, if you report your interpretations with confidence, your readers will quickly recognize your success in making sense of the material you've worked with.

Though the term *research paper,* when a teacher uses the term, usually means "library and internet research paper," because your teacher wants you to learn how to use these traditional and common sources, those aren't, of course, the only places to locate firsthand information. Other likely sources include:

1. Interviews
2. Corporation records
3. Court records
4. City, state, or federal records
5. Museum holdings
6. Letters in your grandparents' attic
7. Films, television shows, radio shows, or transcripts or screenplays for any of these three
8. Old copies of books, magazines, or newspapers in secondhand stores.

First-hand records of the way people behaved and thought in the past pull us into their world in ways we can't imagine until we immerse ourselves in them. Listening to a tape of President Kennedy talking on the phone with Governor Ross Barnett of Mississippi in 1962 while James Meredith was trying to enroll at the University of Mississippi and the state police were trying to stop him, looking at a November 1918 edition of the *San Francisco Chronicle* describing the end of the Great War, or reading the wills of 19th-century farmers in the Public Record office in Evansville, Indiana makes you feel like you're reliving history. That thrill of discovery just isn't available, useful as the sources are, when you look up "McCarthyism" or "The Great Depression" on Wikipedia.

When you are asked to write, to write any paper or memo or report, the first thing that should pop into your head is *research*—you have to search *somewhere* for the facts from which you will draw your inferences. That research can often be completed without the help of the internet or a library. When a student decides to write, for example, about the campus Health Center, he goes there to see what he can see, to find out whom he can interview, to read any newspaper articles about it, to collect any facts about it that are telling. When a book reviewer reads through a book she's just been sent by a publisher, she underlines passages that strike her as good, or bad, or unusual, and then when she starts writing, she looks back at her carefully observed underlinings to find telling quotations to use in her review. When a journalist interviews the trainer of a successful racehorse, he observes carefully how the person acts and what is said or unsaid. Most often, though, when you're assigned a research paper, you'll be doing the bulk of your research using the internet and your library.

The Internet and Its Databases

Available on the internet these days is a wealth of materials that only used to be available in libraries. The Library of Congress, for example, now maintains a free database called American Memory, which contains sound recordings, pictures, short films, and historical maps that can immerse us in our nation's history and creativity. To write a sensible and well informed research paper, your most efficient tools now are the databases, primarily of written materials, that your library subscribes to. You may get some useful background material from Wikipedia or from a Google search, but the professionally most respectable sources will be on databases that are not free on the internet, but must be subscribed to by your school. As a result, you will have access to different databases depending on where you are studying, and your teacher and librarian are the best guides to the databases available to you. Several national databases that my students have found useful in recent years are Academic Search Premier, JSTOR, Lexis-Nexis Academic, New York Times Archive, Opposing Viewpoints Resource Center, Readers Guide Full Text, Project Muse, and Wilson Omnifile. A good place to begin your research is to enter several of these databases, generally through your library home page.

Each of these databases will yield, once you type in some key words, long lists of studies whose authors have seriously researched some part of your topic themselves. First, from those lists you should generate your own list of at least ten sources whose titles sound interesting to you. Next, click to bring up the full text of these studies, and browse through each study long enough to decide whether it is thoughtful enough and clearly written enough for you to want to read it carefully, and therefore to print it up. Once you've printed six or seven database sources, and then combined them with a couple of books on your subject that you've found in your library, and perhaps a survey you can conduct or an interview that you can arrange for, you'll have enough raw material, enough potential telling facts, to write your paper.

Libraries

Research often starts on the internet, but it should also take a writer to a library. The internet is still only skimming the surface of the best of our historical thinking—often it emphasizes only very recent work, and too often only briefer and more superficial treatments of issues. As a person who aspires to be well educated, you ought to feel embarrassed if you have relied only on the internet to research an issue and not dug deeper into your library's riches. Libraries are still, though the gap is slowly closing, the repository of 100 to 1,000 times more of our history—documents, newspapers, magazines, audiotapes, videotapes, books, academic studies—than has been uploaded into cyberspace. In two or three hours in your library you could easily find a wide variety of firsthand information that you will not yet find on the internet:

1. An account of a World War II battle (or of the 1929 stock market crash) in *Time* magazine.
2. Social thinking about birth control in 1911 in *The Yale Review.*
3. *National Geographic* articles about Iran dated 1985, 1980, 1975, 1968, 1960, 1953, 1947, 1943, and 1932
4. Poems giving us a window on a new world by Australian or African poets.
5. Firsthand accounts of life in prison, or in Colorado, or in El Salvador.
6. Local, national, and international newspapers, on microfilm, dating well back into the nineteenth, and occasionally even the eighteenth, century.
7. Videotapes or CD's of 1940s detective films or of films by 1960s experimental French directors.
8. Microfilmed document collections of the most seemingly random subjects, such as *The Archives of George Allen and Company, 1893–1915,* or *Contemporary Newspapers of the North American Indian,* or *Records and Briefs in the United States Cases Decided by the Supreme Court.*

If you get interested in Germans during World War II who tried to overthrow Hitler, or in Europeans who moved to Kenya in the first two decades of the twentieth century, you can probably find sixty books, many of them diaries or autobiographies, in your library on either subject. Some of these books after a brief glance can be flipped quickly to the side, but others you'll find so absorbing that you won't want to stop reading and resume your writing.

Historical Exploring

To sense the pleasures of exploring the information available to you, and not just efficiently finding what you "need," you might try the following exercises (or similar exercises specific to your library). If you are stumped at any point, ask a librarian for help. Librarians know well how complex a research task can be, and they welcome the opportunity to teach us how to use the library efficiently.

Exercise 10-2

1. Look up—on microfilm or in the *New York Times* database if it is available to you— *The New York Times* from the day that one of your parents was born. In class the next day, describe, using two or three examples, the world into which your parent was born.

2. Look up *The New York Times* from the day that *you* were born. Find a subject of interest to you and use *The New York Times* and other historical database sources available to you, particularly Readers Guide Full Text, to write a research paper about the world you were born into. The most natural kinds of papers you could write using this data are an assertion-with-examples in which you offer your judgment (inferences) of the world you were born into, or a problem-solution paper showing how a problem that existed when you were born has now been largely solved or perhaps taken on another form.

   While you're reading any of these articles, take notes, including at least the following:

   a. The author's main points
   b. Assumptions of the author that you can detect
   c. Fact-inference links that the author makes
   d. Inferences you have drawn about the author or the historical time in which he wrote
   e. The page, or the paragraph (if you have no page numbers) in which the material appeared that you want to include, either by quoting or by summarizing

   The notes of this sort that you take will provide you with precisely the raw material you'll need for your paper.

The Research Process in a Nutshell

To make your paper easier to write, and to help you avoid plagiarism, you should complete your paper in stages. As soon as you've chosen your topic and looked through a few useful databases and your library catalogue to select possible sources, you should be ready to write a Research Proposal of 1-2 pages, which should include three sections: 1) what I know now about my topic, 2) what I would like to learn about my topic, and 3) where I think I might find useful information—a list of 10 or more sources that you haven't read yet, but judging from their titles, you think you might use.

Once your teacher has approved your research proposal, your job is to start reading the books and articles you've selected, first printing them, if you've found them on the internet, then highlighting passages you might want to quote and jotting down your inferences about those passages in the margins so your facts and inferences match up and will always be easy to find. Once you've read enough to begin writing, I recommend writing up your research in narrative form, a write-up Ken Macrorie has called an "I-Search" (Macrorie, *Searching Writing* 54). Your "I-Search" should consist of five sections:

1) How and Why I Got Interested in this Topic
2) What I Knew and Didn't Know about my Topic When I Began this Paper (based on the first two sections of your Research Proposal)
3) The Story of my Search Through my Sources—a detailed account of what you learned from each article you read, including quotations from your sources and citations in parentheses following those quotations
4) What I Learned by Doing This Research and What I Still Don't Know after Completing My Research
5) Works Cited List

You'll be surprised how easily you can write 5, 10, or even 15 pages using this "I-Search" format and not having to worry about your organization, or your argument, or a thesis.

After turning in your "I-Search" narrative and having it graded, or at least reviewed, by your teacher, you'll write the final version of your paper in standard introduction/body-paragraphs/conclusion form by looking through your "I-Search" narrative and dividing your information and inferences into several topics, usually following either a problem-solution, a cause-effect, or an assertion-with-examples organization. Somewhere in your "I-Search" narrative should be material you can use in your introductory paragraph, and now you'll need a thesis, topic sentences, transitions from idea to idea, and a thoughtful conclusion. But all your raw material, and your parenthetical citations, and your "Works Cited" list, will already be in one, easily mined, place—your "I-Search" narrative. In this last step of your paper, you'll appreciate how useful your work on organization was in Chapter 5. You'll also notice that the more personal parts of your "I-Search" writeup will fit well into your introduction and conclusion, and even occasionally into your body paragraphs. Those elements will help make this project distinctively yours.

Research Paper Skills

Many constituent skills go into the writing of a research paper. Let's consider several of these one at a time.

1. Note Taking

Writers, like gold diggers, sort through a lot of indifferent material looking for gold, looking for telling facts. The quality of the paper you finally produce will depend to a great extent on your ability to decide what is worth noting and what is not. The notes you take reflect your intellectual achievement as a sorter.

As you read, you'll begin to see facts you'll want to use, quotations you'll want to use, and opinions of others you'll want to use and comment on. Either copy them out in the library, or print them from the internet. *Each time you select or copy out a fact, a quotation, or an opinion, ask yourself, "So what?" Your answers to that question will begin to build your stock of inferences.* Equally important, each time you find a passage to quote or one you want to paraphrase, take down its essential information for your "Works Cited" page so you won't be scrambling to find that information when the paper is due.

2. Drawing Inferences from Your Research Sources

Exercise 10-3

Imagine that the two items below drew your attention while you were doing your research. For each of these items, draw as many inferences as you can about the writers, the issues discussed, and the cultural climate at the time that these pieces are describing. Circle the words you used to draw these inferences.

a. From the *Los Angeles Times*, June 2, 1944, page 5, a caption below a picture:

On Warpath—Sporting mustache and cigar as in his Guadalcanal glory days, when he downed 26 Jap planes, Marine Major Joseph J. Foss of Sioux Falls, South Dakota, is again on duty in the South Pacific. He heads his own squadron of Corsairs which bear the insignia of a royal flush in spades with the joker a winged fighter smoking a large cigar.

b. From a senior thesis of a student, Nam Pham, who with his family, after the U.S. war in Vietnam, endured "re-education" camps there before moving to the United States:

I lay on the floor in the cement cell thinking about my conversation with the prison guard and the report I had written for him. I wondered if they were satisfied with my report. A disturbing thought came to me. What if they ask Thuy Nhu? How could she write down the same thing I had written. That was the trick the prison guards used to interrogate the prisoners. I remembered hearing that one should remember and write exactly the same report at every interrogation for the communists. The communists would check the prisoners by letting them write about the same subject many times. I quickly recalled each detail I had written upstairs for the next time I might have to write.

Compare the inferences you've drawn from these passages with the inferences drawn by your classmates. When you do your own research, use the same method to build the stock of inferences that will yield *your* point of view about the material you have researched.

3. Keeping the Subject Covered to a Reasonable Size

Only time and experience will help you do this easily. It is obviously difficult to cover "The Rise of Al Qaeda," or "The Life of Archbishop Desmond Tutu," in three to ten pages. But that doesn't mean that you have to restrict yourself to Al Quaeda's bombing of the U.S.S. Cole in Yemen at 11:18 am on October 12th, 2000 or to Archbishop Tutu's actions on behalf of Aung San Syu Kii in Myanmar on September 26th, 2007. You can write about large events or whole lives by discussing them through a few typical events or representative examples. Almost any large issue or whole life can be brought within a reasonable compass if you examine in some detail three or four representative examples of how the issue has been raised or of significant milestones in a person's life.

4. Evaluating Your Sources

As a student, you can't always tell whether the sources you quote from are reliable or not. The fact that they've been published and the fact that they've been bought by your library or selected by a good database help establish their reliability, but these criteria are not a sufficient guarantee of either accuracy or sophistication of judgment. As you get to know certain fields (Iraqi history, for example, or computer design), you'll gradually come to realize whom you can trust and whom you can't in those fields. Do try to get to know the political conditions in the fields you write about, but because papers are due early and often, you'll usually, in the meantime, just have to use your own judgment of the *ethos, logos,* and *pathos* employed by the authors you're reading to make your best assessment of their value.

5. Ensuring That Your Work Is Your Own

The point of doing a research paper is to arrive at *your* interpretation of events or of people or of works that people have created. You fail to achieve that interpretation if you rely heavily on someone who has already interpreted the same events or works. When we read a persuasive interpretation of some event, it's difficult in most cases to form an alternative interpretation. The biggest challenge for most students writing a research paper is to get your head above the water of all that you have read and to keep thinking for yourself. To help you continually distinguish your thoughts from those of the experts whose works you're reading, just remember that "Expert A" thinks "B" is, to you, just another piece of evidence, a fact that you must in turn draw your own inference from.

You know you can't use any opinions of others, word for word, as if they were your own. For example, suppose you were writing a paper about ecology and you came across the following passage written by Annie Dillard in *Pilgrim at Tinker Creek*:

> Nature is, above all, profligate. Don't believe them when they tell you how economical and thrifty nature is, whose leaves return to the soil. Wouldn't it be cheaper to leave them on the tree in the first place? (Dillard 65)

In most schools, if you turned in a paper which used the words above without a citation and without quotation marks, you'd be charged with plagiarism, fail your course, and be put on academic probation. You'd be just as guilty, though, if you wrote the following, in an attempt to "change a few words":

> Nature is wasteful. Just because its leaves return to the soil doesn't make it economical and thrifty. Wouldn't it be cheaper if the tree just kept its leaves all year round?

In order to avoid danger, and in order to force yourself to do the thinking that a research paper is supposed to elicit from you, you should (if you want to use this passage) do one of the following:

a. Quote the whole passage, acknowledge your source with a parenthetical reference—(Dillard 65)—and full information in your Works Cited list, and then comment on the quotation from your own point of view.
b. Summarize the quotation in one sentence, acknowledge your source as before—(Dillard 65), and *comment* (as before) on Dillard's point of view from your own point of view.

If you want to incorporate a substantial line of thinking from a source, paraphrase that source, and insert a parenthetical citation—e.g. (Dillard 65)—no less than every three sentences.

A library research paper requires a serious investment of time and thinking. There are no legitimate shortcuts. Shortcuts like plagiarism short-circuit learning, and they are a breach of trust.

6. Incorporating Quotations

One of the recurrent worries of writers of research papers is how to handle quotations: we worry about what to quote, about taking quotations out of the author's context, and about blending quotations into our own writing. Four guidelines, though, will get you through the thicket of worry: (1) you should use quotations as evidence, not as a continuation of your own argument; (2) before each quotation, you should identify the author and introduce the context in which the author wrote the sentence or sentences that you want to quote; (3) you should include a citation in parentheses after every quotation, with the parenthenses following the closing quotation mark and coming *before* the period ending your sentence; and (4) you should follow up each quotation by explaining its significance in your eyes.

7. Punctuating Quotations

Exercise 10-4
in class

To practice the mechanical rules for introducing quotations in your work, answer the questions below, and compare your answers with those of your classmates. You'll find the correct answers to these questions at the beginning of Chapter 14.

1. How would you punctuate your sentence if you were using footnote style and you wanted to quote from page 296 of Ralph Ellison's *Shadow and Act*, where he says that in Harlem "it is possible for talented youths to leap through the development of decades in a brief twenty years"?

2. How would you punctuate this same quotation if you were using not footnotes but parenthetical references with a "List of Works Cited" at the end?

3. If you wanted to quote the words "this is no dream" from page 296, and you knew that "this" referred to Harlem but your reader didn't, how could you use brackets to make that clear to the reader?

4. If you wanted to quote the line "a world so fluid and so shifting that often within the mind the real and the unreal merge, and the marvelous beckons from behind the same sordid reality that denies its existence" from page 296, but you thought the quotation was too long, and you didn't think that the part about the real and the unreal merging was so important, how could you shorten and then punctuate your quotation?

5. If you wanted to quote more than four lines from any source, how would you place the words you were quoting on the page?

8. Acknowledging Sources

You may have the impression that the purpose of writing research papers is to learn the forms for what used to be "footnotes" and "Bibliographies" and what are now "parenthetical citations" and "Works Cited" lists. But that issue looms large only until you become familiar with and comfortable with citations, neither of which takes long once you allow yourself to put your mind to it.

Research papers are assigned so that you can practice investigating a mass of material, determining what is important in that material, coming to a conclusion about the material, and organizing the selected material to help a reader. The purpose of citing itself is to help your reader find and follow up with the sources that you found useful.

Conventions for acknowledging sources have been shifting significantly the past few decades, but they have now settled down, and I'm confident that your children will be using, for the most part, the same "new" forms that you are using now. First in psychology but now in almost all fields, footnotes have been replaced by parenthetical references, and bibliographies by a final list of Works Cited. The official guides to how to acknowledge sources are now the *Publication Manual of the American Psychological Association* (2001) for social science subjects, *Scientific Style and Format* (1994) for sciences, *The Chicago Manual of Style* (2008) for history, and the *Modern Language Association Style Manual* (2006) for humanities subjects except history. In this book we will follow the Modern Language Association guide, but if your teacher expects you to follow one of the others, the changes you'll need to make will be minimal.

The aim of parenthetical citations is to be as simple as possible. The parentheses that enclose your citation are placed just before the final punctuation mark in the sentence in which you refer to the work being acknowledged. In most cases the citation includes just the author's last name and the page on which the material you are referring to originally appeared:

(McCauley 25).

If two books or articles by McCauley appear in your Works Cited list your parenthetical reference must distinguish the two works:

(McCauley, "Pollution Control" 36–37)
(McCauley, "Hospital Costs" 122)

If two McCauleys appear in your works cited list, you must distinguish between the two McCauleys:

(Michael McCauley 36–37)
(Patricia McCauley 16-17)

If you are quoting from an article whose author is anonymous, your parenthetical citation should include the title—shortened—in the usual place of the author:

("Hospital Costs" 14)

If you have mentioned the author in the sentence where your parenthetical citation is to appear, or if you're quoting from only one book in your paper, as is common in literary analysis papers, your citation need only indicate the page or pages:

(36–37)

The system is wonderfully simple, as soon as you get used to seeing numbers without p. or pp. before them and knowing that those numbers refer to pages.

One difficulty we have now in 2010 that has not yet been resolved is how to direct your readers to the page numbers of studies that first appeared in print but which you have read or downloaded online. If you cite a short passage from a 20-page study and you can't tell your reader in your citation where in that study your passage came from, your citation is not much help to him. It would take your reader a lot of searching or a lot of luck to find the passage you've quoted in less than 15 minutes. The best compromise we've come up with so far is for you to *note, and then cite in your parentheses, the paragraph* in which you found any material that is no longer paginated—i.e. (Clinton, para. 12). Perhaps in the next few years, as html technology is refined, we'll come up with a system a little less clumsy and time consuming.

Every parenthetical citation is a promise to the reader that full information about this source will be found in your list of works cited. Therefore, when you've finished your paper, make a list of all the works you've cited, get all the bibliographic information you need, and make up, in alphabetical order by authors' last names, your list of Works Cited.

9. Putting Together Your Works Cited List

Try to follow the guidelines in Table 10-1 that follows when you're listing your Works Cited, but don't get obsessed about them. Remember the reason for citations: to make it easy for your reader to find your sources. Whenever you're in doubt about the "rules," just use your best judgment.

When listing *books* according to the Modern Language Association style, the four principal parts of your entry should be (1) the author's name, (2) the title of the book, (3) the place of publication, publisher, and date of publication, and (4) the word, "Print," which, since 2009, should be included with all print sources. Each of the four principal parts is separated by a period.

McPhee, John. *Basin and Range.* New York: Farrar, Straus, and Giroux, 1981. Print.

Note that the author's last name comes first, that titles are italicized, that a colon comes between the place of publication and the publisher, and that a comma comes between the publisher and the date of publication. When the entry requires more complicated information, the required order is as follows: (1) the author's name, (2) the title of the part of the book written by the author, (3) the title of the whole book, (4) the name of the editor or translator, (5) the edition of the book, (6) the number of volumes in the book, (7) the place of publication, publisher, and date of publication, (8) the pages within the larger work that the author's work covers, and (9) the word "Print."

When you are listing *periodicals* in your Works Cited list, the required order is (1) the author, (2) the title of the article, (3) the name of the periodical,

(4) the volume number of the periodical if it is published no more frequently than quarterly, (5) the date of publication, (6) the pages within the periodical that the author's work covers, and (7) the word "Print." Here is an entry for an unsigned article in *Time* magazine:

"A Fighter Pilot Turned Negotiator." *Time* 10 Oct. 1983: 35. Print.

Note that titles of articles are placed in quotation marks, that the titles of newspapers, magazines, or journals are italicized, that a period follows the title of the article, that no punctuation comes between the magazine and its date, that all months except May, June, and July are abbreviated, and that a colon comes between the date and the page numbers.

When you are listing *articles found on the internet* in your Works Cited list, the expected order is: (1) Author's last name, first name. (2) "Article Title" or *Book Title*. (3) Publication information for any printed version, or subject line of forum or discussion group. (4) Indication of online posting or home page. (5) *Title of Electronic Journal*. (6) Date of electronic publication. (7) Page numbers, or the numbers of paragraphs or sections. (8) Name of institution or organization sponsoring the Website. (9) the word "Web." (10) Date that you electronically accessed the source.

Table 10-1 is a chart that covers the most usual possibilities that you'll come across in your research, but Murphy's Law of research guarantees that you will turn up a source that fits no model that I predict here. When you do, just make your best guess based on the principles explained here. The purpose of systems of acknowledgment is not to drive writers crazy but to serve readers by being clear, convenient, and concise.

Table 10-1   Checklist for Works Cited Format for Your Most Common Types of Sources

Articles Found on the Internet	
Clinton, Bill. "Welfare Should be Reformed." *Opposing Viewpoints: Welfare*. Ed. Charles P. Cozic. San Diego: Greenhaven Press, 1997, Opposing Viewpoints Resource Center. Thirty-six paragraphs. Gale. 28 Feb. 2009. Web. 28 Feb 2009.	

Books	
One Author	Chen, Da. *Colors of the Mountain*. New York, Random House, 2000. Print.
Two authors	Albright, Priscilla, and Rodney Albright, *Short Nature Walks on Long Island*. Guilford, CT: Globe Pequot, 2001. Print.
Editor	Cooper, Lane, ed. *The Rhetoric of Aristotle*. New York: Appleton, Century, Crofts, 1932. Print.

(Continued)

**Table 10-1   Checklist for Works Cited Format for Your Most
Common Types of Sources (Continued)**

	Books
Author and Editor	Miller, Kate. *Poems in Black and White*. Ed. Helen Robinson. Honesdale, PA: Wordsong, 2007. Print.
No Author Identified	*College Park Grammar Review Worksheets*. Raleigh, NC: Contemporary Publishing, 1980. Print.
Second or Later Edition	Strunk, William, and E.B. White. *The Elements of Style*. 4th ed. New York: Allyn & Bacon, 2000. Print.
One of Several Volumes	Keller, Helen Rex. *The Dictionary of Dates*. 2 vols. New York: Macmillan, 1934. Print.
Article that is Included in a Book	Babbitt, Irving. "Burke and the Moral Imagination." In *The Burke-Paine Controversy*. Ed. Ray B. Browne. New York: Harcourt, Brace, & World, 1963: 149–156. Print.
	Magazines and Newspapers
Signed article in a journal appearing quarterly or less frequently	Lindblom, Ken. "'Once More unto the Breach, Dear Friends': Beginning Another Year." English Journal 98 (2008): 11–12. Print.
Unsigned article in a magazine appearing monthly or more often	"A Fighter Pilot Turned Negotiator." *Time* 10 Oct. 1983: 35. Print.
Signed newspaper article	Roberts, Sam. "Celebrating 400th Anniversary of Henry "Hudson's Historic Voyage." *The New York Times* 29 Mar. 2009: A25. Print.
Unsigned newspaper article	"Another Icy Blast Moves In." *Houston Chronicle* 19 Jan. 1984: 1. Print.
Newspaper editorial	"Border Control." Editorial. *The New York Times* 28 Mar. 2009: A20. Print.
Book review	Wood, James. Review of *War and Peace*, by Leo Tolstoy. Trans. Richard Pevear and Larissa Volokhonsky. *The New Yorker* 26 Nov. 2007: 158–166. Print.
	On-Line Encyclopedia Articles
Signed Article	Hore-Lacy, Ian. "Uranium." *Encyclopedia of Earth*. 12 Feb. 2008. Seven sections. Web. 3 May 2009.
Unsigned Article	"Block Quotation." *Wikipedia*. 2 Apr. 2009. Six sections. Web. 3 May 2009.

(continued)

Table 10-1   Checklist for Works Cited Format for Your Most Common Types of Sources (*Continued*)

	Unpublished Materials
Photocopy	Walsh, Mark, and Martha Walsh. "The Farm." Unpublished manuscript, 2009.
Lecture	Ellison, Ralph. "A Writer's Life." University of Notre Dame, 4 Apr. 1968.
Interview	Hubert Miller. Email Interview. 3 Nov. 2007.
Television or Radio program	Robertson, Pat. "The 700 Club." WTTG, Washington, D.C. 15 Feb. 1998. Video.

To keep works-cited conventions from taking on greater importance than they deserve, I'd like to conclude this chapter not with talk about those conventions, but with a comment on inferences. We consider our research papers finished, and we begin to feel genuine pride in them, when we are confident of our inferences, confident, that is, of our interpretations. It is those thoughtful interpretations, and the well-selected information on which we have based our interpretations, that mark the difference between drudgery (halfhearted term papers) and challenging, satisfying intellectual work.

11

Research through Interviewing

At first I was scared, but I enjoyed interviewing someone. It made me and him feel important.

STUDENT

Nothing so animates writing as someone telling what he thinks or what he does—in his own words.

WILLIAM ZINSSER

Exercise 11-1   Review

on your own

Answer the following question in your notebook:

> What qualities would you expect to find in a good interviewer?

In most kinds of writers' research, the first steps are the easiest: surfing through possible sites you can use, browsing through books related to your topic, sitting back to watch a movie before you review it more carefully, walking through a farmers' market watching the customers and the sellers while jotting notes in a notebook. But when your writing is to be based on an interview, the hardest step comes first—asking a stranger to set aside an hour to sit and talk with you. (Asking for the first interview of your life is also harder than asking for any later ones.) Once you've screwed up your courage to ask for an interview, though, the interview itself and writing a paper based on it will come more easily. The interview, if you have well-prepared questions, is almost always more enjoyable than you would have guessed, and writing a character sketch or an analysis of a person's views based on an interview (the two most common uses of interview research) involves, as usual, selecting the best material, drawing inferences, searching for a focus and organization, testing your ideas in a first draft, and revising that draft until it makes good sense.

Before you ask for an interview, stop to ask yourself whether you have picked up some bad habits without even having started writing. First of all, most published interviews are interviews of "famous" people, and as readers we're not very demanding about what we're willing to listen to from them. If an interviewer can get Denzel Washington to say anything, we'll probably pay money to read it. The writer doesn't have to ask skillful questions or select very carefully what she'll print and what she'll edit out. Writers of interviews with famous people often earn their salaries more for their ability to "get" interviews than for their ability to write or edit them well. The person you interview for this class will *not* be a celebrity, so you'll have to ask good questions, and you'll have to select very carefully what to present your readers with. You'll have to both interview and write well.

The second bad habit you may have picked up is the laziness of printing an interview as a disjointed set of questions and answers, as in the following excerpt from an interview with British novelist E. M. Forster (Cowley 28):

INTERVIEWERS: While we are on the subject of the planning of novels, has a novel ever taken an unexpected direction?

FORSTER: Of course, that wonderful thing, a character running away with you—which happens to everyone—that's happened to me, I'm afraid.

INTERVIEWERS: Can you describe any technical problem that especially bothered you in one of the published novels?

FORSTER: I had trouble with the junction of Rickie and Stephen. [The hero of *The Longest Journey* and his half brother.] How to make them intimate, I mean. I fumbled about a good deal. It *is* all right once they are together. . . . I didn't know how to get Helen to Howards End. That part is all contrived. There are too many letters. And again, it is all right once she is there. But ends always give me trouble.

INTERVIEWERS: Why is that?

FORSTER: It is partly what I was talking about a moment ago. Characters run away with you, and so won't fit on to what is coming.

INTERVIEWERS: Another question of detail. What was the exact function of the long description of the Hindu festival in *A Passage to India?*

FORSTER: It was architecturally necessary. I needed a lump, or a Hindu temple if you like—a mountain standing up. It is well placed; and it gathers up some strings. But there ought to be more after it. The lump sticks out a little too much.

INTERVIEWERS: To leave technical questions for a moment, have you ever described any type of situation of which you have had no personal knowledge?

FORSTER: The home-life of Leonard and Jacky in *Howards End* is one case. I knew nothing about that. I believe I brought it off.

INTERVIEWERS: How far removed in time do you have to be from an experience in order to describe it?

This form doesn't require the interviewer to be a writer; it only requires that the interviewer own a recording device. Such an interviewer may well have asked good questions, but he's provided no writer's consciousness to guide us along, helping us see connections, highlighting the interviewee's most important character traits. Although you're practicing a new research technique in this chapter (interviewing), you'll bring to what you finally write all the writing skills you've shown in your earlier work—selecting and organizing your material, interesting your reader in the subject, showing that you understand the implications of what you've written.

Your first step is to choose the person you'd like to interview. Start thinking of possibilities now, and tell someone—soon—whom it is you plan to interview so that you will begin to believe that you will actually do it. If you're writing a character sketch, your interview will work best (believe it or not) if you don't know the interviewee at all, or if at all, only by sight. Also, you should probably interview a person at least 40 years old—old enough to have developed a perspective about what life means to her, or to him. I recommend that you interview someone who has chosen a path you don't plan to follow— a roofer, a bus driver, a mother of seven, a fire fighter, someone who has grown up in another country.

No matter whom you interview, though, you'll be surprised how often people respond enthusiastically to the idea of talking about themselves. If the first person you ask doesn't want to talk or doesn't want to take the time, just thank her anyway and try someone else. You're not a reporter whose story will be incomplete until he has talked to a key witness. Another interviewee will do just, or almost, as well. If your first try results in a refusal, your second one is not likely to.

In class, before you actually face your interviewee, you can practice several techniques that will make the process of interviewing and writing easier and more effective.

Preparing Questions for an Interview

Exercise 11-2
in class

Bring to class ten sample questions that you might bring to an interview. When class begins, pass your list to a neighbor and take a list from a neighbor. Choose the three questions of those ten that you think will elicit the most interesting answers. Pass the list along again, and take a different list. See if you'd choose the same three questions as the person who reviewed the list before you. Then, with your classmates, share the best questions and explain, in each case, *why* those questions were designed to bring out the best information. Take good notes, and feel free to use any of these questions that others in the class came up with in your own interview.

Practice Interview

Exercise 11-3
in class

Practice interviewing your teacher. (Instead of, or in addition to, interviewing the teacher, you and your classmates may want to interview each other or a person selected by your teacher.)

Use the expanded question list you now have to conduct a group interview of your teacher. Take notes on all questions asked, not just your own. Note how your teacher responds, just as any interviewee will respond. Some questions she will refuse to answer, some she will answer matter-of-factly, some she will enjoy talking about. When you note an area that she is interested in, abandon your question list and ask more detailed follow-up questions about the areas of her greatest interest.

When the interview is over, write up (either in class or at home) a character sketch of your teacher. If all the sketches are compared, you will see a variety of choices—for introductions, conclusions, quotations, organization. The following are some instructive samples of a variety of student choices from a teacher interview:

1. *Opening sentences:* Do these start the reader off well?

   - Cristina Cheplick left her friends and family to come to America to live with her husband.

   - Many questions come to mind when you talk to someone who has emigrated from another country.

   - "My parents wanted me to be a doctor, but I wanted to teach," said Cristina Cheplick.

   - "Life is a series of hassles," C. Cheplick said about life in Romania.

   - Cristina Cheplick began to learn English in 5th grade, and read her whole book in a week.

   - In 5th grade, Cristina was introduced to the English language; consequently, at the age of 28, she is an English teacher.

   - Cristina Ionescu was born in a hospital in the Romanian town [*sic*] of Transylvania, which is near her hometown of Cluj.

   - Cristina Cheplick is a woman who has already experienced more then most people have.

   - Cristina Cheplick has chosen the lifestyle of the U.S. instead of the one in Romania.

2. *Telling facts:* Are these good ones?

   - When she talks to friends from Romania, they don't ask about the government here but about food: "Do you have to stand in line for cheese?"

   - Cristina smiled when she showed off the Romanian valentines her friends sent.

- Even though her own country has its problems, she still looks back on it with fondness.
- She saw *The Sound of Music* ten times, and even knows the dialogue by heart.
- It was a zip for her to read an English novel, she was so taken by the language.
- She went to all the movies she could and learned everything that she could about English culture. She met a visiting American and married him.
- In Romania, she lived in a two-bedroom apartment with the rest of her family.

3. *Using quotations:* Are these well chosen?

   - "It's a land where people vote with their feet," said Mrs. Cheplick, quoting her husband, "everyone wants to leave."
   - Eight years of English and college gave her a good background to come here: "Everyone is poor and has to stand in line."
   - "My marriage enabled me to leave, but that's not why I married."
   - The national paper is only five pages long, due to government censorship. "When my mother saw the *Washington Post*, she thought it was the news for the entire year."
   - The question most people wanted an answer to was: "How are people in America different from the people in your country?" She replied that "the biggest difference is in the demeanor of the people."
   - She emphasized her happiness with teaching English in America through her enthusiasm and detailed descriptions. "Romania," she says, "is a very poor country."

4. *Paragraphing:* Would these paragraphs make a substantial contribution to a paper?

   - She took the bus to her teaching job every morning, and returned in the evening. On her return trip, she witnessed the long line of citizens already waiting in line for the morning bread, cheeses, and other needs. When she retired for the night, she would sit up in bed, and read the 5-page *Scinteia* published by the gov't.
   - C. Cheplick is an English teacher at the University of Maryland. She used to live in Romania until her marriage. She hopes to be an American citizen soon. She dresses in sweaters and slacks and ruffly blouses. The main difference she sees is the carefree attitude of Americans. America is a completely different world. Cristina smiled when she showed off her Romanian valentines.
   - Her college education was free, with an agreement to work for the government. She took eight years of it in grade school and four in college. What a life!

5. *Choosing a focus:* Note how many choices you have.

   - *Being practical:*

Mrs. Cheplick picked her occupation in Romania, knowing that teachers and doctors made the same amount of money.

■ *The linguist:*

All of her life, she has had a love for different languages. Many a time, she would go to the movies to try and pick up some of the languages. Many times in class she would read ahead, just for the fun of it.

■ *The happy teacher:*

An English teacher from Romania? Sounds like a contradiction in terms, but C. Cheplick, Freshman English teacher at the University of Maryland, is very happy in America teaching English. She emphasized it through her enthusiasm and detailed descriptions.

■ *Seeking a new life:*

She was refused entrance to the party government. She left her family and friends to try to make a new life with her husband in a strange new country. She knew she would never have a successful career in Romania.

■ *Appreciating the new life:*

Cristina left Romania to come to teach in America. She has much more freedom and enjoys the freedom of expression. Also, she does not have the everyday worry of where the next meal is coming from.

■ *Hard times:*

Mrs. Cheplick recalls the time when she was on a bus in Romania, and "the driver shut the doors on a person." People are rude and discourteous.

■ *Hard worker:*

C. Cheplick began to learn English in the 5th grade and read the whole book in a week. She was always ahead of her class and studied for two years solid to get into college to study English.

Comparing Written and Video Interviews

Exercise 11-4

on your own

Use video sources to learn interviewing techniques. Like the papers you'll write for this class, segments from Charlie Rose, the Book Channel, and *60 Minutes* are successful because they are written to inform and entertain audiences—several of these twenty- to thirty-minute segments on these shows try to reveal the predominant character trait of a person, making that person come alive for the viewer.

1. View a CD or videotape which features a particular individual (the person does not have to be famous). If possible, get a copy of the script.
2. As you watch, keep in mind the following questions:

- How does the introduction try to gain your interest?
- What is the scriptwriter's focus?
- How does the interviewer move (i.e. make transitions) from one subject to the next?
- Note the three quotations from the interviewee that you found most telling.
- Why is the ending provocative (if it is)?

The writing process is very much the same for a television script and for a written article. Writing for presentation on paper must, however, be more descriptive than writing for a television script, because a camera can capture for the viewer what a reader—unless told—never sees. Note, in the tape you've chosen, how the camera shots (description) aid in emphasizing points made by the narrator.

If you've done Exercises 11–2 and 11–3, you should be well prepared to start now on your interview. Take your master list of questions and meet your interviewee at a scheduled time and place. Bring a small recording device if you wish and if your interviewee doesn't mind. A recorder will give you much (perhaps too much) raw material to work with and prune. But don't feel that you need a recorder; you'll probably be better off without one. You'll be well prepared for writing, and you'll save yourself hours of listening time later, if you just bring two or three pencils and plenty of paper. Since you won't want to write down everything, your pencil will serve as a natural instrument of selection. Inevitably, both you and the interviewee will be nervous for the first few minutes, but soon you'll be talking freely. The questions you'll ask will depend on you and your interviewee and on the quality of the question-list selection you did in class, but there are some general guidelines you can follow:

1. Be sure to ask not only *what* the person has done but also *why* she has done it. You can be sure that the reader reading your sketch will consistently be asking, "Why?" Anticipate the question.
2. When you come upon any area that your interviewee is clearly interested in, ask more questions about that area. It may well be a key to the person's character.
3. Don't be afraid to stop and write something down to keep it from being lost. Your interviewee won't feel ignored. He'll be glad that you're being careful.
4. When you run out of good questions, thank your interviewee and leave, even if you think you'll need more information later. You can plan on being back in touch, at least by phone. You haven't had your last chance at research yet.
5. As soon as you're on your own, fill out your abbreviated notes so that you can understand them. Two hours after the interview, your notes will be puzzling. Two days later, they'll look like hieroglyphics.

When writing time comes, remember that, as with any other assignment, you are both a researcher and a writer. In this assignment, specifically, you are both an interviewer and a writer. Now that you have the raw material for a paper, it's your job to pull that material into shape: to *select* (don't fill your pages with everything you heard); to draw inferences from the facts you've discovered; to decide on a focus, an introduction, and a conclusion; to find a scheme of organization; to introduce your quotations skillfully and balance your emphases on quotations and commentary; to make sure you've provided enough breadth and depth of information; to omit irrelevant biographical details; to check for inaccuracies. As your draft begins to take shape, you'll find that you can't do all these tasks yourself, that your interviewee is still necessary. If you return to the interviewee, you can, in ten to fifteen minutes, ask the questions that you now know are important, though you didn't see their importance when you were only a first-time interviewer.

As you rework the final draft, there are some larger questions well worth asking. Have you found something that your readers wouldn't expect? Have you challenged your readers' assumptions? Have you told us something about human nature? If you have, we can now see a little better behind our human masks.

12

Research through Careful Reading

Reading is not simply a matter of gathering data, but also, and simultaneously, a matter of going through a sequence of moves that the writer has controlled for the purpose of leading the reader to assent. The skill of critical reading, it goes without saying, is one of understanding when one's assent has been earned.

JOHN T. GAGE

Writing is both knowing conventions and knowing where to flaunt them. Reading is knowing conventions and knowing how to recognize when, how, and why they have been broken.

ALAN C. PURVES

I have been told that reading helps.

STUDENT

Review of Your Reasons for Reading

Exercise 12-1
on your own

Before you begin this chapter, answer the following question in your notebook:

When you casually pick up a book or a magazine, what is it that makes you keep reading?

Drawing Inferences While Reading (Reading between the Lines)

Whenever we read, we expect our writer to take us a step beyond our current situation. (When we're writing, of course, we should keep the same in mind—that we are trying to take *our* readers a step beyond *their* current situation.) Reading, like writing, is a naturally reflective activity. Rarely do we just soak in something that we're reading. Most of the time we implicitly comment to ourselves on what we read while we read. Of course, when we're distracted or tired, our eyes may be running over the pages, but in those cases we're not really reading.

Your reading has been becoming more thoughtful throughout this course. In Exercise 3–5, you read Sister Rebecca's advertisement and drew inferences about her. In Chapter 5 you read several excerpts from textbooks noting the patterns by which they organized their material. In Chapter 7 you wrote a one-sentence-per-paragraph outline of a Robertson Davies essay. Throughout this writing course you've been reading and judging your classmates' drafts. And throughout the course, you've been reading and judging your own work as you revise. In addition, you may frequently have been asked to write in class about your reading assignments. Perhaps you've even kept a journal of notes on what intrigued or puzzled you about your reading during the semester. All these exercises have helped to make you a more active reader. In this chapter, though, we'll try to dig deeper by becoming more self-conscious of what we do when we read thoughtfully.

Any piece of writing you pick up will consist primarily of facts (selected by the writer) and inferences (made by the writer). Here are two examples from Rachel Carson's book, *Silent Spring* (1962):

> *Fact Rachel Carson collected:* Since the mid-1940s over 200 basic chemicals have been created for use in killing insects, weeds, rodents, and other organisms described in the modern vernacular as "pests."
>
> *Inference Rachel Carson drew:* To adjust to these chemicals would require time on the scale that is nature's; it would require not merely the years of a man's life but the life of generations.

As readers, we can simply take all this in, adding the facts to our memories and accepting the inferences as helpful insights. *Or we can do our own thinking, our own drawing of readers' inferences about the facts and inferences as we read. (See Table 12–1 on the next page.) Our inferences are called "readers' inferences" because we are drawing inferences not about the author's subject but about the author as a writer: her interests, her aims, her prejudices, the reading and research that prepared her to write, the cultural expectations of her society, the readers she intended to write for.* The author's fact and inference above become, for the reader, two facts about the author from which the reader can draw inferences.

Table 12-1   Drawing Readers' Inferences

Author's Fact
Since the mid-1940s over 200 basic chemicals have been created for use in killing insects, weeds, rodents, and other organisms described in the modern vernacular as "pests."

Reader's Fact (About the Author)	Reader's Inference (About the Author)
The author has checked government records to get these statistics.	The author has been responsible about providing evidence. She probably decided to use statistics because that's the only language that is persuasive to those who don't seem to care about environmental issues.

Author's Inference
To adjust to these chemicals would require time on the scale that is nature's; it would require not merely the years of a man's life but the life of generations.

Reader's Fact (About the Author)	Reader's Inference (About the Author)
The author makes a bold predictive inference here about the future.	The author is trying to use her expertise as a biologist and her sensitivity to biological time to scare us. Her statement is so extreme that perhaps she is exaggerating.

Drawing Readers' Inferences

Exercise 12-2

on your own, then in class

An active reader draws a large number of readers' inferences while reading. See if you can draw ten such inferences as you read the following preface adapted from one that appeared in a self-published plumbing guidebook in 1963. Bring your list to class. You and your classmates can compare lists—either in small groups or as a class. You should be able to refer to sentences, words, or phrases in the article to back up your inferences.

■   ■   ■

The purpose of this book is not to make a Plumber out of the Home Owner or Tenant, but to give the necessary information on the Care and Repair of the Plumbing and Heating System, etc., WHETHER YOU EVER DO

ANY OF YOUR OWN REPAIRING OR NOT. THIS BOOK SHOULD BE READ by the Home Owner, Tenant, Housewife, Maid, etc., in fact anyone left to care of the Home during the Summer as well as the Winter seasons. If the instructions are carefully followed, you will, no doubt, find it a WONDERFUL HELP IN CASE OF SUDDEN OR UNEXPECTED REPAIRS, in eliminating accidents, damaging property, unnecessary expense, etc.

DO NOT THINK THAT PARTS IN THIS BOOK ARE OLD-FASHIONED, or behind the times, DO YOU KNOW this book is being sold all over the Country. About one third of the population live in Small Towns, Farms, Villages, etc., and have no City Sewer, Gas, City Water, etc., U.S. official Census 1960, Urban 125,268,759, Rural 54,054,425, Total Population 179,323,175. Where the majority have Gas or Oil for fuel, others have to use Coal or Wood . . .

The author in a total of many years of experience, has come across some very sad accidents, and the remark that is usually made with a regretting sigh, "IF I HAD ONLY KNOWN." There are many serious accidents that occur every year, especially DURING THE WINTER MONTHS, simply because of the ignorance of the fact that the proper precautions should have been taken, or because of the carelessness commonly called "TAKING A CHANCE." Do not wait until the auto is missing before locking the garage door. Be prepared when it comes to looking after your Plumbing, Heating, Ventilation, etc. . . .

This book is written from practical experience (not technical or trade school experience) having been in the Plumbing and Heating business for many years in Chicago, Chicago Suburbs, Colorado, Kansas, Wyoming, and Canada, so became acquainted with the many different State Laws, License, Examination Tests, Codes, Sanitary Engineering, etc.

You will find this book placed in many Libraries in the U.S., in the world's largest, in Washington, D.C.

MEMORIAL; The net proceeds from this book is being given to Orphan Homes, Blind, Mental Institutions, Missionary Work. If you only followed one of the many items in this book, what you save on, for instance, on fuel alone during the Winter season (25-50 dollars) not saying anything about the healthful results received, what you save, remember just a little for some charitable work.

This book is written in the hope of helping and assisting the reader along the lines for which it is intended.

See whether your class as a whole can come up with at least 15 distinct inferences about this writer's character and attitudes.

Drawing Inferences from a Writer's Facts

Writers of non-fiction freely offer their opinions along with the facts they have gathered. As readers of such works, we draw our own inferences, but as we do, we compare them with those of these authors. Other authors, particularly writers of fiction, prefer to engage their readers by using only telling details and then allowing readers to draw their own inferences not only about the author as a writer but about the subject of the writing itself.

Exercise 12–3
on your own, then in class

See how many inferences you can draw about the family and the society described in the passage below, the opening pages of Richard Wright's novel, *Native Son*. Again, bring your list of inferences to class, and compare your results with those of your classmates. As always, be prepared to point to the evidence for your inferences (you probably ought to underline or circle such evidence).

■ ■ ■
From Native Son *(1940)*

Richard Wright

Brrrrrrriiiiiiiiiiiiiiiiiiiinng!   1

An alarm clock clanged in the dark and silent room. A bed spring   2
creaked. A woman's voice sang out impatiently:

"Bigger, shut that thing off!"   3

A surly grunt sounded above the tinny ring of metal. Naked feet swished   4
dryly across the planks in the wooden floor and the clang ceased abruptly.

"Turn on the light, Bigger."   5

"Awright," came a sleepy mumble.   6

Light flooded the room and revealed a black boy standing in a narrow   7
space between two iron beds, rubbing his eyes with the backs of his hands.
From a bed to his right the woman spoke again:

"Buddy, get up from there! I got a big washing on my hands today and I   8
want you-all out of here."

Another black boy rolled from bed and stood up. The woman also rose   9
and stood in her nightgown.

"Turn your heads so I can dress," she said.   10

The two boys averted their eyes and gazed into a far corner of the room.   11
The woman rushed out of her nightgown and put on a pair of step-ins. She
turned to the bed from which she had risen and called:

"Vera! Get up from there!"   12

"What time is it, Ma?" asked a muffled, adolescent voice from beneath a   13
quilt.

"Get up from there, I say!"   14

"O.K., Ma."   15

A brown-skinned girl in a cotton gown got up and stretched her arms   16
above her head and yawned. Sleepily, she sat on a chair and fumbled with her
stockings. The two boys kept their faces averted while their mother and sister
put on enough clothes to keep them from feeling ashamed; and the mother
and sister did the same while the boys dressed. Abruptly, they all paused,
holding their clothes in their hands, their attention caught by a light tapping
in the thinly plastered walls of the room. They forgot their conspiracy against
shame and their eyes strayed apprehensively over the floor.

"There he is again, Bigger!" the woman screamed, and the tiny one-room   17
apartment galvanized into violent action. A chair toppled as the woman, half-
dressed and in her stocking feet, scrambled breathlessly upon the bed. Her
two sons, barefoot, stood tense and motionless, their eyes searching anxiously
under the bed and chairs. The girl ran into a corner, half-stooped, and gathered the hem of her slip into both of her hands and held it tightly over her
knees.

"Oh! Oh!" she wailed.   18
"There he goes!"   19
The woman pointed a shaking finger. Her eyes were round with fasci-   20
nated horror.
"Where?"   21
"I don't see 'im!"   22
"Bigger, he's behind the trunk!" the girl whimpered.   23
"Vera!" the woman screamed. "Get up here on the bed! Don't let that   24
thing *bite* you!"
Frantically, Vera climbed upon the bed and the woman caught hold of   25
her. With their arms entwined about each other, the black mother and the
brown daughter gazed open-mouthed at the trunk in the corner.
Bigger looked round the room wildly, then darted to a curtain and swept   26
it aside and grabbed two heavy iron skillets from a wall above a gas stove. He
whirled and called softly to his brother, his eyes glued to the trunk.
"Buddy!"   27
"Yeah?"   28
"Here; take this skillet."   29
"O.K."   30
"Now, get over by the door!"   31
"O.K."   32
Buddy crouched by the door and held the iron skillet by its handle, his   33
arm flexed and poised. Save for the quick, deep breathing of the four people,
the room was quiet. Bigger crept on tiptoe toward the trunk with the skillet
clutched stiffly in his hand, his eyes dancing and watching every inch of the
wooden floor in front of him. He paused and, without moving an eye or muscle, called:
"Buddy!"   34
"Hunh?"   35

"Put that box in front of the hole so he can't get out!"   36

"O.K."   37

Buddy ran to a wooden box and shoved it quickly in front of a gaping   38
hole in the molding and then backed again to the door, holding the skillet
ready. Bigger eased to the trunk and peered behind it cautiously. He saw nothing. Carefully, he stuck out his bare foot and pushed the trunk a few inches.

"There he is!" the mother screamed again.   39

A huge black rat squealed and leaped at Bigger's trouser-leg and   40
snagged it in his teeth, hanging on.

"Goddamn!" Bigger whispered fiercely, whirling and kicking out his leg   41
with all the strength of his body. The force of his movement shook the rat
loose and it sailed through the air and struck a wall. Instantly, it rolled over
and leaped again. Bigger dodged and the rat landed against a table leg. With
clenched teeth, Bigger held the skillet; he was afraid to hurl it, fearing that he
might miss. The rat squeaked and turned and ran in a narrow circle, looking
for a place to hide; it leaped again past Bigger and scurried on dry rasping feet
to one side of the box and then to the other, searching for the hole. Then it
turned and reared upon its hind legs.

"Hit 'im, Bigger!" Buddy shouted.   42

"Kill 'im!" the woman screamed.   43

The rat's belly pulsed with fear. Bigger advanced a step and the rat emit-   44
ted a long thin song of defiance, its black beady eyes glittering, its tiny forefeet
pawing the air restlessly. Bigger swung the skillet; it skidded over the floor,
missing the rat, and clattered to a stop against a wall.

"Goddamn!"   45

The rat leaped. Bigger sprang to one side. The rat stopped under a   46
chair and let out a furious screak. Bigger moved slowly backward toward
the door.

"Gimme that skillet, Buddy," he asked quietly, not taking his eyes from   47
the rat.

Buddy extended his hand. Bigger caught the skillet and lifted it high in   48
the air. The rat scuttled across the floor and stopped again at the box and
searched quickly for the hole; then it reared once more and bared long yellow
fangs, piping shrilly, belly quivering.

Bigger aimed and let the skillet fly with a heavy grunt. There was a shat-   49
tering of wood as the box caved in. The woman screamed and hid her face in
her hands. Bigger tiptoed forward and peered.

"I got 'im," he muttered, his clenched teeth bared in a smile. "By God, I   50
got 'im."

He kicked the splintered box out of the way and the flat black body of   51
the rat lay exposed, its two long yellow tusks showing distinctly. Bigger took
a shoe and pounded the rat's head, crushing it, cursing hysterically:

"You sonofa*bitch*!"   52

The woman on the bed sank to her knees and buried her face in the 53
quilts and sobbed:

"Lord, Lord, have mercy. . . ."   54

"Aw, Mama," Vera whimpered, bending to her. "Don't cry. It's dead 55
now."

_____

Locating Assumptions While Reading

Editorial writers, especially those who have come to be regarded as authorities, use fewer facts than you've noticed in the two previous readings.
A writer who has become an authority (by showing in his earlier work a
command of facts) tends to rely more on judgments (inferences) based on
experience, and often on the clever use of language as well. As readers,
when we read such writers, we should be alert for assumptions guiding the
writer's thinking but not explicitly written down, and for words the writer
is deliberately using in unconventional ways. By noting these words and by
discovering these assumptions, we can better understand the writer's point
and make a better-informed decision about whether or not we agree.

_____

Exercise 12-4
on your own, then in class

Read the following editorial written by Ellen Goodman of the *Boston Globe*. Circle
all the words that are used in an unusual way, and when you've finished, try to explain,
for each circled word, the difference between the usual meaning of the word and the
meaning implied by the author. Also, try to locate any assumptions the author has about
relations between men and women that are not stated but that clearly influence the author's point of view. Bring your notes to class, and compare your results with those of
your classmates.

■ ■ ■

When Grateful Begins to Grate (1979)

Ellen Goodman

I know a woman who is a grateful wife. She has been one for years. In   1
fact, her gratitude has been as deep and constant as her affection. And together they have traveled a long, complicated road.

In the beginning, this young wife was grateful to find herself married to 2
a man who let her work. That was in 1964, when even her college professor

said without a hint of irony that the young wife was "lucky to be married to a man who let her work." People talked like that then.

Later, the wife looked around her at the men her classmates and friends   3
had married and was grateful that her husband wasn't threatened, hurt, neglected, insulted—the multiple choice of the mid-'60s—by her job.

He was proud. And her cup overran with gratitude. That was the way it   4
was.

In the late '60s, when other, younger women were having consciousness-   5
raising groups, she was having babies and more gratitude.

You see, she discovered that she had a Helpful Husband. Nothing in her   6
experience had led her to expect this. Her mother was not married to one; her
sister was not married to one; her brother was not one.

But at 4 o'clock in the morning, when the baby cried and she was ex-   7
hausted, sometimes she would nudge her husband awake (wondering only
vaguely how he could sleep) and ask him to feed the boy. He would say sure.
And she would say thank you.

The Grateful Wife and the Helpful Husband danced this same *pas de*   8
deux for a decade. When the children were small and she was sick, he would
take charge. When it was their turn to carpool and she had to be at work early,
he would drive. If she was coming home late, he would make dinner.

All you have to do is ask, he would say with a smile.   9

And so she asked. The woman who had minded her p's and q's as a   10
child minded her pleases and thank yous as a wife. Would you please put the
baby on the potty? Would you please stop at the store tonight for milk? Would
you please pick up Joel at soccer practice? Thank you. Thank you. Thank you.

It is hard to know when gratitude first began to grate on my friend. Or   11
when she began saying please and thank you dutifully rather than genuinely.

But it probably began when she was tired one day or night. In any case,   12
during the car-time between one job and the other, when she would run lists
through her head, she began feeling less thankful for her moonlighting job as
household manager.

She began to realize that all the items of their shared life were stored in   13
her exclusive computer. She began to realize that her queue was so full of
minutiae that she had no room for anything else.

The Grateful Wife began to wonder why she should say thank you when   14
a father took care of his children and why she should say please when a husband took care of his house.

She began to realize that being grateful meant being responsible. Being   15
grateful meant assuming that you were in charge of children and laundry
and running out of toilet paper. Being grateful meant having to ask. And
ask. And ask.

Her husband was not an oppressive or even thoughtless man. He was   16
helpful. But helpful doesn't have to remember vacuum cleaner bags. And
helpful doesn't keep track of early dismissal days.

Helpful doesn't keep a Christmas-present list in his mind. Helpful   17
doesn't have to know who wears what size and colors. Helpful is reminded;
helpful is asked. Anything you ask. Please and thank you.

The wife feels, she says, vaguely frightened to find herself angry at say-   18
ing please and thank you. She wonders if she is, indeed, an ingrate. But her
wondering doesn't change how she feels or what she wants.

The wife would like to take just half the details that clog her mind like   19
grit in a pore and hand them over to another manager. The wife would like
someone who would be grateful when she volunteered to take *his* turn at the
market or *his* week at the laundry.

The truth is that after all those years when she danced her part perfectly,   20
she wants something else. She doesn't want a helpful husband. She wants one
who will share. For that, she would be truly grateful.

Thoughtful Reading

Exercise 12-5

In your reading thus far in this chapter I've guided you in what to look for as you read. But each of us reads in an individual way, based on past reading experience and on past experience in general. Consequently, each of us draws unique inferences (you might prefer the term *insights*) from any work we read with care. While reading the following selections—a brief poem and a description of a coal mine—underline or circle in each whatever *you* think is important, and make at least five comments in the margins. (Your underlining indicates that you regard the author having written those words as a fact worth noting. Your marginal comments are readers' inferences that you're drawing.) In class, then, compare your comments with those of your classmates. How different was what you chose to mark from what they marked? What inferences were the most thoughtful in the class? What was it that made those inferences stand out from the crowd?

In completing this exercise, you will see more clearly what you value when you read, and you will begin to discover what other readers, including your teacher, look for. Are some ways of reading better than others?

■ ■ ■

Airport: A Takeoff on a Poem (1980)

E. Ethelbert Miller

sitting in the airport
for about two hours
i finally landed a conversation
with an old white lady who looked

mulatto
she asked me if i was a student
at the university
i told her no
she asked me what i did
i told her i wrote poetry
she asked me what i wanted to do
i told her i had always
wanted to kill a large number of people
i told her of my desire to climb into
clocktowers and be a sniper
i told her that i had missed the draft
and was too proud to enlist
i told her about all the audie murphy
films i had ever seen
i told her that i was the type
that carried bombs inside luggage
when making short trips
i watched the old mulatto lady
turn white
there was no mistaking it now
she was a white lady and i...

well i have been sitting in this
airport for over two hours more
listening to the soft ticking sounds
coming from the case i carry my poems in

■ ■ ■

From The Road to Wigan Pier *(1937)*

George Orwell

Our civilization . . . *is* founded on coal, more completely than one real-izes until one stops to think about it. The machines that keep us alive, and the machines that make the machines, are all directly or indirectly dependent upon coal. In the metabolism of the Western world the coal miner is second in importance only to the man who ploughs the soil. He is a sort of grimy cary-atid upon whose shoulders nearly everything that is *not* grimy is supported. For this reason the actual process by which coal is extracted is well worth watching, if you get the chance and are willing to take the trouble. . . .

It is impossible to watch the "fillers" at work without feeling a pang of envy for their toughness. It is a dreadful job that they do, an almost superhuman job by the standards of an ordinary person. For they are not only shifting monstrous quantities of coal, they are also doing it in a position that doubles or trebles the work. They have got to remain kneeling all the while—they could hardly rise from their knees without hitting the ceiling—and you can easily see by trying it what a tremendous effort this means. Shoveling is comparatively easy when you are standing up, because you can use your knee and thigh to drive the shovel along; kneeling down, the whole of the strain is thrown upon your arm and belly muscles. And the other conditions do not exactly make things easier. There is the heat—it varies, but in some mines it is suffocating—and the coal dust that stuffs up your throat and nostrils and collects along your eyelids, and the unending rattle of the conveyor belt, which in that confined space is rather like the rattle of a machine gun. But the fillers look and work as though they were made of iron. They really do look like iron—hammered iron statues—under the smooth coat of coal dust which clings to them from head to foot. . . .

Probably you have to go down several coal mines before you can get much grasp of the processes that are going on round you. This is chiefly because the mere effort of getting from place to place makes it difficult to notice anything else. In some ways it is even disappointing, or at least is unlike what you have expected. You get into the cage, which is a steel box about as wide as a telephone box and two or three times as long. It holds ten men, but they pack it like pilchards in a tin, and a tall man cannot stand upright in it. The steel door shuts upon you, and somebody working the winding gear above drops you into the void. You have the usual momentary qualm in your belly and a bursting sensation in the ears, but not much sensation of movement till you get near the bottom, when the cage slows down so abruptly that you could swear it is going upward again. In the middle of the run the cage probably touches sixty miles an hour; in some of the deeper mines it touches even more. When you crawl out at the bottom you are perhaps four hundred yards under ground. That is to say you have a tolerable-sized mountain on top of you; hundreds of yards of solid rock, bones of extinct beasts, subsoil, flints, roots of growing things, green grass and cows grazing on it—all this suspended over your head and held back only by wooden props as thick as the calf of your leg. But because of the speed at which the cage has brought you down, and the complete blackness through which you have traveled, you hardly feel yourself deeper down than you would at the bottom of the Piccadilly tube. . . .

When you think of a coal mine you think of depth, heat, darkness, blackened figures hacking at walls of coal; you don't think, necessarily, of those miles of creeping to and fro. There is the question of time, also. A miner's working shift of seven and a half hours does not sound very long, but one has got to add on to it at least an hour a day for "traveling," more often two hours and sometimes three. Of course, the "traveling" is not technically work and the miner is not paid for it; but it is as like work as makes no difference. It is easy to say that miners don't mind all this. Certainly, it is not the same for them as it would be for you or me. They have done it since childhood, they have the right muscles hardened, and they can move to and fro underground with a startling and rather horrible agility. A miner puts his head down and *runs*, with a long swinging stride, through places where I can only stagger. At the workings you see them on all fours, skipping round the pit props almost like dogs. But it is quite a mistake to think that they enjoy it. I have talked about this to scores of miners and they all admit that the "traveling" is hard work; in any case when you hear them discussing a pit among themselves the "traveling" is always one of the things they discuss. It is said that a shift always returns from work faster than it goes; nevertheless the miners all say that it is the coming away, after a hard day's work, that is especially irksome. It is part of their work and they are equal to it, but certainly it is an effort. It is comparable, perhaps, to climbing a smallish mountain before and after your day's work. . . .

Watching coal miners at work, you realize momentarily what different   10 universes different people inhabit. Down there where coal is dug it is a sort of world apart which one can quite easily go through life without ever hearing about. Probably a majority of people would even prefer not to hear about it. Yet it is the absolutely necessary counterpart of our world above. Practically everything we do, from eating an ice to crossing the Atlantic, and from baking a loaf to writing a novel, involves the use of coal, directly or indirectly. For all the arts of peace coal is needed; if war breaks out it is needed all the more. In time of revolution the miner must go on working or the revolution must stop, for revolution as much as reaction needs coal. Whatever may be happening on the surface, the hacking and shoveling have got to continue without a pause, or at any rate without pausing for more than a few weeks at the most. In order that Hitler may march the goosestep, that the Pope may denounce Bolshevism, that the cricket crowds may assemble at Lord's, that the Nancy poets may scratch one another's backs, coal has got to be forthcoming. But on the whole we are not aware of it; we all know that we "must have coal," but we seldom or never remember what coal-getting involves. Here am I, sitting writing in front of my comfortable coal fire. It is April but I still need a fire. Once a fortnight the coal cart drives up to the door and men in leather jerkins carry the coal indoors in stout sacks smelling of tar and shoot it clanking into the coal-hole under the stairs. It is only very rarely, when I make a definite mental effort, that I connect this coal with that far-off labor in the mines. It is just "coal"—something that I have got to have; black stuff that arrives mysteriously from nowhere in particular, like manna except that you have to pay for it. You could quite easily drive a car right across the north of England and never once remember that hundreds of feet below the road you are on the miners are hacking at the coal. Yet in a sense it is the miners who are driving your car forward. Their lamp-lit world down there is as necessary to the daylight world above as the root is to the flower.

It is not long since conditions in the mines were worse than they are now.   11
There are still living a few very old women who in their youth have worked underground, with a harness round their waists and a chain that passed between
their legs, crawling on all fours and dragging tubs of coal. They used to go on
doing this even when they were pregnant. And even now, if coal could not be
produced without pregnant women dragging it to and fro, I fancy we should let
them do it rather than deprive ourselves of coal. But most of the time, of course,
we should prefer to forget that they were doing it. It is so with all types of manual work; it keeps us alive, and we are oblivious of its existence. More than anyone else, perhaps, the miner can stand as the type of the manual worker, not only
because his work is so exaggeratedly awful, but also because it is so vitally necessary and yet so remote from our experience, so invisible, as it were, that we are
capable of forgetting it as we forget the blood in our veins. In a way it is even hu-
miliating to watch coal miners working. It raises in you a momentary doubt
about your own status as an "intellectual" and a superior person generally. For it
is brought home to you, at least while you are watching, that it is only because
miners sweat their guts out that superior persons can remain superior. You and I
and the editor of the *Times Literary Supplement*, and the Nancy poets and the
Archbishop of Canterbury and Comrade X, author of *Marxism for Infants*—all of
us *really* owe the comparative decency of our lives to poor drudges underground, blackened to the eyes, with their throats full of coal dust, driving their
shovels forward with arms and belly muscles of steel.

From Drawing Inferences to Evaluating

When you write a paper or an essay exam about something you've read,
your responsibility is not simply to summarize it but to do what we've been
practicing throughout this chapter: draw inferences about it. But the inferences you'll be expected to draw in academic papers will be restricted a bit.
They can no longer be about the author, but must be about the author's craft.

You may have inferred from George Orwell's writing, for example, that he
was physically strong himself, even if he just accompanied the miners at their
work for a few days as he did his research. When we analyze reading in school,
though, this kind of inference takes a secondary role to inferences about how
well the writer has used the tools at his or her disposal. Words are of course the
primary tools of a writer; every word and phrase has a history of use by others
behind it and therefore a set of emotional meanings that we can interpret and
comment on. But more abstract tools, the tools that you have been sharpening
yourself during this course—*ethos, logos, and pathos*—are also at every writer's
disposal, of course, and the words that the writer puts on the page can be used
by us as evidence of the writer's greater or lesser effectiveness in using *ethos,
logos,* and *pathos.* One of the most straightforward ways to evaluate any piece of
writing is to examine, using the questions in Chapter 6 on p. 94, how effectively

the author has used these three means of affecting readers. Your textbooks, your mail, and everything else you "read" (including ads, films, political speeches, and popular songs) can be judged by the same standards.

Rhetorical Analysis

Exercise 12-6
on your own, then in class

In the 19th century, crowds of thousands would gather in small towns throughout the United States, paying a good chunk of their salaries, to hear speeches by famous Europeans like Charles Dickens, Richard Wagner, and Winston Churchill. With radio, television, and the internet, we are no longer so hungry for good speeches, but we are still very susceptible to being influenced by a good speech. Read a recent speech suggested by your teacher (you can easily find one on the internet) and perhaps the one following given by the novelist Robertson Davies to the graduates of Bishop Strachan School in Ontario, Canada, in 1973. Read each carefully, noting, again using the questions on p. 94, how effectively you think it employs *ethos, logos,* and *pathos.* Circle the evidence you find for every conclusion (inference) you draw about *ethos, logos,* or *pathos.* Decide how well crafted you think each speech is, and compare your results, and the evidence you have used to arrive at your results, in class.

■ ■ ■

What Every Girl Should Know (1973)

Robertson Davies ·

As a schoolboy I listened to many speeches on Prize Days from older persons whose good intentions were impeccable, but whose manner and matter were tediously patronizing and stuffy. When my own turn came I determined to be as honest as possible, not to talk down, and if possible to say something that was not usually said in schools. This is what I said to the girls of the Bishop Strachan School in June 1973.

During the years when my own daughters were pupils in this school I attended many of these gatherings, and heard many speeches made by men who stood where I stand at this moment. They said all sorts of things. I recall one speaker who said that as he looked out at the girls who were assembled to receive prizes, and to pay their last respects to their school, he felt as though he were looking over a garden of exquisite flowers. He was drunk, poor man, and it would be absurd to treat his remark as though he were speaking on

1

oath. I am not drunk, although I have lunched elegantly at the table of the Chairman of your Board of Governors; I have had enough of his excellent wine to be philosophical, but with me philosophy does not take the form of paying extravagant and manifestly untruthful compliments. Let me put myself on record as saying that I do *not* feel as though I were looking over a garden of exquisite flowers.

On the contrary, I feel as though I were looking into the past. You look   2
uncommonly as the girls of this school looked when my daughters were of your number. And in those days I used to think how much you looked like the girls who were in this school when I was myself a schoolboy, just down the road, at Upper Canada College.

I remember that boy very well. He was a romantic boy, and he thought   3
that girls were quite the most wonderful objects of God's creation. In these liberated days, when it is possible for anyone to say anything on any occasion, I may perhaps make a confession to you, and this is it: I never liked anything but girls. Nowadays it is accepted as gospel that everybody goes through a homosexual period of life. I cannot recall any such thing: I always regarded other boys as rivals, or nuisances, or—very occasionally—friends. I am rather sorry about it now, because in the eyes of modern psychologists and sociologists it marks me as a stunted personality. Nowadays it appears that there is something warped about a man who never had a homosexual period. But there it is. I stand before you with all my imperfections weighing heavily upon me. I always liked girls, and simply because of geography, the girls I liked best were the girls of BSS.

I have recovered from this folly. I have myself achieved some knowl-   4
edge of psychology and sociology, and it tells me significant but not always complimentary things about you. I don't know how many of you are here today, but statistically I know that during the next ten years 58.7 per cent of you will marry, and that of that number 43.4 per cent will have two and a half children apiece, and that 15.3 per cent will be divorced. Of the remainder, 3.9 per cent will be dead, 14.5 per cent will have been deserted, 24.2 per cent will have spent some time in jail. One hundred per cent of those who have married will have given up splendid careers in order to do so, and of this number 98.5 per cent will have mentioned the fact, at some time, to their husbands. These statistics were compiled for me by a graduate student at OISE, and if you doubt them, you must quarrel with her, and not with me. I accept no responsibility for statistics, which are a kind of magic beyond my comprehension.

I have said that when I was a boy I entertained a lofty, uncritical admira-   5
tion for the girls of this school. Our romantic approach in those days was more delicate than it is today, when sexual fervour has achieved almost cannibalistic exuberance, and I thought I was lucky when I had a chance simply to talk to one of the girls from this school. I never had enough of that pleasure; I yearned for more. Now here I offer my first piece of good advice to you: be

very careful of what you greatly desire, in your inmost heart, because the chances are very strong that you will get it, in one form or another. But it will never be just the way you expected. You see what has happened? As a boy I wanted to talk to the girls of BSS, and I always thought of doing this to one girl at a time, in shaded light, with music playing in the distance. And here I am today, talking to all of you, in broad daylight. The things I planned to say when I was a boy would be embarrassingly inappropriate if I were to say them now. Indeed, I don't want to say them; they have ceased to be true or relevant for you or for me. I know too much about you to compliment you, and in your eyes I am not a romantic object. Or if I am, you had better put yourself under the treatment of some wise psychiatrist.

Here I am, after all these years, and Fate has granted one of my wishes, in the way Fate so often does—at the wrong time and in whole-sale quantity. What am I to say to you?   6

The hallowed custom, at such times as these, is that I should offer you some good advice. But what about? It was easier in the days when girls like yourselves thought chiefly about marriage. Nowadays when little girls play   7

Rich man, poor man, beggar man, thief,
Doctor, lawyer, Indian chief,

they are trying to discover their own careers, not those of their husbands. Quite recently a very young girl told me that she did not intend to bother with a husband; she would be content with affairs, because they would interfere less with her career. That remark showed how much she knew about it. A girl who thinks love affairs are less trouble than a marriage is probably also the kind of girl who thinks that picnics are simpler than dinner-parties. A first-class picnic, which has to be planned to the last detail, but which must also pretend to be wholly impromptu, is a vastly more complicated undertaking than a formal dinner for twenty guests, which moves according to a well-understood pattern. Personally I have always greatly liked dinner-parties, and hated picnics. But then I am a classicist by temperament, and I think the formality and the pattern, either in love or in entertaining, is half the fun.

But you may have different views, so we won't talk about that. Let us talk about something that will be applicable to your life, whether the love aspect of it takes the dinner-party or the picnic form. Let us talk about enjoying life.   8

Don't imagine for a moment that I am going to talk about that foolish thing happiness. I meet all kinds of people who think that happiness is a condition that can be achieved, and maintained, indefinitely, and that the quality of life is determined by the number of hours of happiness you can clock up. I hope you won't bother your heads about happiness. It is a cat-like emotion; if you try to coax it, happiness will avoid you, but if you pay no attention to it it will rub against your legs and spring unbidden into your lap. Forget happiness, and pin your hopes on understanding.   9

Many people, and especially many young people, think that variety of   10
sensation is what gives spice to life. They want to do everything, go everywhere, meet everybody, and drink from every bottle. It can't be done. Who-
ever you are, your energies and your opportunities are limited. Of course you
want to try several alternatives in order to find out what suits you, but I hope
that ten years from today you will agree with me that the good life is lived not
widely, but deeply. It is not doing things, but understanding what you do, that
brings real excitement and lasting pleasure.

You should start now. It is dangerously easy to get into a pattern of life,   11
and if you live shallowly until you are thirty, it will not be easy to begin living
deeply. Whatever your own desires may be, the people around you won't put
up with it. They know you as one sort of person, and they will be resentful if
you show signs of becoming somebody else. Live shallowly, and you will find
yourself surrounded by shallow people.

How are you to avoid that fate? I can tell you, but it is not a magic secret   12
which will transform your life. It is very, very difficult. What you must do is to
spend twenty-three hours of every day of your life doing whatever falls in
your way, whether it be duty or pleasure or necessary for your health and
physical well-being. But—and this is the difficult thing—you must set aside
one hour of your life every day for yourself, in which you attempt to understand what you are doing.

Do you think it sounds easy? Try it, and find out. All kinds of things will   13
interfere. People—husbands, lovers, friends, children, employers, teachers,
enemies, and all the multifarious army of mankind will want that hour, and
they will have all sorts of blandishments to persuade you to yield it to them.
And the worst enemy of all—yourself—will find so many things that seem attractive upon which the hour can be spent. It is extremely difficult to claim
that hour solely for the task of understanding, questioning, and deciding.

It used to be somewhat easier, because people used to be religious, or   14
pretended they were. If you went to the chapel, or the church, or a praying-
chamber in your own house, and fell on your knees and buried your face in
your hands, they might—not always, but quite often—leave you alone. Not
now. "Why are you sitting there, staring into space?" they will say. Or "What
are you mooning about now?" If you say "I am thinking" they may perhaps
hoot with laughter, or they will go away and tell everybody that you are intol-
erably pretentious. But you are doing very much what you would have been
doing if you were your great-grandmother, and said that you were praying.
Because you would be trying your hardest to unravel the tangles of your life,
and seek the aid of the greatest thing you know—whatever you may call it—
in making sense of what will often seem utterly senseless.

I am not going to advise you to pray, because I am not an expert on that   15
subject. But I do know that it is rather the fashion among many people who do
pray to think that it is pretentious to pray too much for yourself; you are supposed to pray for others, who obviously need Divine assistance more than

you do. But when I was a boy at the school down the road, we were taught that prayer has three modes—petition, which is for yourself; intercession, which is for others; and contemplation, which is listening to what is said to *you*. If I might be permitted to advise you on this delicate subject, I would suggest that you skip intercession until you are a little more certain what other people need; stick to petition, in the form of self-examination, and to contemplation, which is waiting for suggestions from the deepest part of you.

If I embarrass you by talking about praying, don't think of it that way. 16 Call it "pondering" instead. I don't know if you still learn any Latin in this school, but if you do, you know that the word ponder comes from the Latin *ponderare*, which means "to weigh". Weigh up your life, and do it every day. If you find you are getting short weight, attend to the matter at once. The remedy usually lies in your own hands. And in that direction the true enjoyment of life is to be found.

There you are. I promised your Headmaster I would not speak for too 17 long. But I have done what a speaker on such occasions as this ought to do. I have given you good advice. It is often and carelessly said that nobody ever takes advice. It is not true. I have taken an enormous amount of advice myself, and some of it was extraordinarily helpful to me. I have passed on some of the best of it to you this afternoon, and I have enjoyed doing so. Because, as I told you, it was my ambition for years to have a chance to talk to every girl in BSS and today I have achieved it. Not quite as I had hoped, but then, in this uncertain world, what ever comes about quite as one hopes? I have enjoyed myself, and for what I have received from you I am truly thankful.

Reading, and Writing about, Fiction

Literature, for the most part, consists of stories invented (with more or less truth behind them) by their authors to entertain us and to make us think about what it means to be human. Fiction writers often select their materials the same way nonfiction writers do: they look for the facts that will most readily convey their intentions to the reader. (They have the advantage over nonfiction writers, of course, of being able to invent facts if the facts they want are not available.) And works of fiction can be judged, like works of nonfiction, by assessing the *ethos*, *logos*, and *pathos* that comes through as we read. More commonly, though, when we think of the tools of the fiction writer, we use a different vocabulary: character, setting, plot, tone of voice, distinctive uses of language, and theme. Since fiction writers immerse us in a world in order to make us think about their meaning, we rarely hear from them what the "thesis" of their work is. Even their titles are often meant to be intriguing rather than self-explanatory. Therefore, deciding what we think the theme or thesis of a work might be is an important aim of any paper about a work of fiction. And deciding on that theme is done in precisely the way we have done it with nonfiction materials throughout this course: by looking at the words (facts), drawing inferences about them, and summarizing (with qualifications) those inferences in a thesis.

Papers about literature usually take one of three forms:

1. An explanation of several devices used by the author to achieve his or her overall effect.
2. An explanation of how one portion of the story helps the author to achieve his or her overall effect.
3. A comparison of one aspect of a story, for example, the theme or the setting, with the same aspect of another story.

All these tasks ask you, as you did in writing about nonfiction, to draw inferences about the writer's craft. As with nonfiction, the more carefully you've read and the more you know about the tools writers use to build their works, the better a paper you can write.

Drawing Inferences about Works of Fiction

Exercise 12-7

Read a pair of stories selected by your teacher and draw two or three inferences (with quotations from the texts to substantiate them) about each of the major tools of the fiction writer's craft: character, setting, plot, tone of voice, and distinctive uses of language. Then give your best judgment of what you think the themes of the two stories were meant to be.

Without the art produced by people who have come before us and by people who live in parts of our country and our world that we're very little familiar with, we would all be trapped in our own local towns and neighborhoods. Films can take us to different countries and times, but the reading of fiction, biography, and history can do so with much greater detail and psychological depth. Use your reading in this writing class as a stepping stone to a lifelong habit of reading that will continue to expand and enrich your life for as long as you're able to do it.

13

The Writing Process: An Overview

English has always been a difficult subject, in that words get lost between the mind and the hand.

STUDENT

Books always amaze me, due to the fact that so many people can express themselves in writing without much difficulty.

STUDENT

The fun is not in writing; the fun is in HAVING WRITTEN.

GENE OLSON

Writing is easy. All you do is stare at a blank sheet of paper until drops of blood form on your forehead.

GENE FOWLER

I now write my first drafts like an optimist, assuming that people are interested in anything I have to say. I revise like a pessimist who figures that none of my ideas will get through.

STUDENT

Now when I know I have to write, I don't feel the task is against me, but on my side.

STUDENT

Reflections on the Writing Process

In this chapter, I'd like to give you some general advice about writing strategies gleaned from what I've learned from students, colleagues, and

207

professionals. Much of this advice you will have found elsewhere in the book, but all of it is here, too, in this single chapter to which you can return as often as you wish. You may want to read it early in your course to get your bearings, but if you read it again later in the course, it will mean more to you since you can then compare it with your own experience writing.

Review of Your Writing Habits

Exercise 13-1
on your own

Your attention will be sharpened if, before we begin, you write out answers to these two questions:

1. What do you hate most about writing?
2. What are the main differences you imagine between a professional writer and yourself?

I don't know anyone who thinks he or she has found the most efficient way to write. In fact, most of us are a little embarrassed about the way we go about it, procrastinating often and being irrationally attached to a special pen, or a desk in a certain place, or starting after midnight, or having Oreo cookies at hand. We also have never admitted to ourselves, much less told our teachers or our classmates, the details of our alternating despairs and satisfactions as we work on a paper.

Your Writing Process

Exercise 13-2
on your own, then in class

The most effective way to get over a vague fear of writing is to admit it, and to spell out exactly what its sources are. Think of something you've written that you're proud of—a report from high school, a paper from this course, a difficult letter, something you've written on the job. Think about *how* you went about writing. What did you do while preparing for and writing it? What problems did you have? Record both the *physical* and the *emotional* steps you went through from the time you first thought about writing to the time you gave your work to someone. If you've never written anything you're proud of, make a record of how you went about writing some piece that you hated doing. In class, read your account of your writing process aloud, and listen to the accounts of several of your classmates. What do you all have in common? What new ideas have you picked up?

Your writing process may seem annoyingly complex to you, but that process will seem miraculously simple if you compare it with the filming process that any film director is faced with. Here is Satyajit Ray, the most admired Indian filmmaker of the 1950s and 60s, explaining the process of creating just one short scene for *Pather Panchali* (Geduld 269–70):

> To me it is the inexorable rhythm of its creative process that makes filmmaking so exciting in spite of the hardships and the frustrations. Consider this process: you have conceived a scene, any scene. Take the one where a young girl, frail of body but full of some elemental zest, gives herself up to the first monsoon shower. She dances in joy while the big drops pelt her and drench her. The scene excites you not only for its visual possibilities but for its deeper implications as well: that rain will be the cause of her death.
>
> You break down the scene into shots, make notes and sketches. Then the time comes to bring the scene to life. You go out into the open, scan the vista, choose your setting. The rain clouds approach. You set up your camera, have a last quick rehearsal. Then the "take." But one is not enough. This is a key scene. You must have another while the shower lasts. The camera turns, and presently your scene is on celluloid.
>
> Off to the lab. You wait, sweating—this is September—while the ghostly negative takes its own time to emerge. There is no hurrying this process. Then the print, the "rushes." This looks good, you say to yourself. But wait. This is only the content, in its bits and pieces, and not the form. How is it going to join up? You grab your editor and rush off to the cutting room. There is a grueling couple of hours, filled with aching suspense, while the patient process of cutting and joining goes on. At the end you watch the thing on the moviola. Even the rickety old machine cannot conceal the effectiveness of the scene. Does this need music, or is the incidental sound enough? But that is another stage in the creative process, and must wait until all the shots have been joined up into scenes and all the scenes into sequences and the film can be comprehended in its totality. Then, and only then, can you tell—if you can bring to bear on it that detachment and objectivity—if your dance in the rain has really come off.

Most beginning writers want to skip this patient "editing" stage that is so important to the success of a film. They feel that "planning" and "shooting" a paper is the most they should be expected to do.

Another art closely related to writing is sculpture—listen to these descriptions of the French sculptor Auguste Rodin at work (Descharnes and Chabrun 236, 238):

> Nothing in Rodin's surroundings resembles the society studios of fashionable sculptors; no knick-knacks, no art objects calculatingly displayed for sale. Everything here reminds one of the craftsman, wearing wooden shoes, with dust and smears of clay on his garments.
>
> Rodin always carried some clay and something to draw with in his pocket and never seemed to spend more than five minutes, even while talking or eating, without either sketching or modeling some shape with his busy fingers.
>
> Rodin appeared to work slowly. When in 1898 he had to part with his *Balzac* to meet the Salon's deadline (he had put off the delivery of the statue as long as he could) he felt he was being hurried and was greatly upset. "They're snatching the work out of my hands," he grumbled, as the statue was removed from the Dépôt des marbres. "When will those idiotic officials understand that in order to turn out something good, one must have time to forget it?"

A careful writer gets his hands just as dirty as Rodin did, is just as alert to new ideas for his work, and is just as aware that the paper finally turned in could still use a little work.

Stages of the Writing Process

The writing process is never as neat and orderly as a cookbook process, but it can be usefully described in terms of stages. Every writing specialist will give you a different version of these stages. Their versions are more or less specific (four are shown below), and their categories overlap, but you'll find many different versions useful.

Richard Gebhardt (21)

1. Generating and focusing
2. Drafting
3. Revising

Michael Adelstein (120)

1. Worrying (15 percent)
2. Planning (10 percent)
3. Writing (25 percent)
4. Revising (45 percent)
5. Proofreading (5 percent)

Kenneth Dowst (4.2, 4.14)

1. Invention writing
2. Revision writing

Sharon Pianko (275–78)

1. Prewriting
2. Planning
3. Composing

4. Writing
5. Pausing
6. Rescanning
7. Rereading
8. Stopping
9. Contemplating the finished product
10. Handing in the finished product

The variety in these lists should remind us that even in this chapter, we should be looking not for a single writing strategy but, rather, for "workable strategies." Every writing assignment and every writing situation is slightly different; no advice about the writing process can give us ironclad, step-by-step instructions. All we can say of even the best advice is that it is *often* fruitful.

Collecting and Selecting

Everyone seems to agree that a person can't just start writing: writing requires preparation. But what that preparation should consist of is a matter of some dispute. Many student writers have been scared or misled by the rhetorical term for prewriting: *invention.* How am I to "invent" a whole five-page paper out of nothing? But *invention* (from the Latin verb *invenire*) means not "to invent," but "to find," or "to discover." Our task is more manageable if we realize that we only have to *find* things. We are all capable of that. Or are we? If we have to find *ideas*, that's still a mystical task.

In many traditional writing courses, you practiced that mysticism, finding a topic (finding a topic meant finding the right-sized topic) and then choosing a pattern of organization to "develop" that topic. But this mysticism is quite unnecessary. Prewriting should begin not with topic analysis but with information. It then continues with interpretation of the information we want to pass on. Once we "find" the information, our creativity, our "invention," comes into play as we draw inferences from the information we have.

Once you've been given a problem or area to research, then, "invention" begins with observation, with a search for telling details. Writing is not worth reading if its subject has not been carefully observed. Why should any of us, even if we are teachers, go to the trouble of reading a piece by a writer who doesn't know his or her subject? The search for details, depending on the assignment, may begin with a careful look at a place, with research in a laboratory, with an interview, with the underlining of passages in books, or with xeroxing or printing from internet or library sources. No matter where this fact collecting takes place, though, the writer will have along the tools of our trade—a pen (or pencil), plenty of paper, and usually a computer—to note whatever facts (details, statistics, quotations) seem pertinent. When drafting time comes, a fact on paper or in a computer file is worth ten in the writer's leaky memory. While collecting facts, a writer should also note *any* ideas about those facts that come to mind. Ideas are even more slippery than facts we observe—they fly out of our heads as fast as they fly in—so they must be written down or typed in. Most people need to practice this crucial step, for it isn't often natural—we're not used to listening to ourselves think. If we later decide that an idea is harebrained or exaggerated, we can always discard or qualify it. Once we have maybe twenty-five telling details and maybe six or seven good ideas, we have the foundation for a three- to four-page paper, and we can consider beginning to write.

Such note taking requires starting early—no one can write an information-rich paper the night before it's due. As often as possible, you should start your work early enough so that you can bring your notes—not yet in the form of a first draft—to class and have them discussed for their value. Which of your notes would the teacher and other students like to see in a paper? Which would elicit, in a final paper, the praise "interesting information" or "well thought through"? If you bring no raw material that's provoking to this session, no amount of coherence you can add will glue a decent paper together by the due date.

Once you've taken some notes, you may want to try some timed writing like that you practiced in Chapter 4 to see what direction your writing might take. Setting a timer forces you to get a page or two or three written, and you may well discover in this kind of writing new aspects of your subject that you'd like to explore. Writing with a timer often allows us to see what we really want to say about a subject—and not just what we think we should say. Writing quickly but honestly temporarily frees our conscious minds from social restraints which cause us to fall into patterns rather than to make a mark for ourselves. Later on, we may not be satisfied with what we've drafted, but we now have some raw material that we can work with.

Another technique that can help us get our information and ideas on paper is called *clustering*. Clustering is a bit like outlining in that it is a record of what we might say, but it is not nearly as rigid as an outline and doesn't commit us to the order in which we will present our ideas. To begin a cluster, just write the only idea you have (if you have only one) on a sheet of paper and then circle it. The author of an analysis of an *Everywoman* magazine from 1944, for example, may have started a cluster, after reading once through the magazine, as follows:

Then he might proceed with his cluster, one circle at a time, until it looked like this:

Such a cluster helps you see how many ideas you have, and it gives you plenty to work with when you start writing.

After collecting facts and inferences, doing some timed writing (if you wish), and building up a cluster (if you wish), you can look over the chaos of facts and ideas on the page and consider your first step well done. We can't begin unless we have some chaos to work with, as we're reminded by Mary Shelley, the author of *Frankenstein*: "Invention, it must be humbly admitted, does not consist in creating out of a void, but out of chaos" (7). To live with this chaos for a while severely tests the patience of most writers: "The mind doesn't like chaos; ordering is its natural activity." But "the aim of composing is not to tolerate chaos for its own sake but to learn to put up with it while you discover ways of emerging" (Berthoff 65).

The writer should now find, among the chaos of facts and ideas, the kernels she likes, and she should then ask some questions. For any isolated facts in the paper, she ought to anticipate a reader's asking "So what?" For any ideas or generalizations, she ought to anticipate a reader's asking "For instance?" Short written answers to these questions should (when combined with the original notes) start giving shape and density to the paper.

Incubation (Waiting)

Fortunately, not all our writing decisions need to be conscious. After doing some spadework for an essay, we can go play ball, do housework, or just go to sleep without feeling guilty, because we are allowing our subconscious mind to take its turn while the conscious mind goes fishing. Both our conscious and our subconscious minds have plenty to contribute to a paper. A paper written by choosing a thesis, writing an outline, and filling out the paragraphs is completed entirely by the conscious mind—the paper may be good, and time limits may occasionally make this way of writing necessary, but it is not the best we can do.

Donald Murray, a Pulitzer-prize-winning writer, has shown how we can put our intuitive strengths to work when we write. When we begin to see a shaping idea for a paper, we should pull away from it for a while, partly to see how new evidence that we come across fits with that idea, but partly just to await the ordering process of our mind, as it sifts and resifts the data we've collected in the light of this new "idea." We don't immediately make judgments about the idea—we test it, half consciously, half unconsciously.

The temptation, of course, is to let this part of the process go on indefinitely: "Writing which can be delayed, will be" (Murray, "Write" 375). Research is more fun than sharing research. It's a great pleasure to have our heads full of ideas, but it doesn't do anyone any good but ourselves. Murray suggests that at this point only force—a waiting audience or an approaching deadline—can make a writer write, can pull the writer out of this very satisfying state. I do think *ego* will also do it; fortunately for us as writers, our egos want credit for the ideas we have. Of all the kinds of force, though, deadlines are the most effective. Don't curse them. They are there to bring out the best in you. Satisfaction doesn't come until late in the writing process—though the pleasures of research come early. Without a deadline, most writers would prefer to bask in the early pleasure of learning. But when we allow ourselves to do so, we deny ourselves the opportunities for the genuine satisfaction that comes from presenting what we've found to others.

Ordering

Let's assume now that we're faced with a writer's dream—we have plenty of notes, and we've stopped for a day or two to think about them. What are we going to do with the information now that we have it? How are we going to organize it? The next steps we take are going to commit us in ways that are difficult to retrace, so this is the time to make sure of our own commitment. I find it useful to make, at this point, a statement of commitment for myself:

I plan to [aim] for [readers] by [methods].

This statement sets our tone, our pace, our level of difficulty, and the question of whether we want to inform, judge, or persuade in our paper. This commitment statement should help us see whether and what kind of further research is necessary. But if we have completed the necessary research, we can now simply sort through the information we've collected and see what inferences (assertions, claims) we want to make and can justify. A simple diagram based on those inferences, perhaps as they appeared in our cluster, can then serve as a provisional outline, which is all we want at this stage. The outlines we form now should only be rough sketches—outlines will play a larger part later in the writing process when we check our draft to see whether we've been systematic and whether we've kept our sense of proportion.

The structure we create in this way should not be considered a complete map of our finished paper. Much will be added during the actual writing. But if the structure seems only half or less than half complete, a writer might refer to some list of common organizing principles, or ways of filling out the plan:

1. Do I have enough information to justify each assertion?
2. Have I drawn as many inferences as I can safely draw from my information? Are my inferences bold enough? thoughtful enough?
3. Are there any contrasts that might highlight my subject?
4. Would some analogy or brief story make any of my points clearer to my intended readers?
5. Would my readers appreciate a historical context?
6. Do any of my key terms need defining?
7. Have I taken sufficiently into account the way that people who disagree with me would feel about my subject?
8. Have I explained how things will be improved if people listen to my argument?
9. Have I answered the six typical readers' questions—Who? What? When? Where? (these four are important, but rapidly answered) and, more important, Why? and How?

Thus, the invention process continues, and it is perhaps more imaginative at this point than it is in the beginning of our work on a paper. By considering (and often rejecting) these options, we not only may stumble onto an organizing principle that sorts out the difficulties we've been having; we also may discover what we don't yet know about our subject.

Planning at this point increases efficiency. An utterly unplanned draft may take so long to sort out that its value as "something on paper" is more than offset by the revision time it requires. A plan that we can refer to while drafting reduces the load on our memories, leaving our minds free to deal with each sentence as it comes.

Drafting

With rare exceptions, all of us would rather do anything than begin to write: no matter how many times a person has written and succeeded before, each time he starts, he faces a fear that nothing of quality will come out this time. In the face of this fear, our best ally is determination: we must make ourselves do what we have to do, when it ought to be done, whether we like it or not. But when we have done all the gathering and planning mentioned in the previous few pages, summoning the determination to begin should be much less traumatic. We face no blank page. We have more than enough notes to complete our assignment.

Three other things can help. First, we must realize that there is *no* rule in writing that can't be broken. Our materials, our purpose, or our intended readers may each require a strategy that we haven't yet heard of. It can't hurt to try. We can always revise later. Second, as we write out our first draft, we must not even think about trying to make it perfect—"decent" is all we want; "playful," perhaps, but "decent" will do. We shouldn't allow ourselves to be slowed down by an attempt to find the "perfect" word or by a worry over a matter of grammar or spelling. Third, we need a deadline—if the teacher hasn't given us one, then we must impose one ourselves. Unless we're in the position of having readers waiting for our results, we won't very often start without a deadline. Flexible deadlines, when they exist, are huge contributors to writer's block on our college campuses.

The other cause of writer's block is a fear that "style"—indeterminate, indefinable "style"—is what makes or breaks a paper. It's very difficult to write when we don't understand the grounds by which we might be judged. If we feel secure, though, that the quality of a piece of writing depends primarily on the quality of the facts we have selected and the quality of the inferences we have drawn from those facts, then much of the quality of a paper is established before the first draft begins to appear on the page—the first draft has thus shrunk to its proper dimensions.

Once writer's block has been shuttled aside, drafting becomes one of the easiest steps in the writing process. We should allow ourselves *some* revision during this stage. One good sentence often produces better sentences after it. One good paragraph often produces better paragraphs following. But it is important to remember that this is "only" a draft, so it's most important that we take some risks and try to convey to our readers the clear voice of a writer enjoying writing (revision is always waiting, prudently, to rescue us). We must be willing, too, to write much more than we will eventually need (thus allowing the reviser in us to distinguish later between our better efforts and our worse). As we write, we must keep in mind not only our subject but the questions our readers will have for us about our subject. The difficulties we can expect while drafting are that we'll have to start earlier than we want to, that our hands and fingers will get tired, that our ideas will tend to come faster than we can express them, and, worst of all, that we'll get discouraged because we'll lose faith that our work is original or that anyone will want to read it. All four difficulties are normal: but when we expect them, they don't hurt so much.

We should think seriously about completing this drafting step at a computer, if at all possible. Some writers disagree with me here. Paul Theroux, author of *The Great Railway Bazaar*, argues that writing by hand is slower and thus allows more time for thought and for surprise. Some writers say they can think better with pen and paper than they can at the computer. But the advantages of working at a computer are numerous. A typed draft is much easier to read objectively, much easier to make changes on while still remaining readable. Our typed draft gives us our first opportunity to really read our work carefully.

The most important thing to note about a draft, though, is not whether it's typed or handwritten but whether our minds are engaged while it's coming into being. Donald Murray says that "the most accurate definition of writing, I believe, is that it is the process of using language to discover meaning in experience and to communicate it" ("Internal Revision" 86). Thus he calls our first draft a "discovery draft," a very useful term. The writer has a plan before beginning that "discovery draft," but she is open to new ideas as she executes it, and she is disappointed if she hasn't "discovered" something as she's worked her way through it. We need room to breathe while writing. We begin with a sense of direction, yes, but we rarely know our final intention before we have finished the paper. If a writer doesn't learn much in writing a paper, the reader isn't likely to learn much from reading it either.

Revising (Making the Work Readable)

When I say writing, O believe me, it is rewriting I have chiefly in mind.
— Robert Louis Stevenson

Revising begins almost as soon as a paper is first conceived, with the writer's first shift in ideas about what to include in the paper or how to organize it. Revising continues with changes in the writer's first written sentence and with pauses for reflection and rereading as the draft is taking shape. But concentrated revising, beginning *after* a first draft, is the point at which a work either comes to life or falls dead. All the preceding steps of writing are relatively easy; the hard work begins here. The British writers Robert Graves and Alan Hodge tell us that "there should be two main objects in ordinary prose writing: to convey a message, and to include in it nothing that will distract the reader's attention or check his habitual pace of reading" (154). Collecting, selecting, waiting, and drafting focus on coming up with a message; *revising focuses on getting that message, as clearly as possible, to the reader*. Only when we have gathered and written out something both thoughtful and informative are we willing to go through this final process, which demands (admittedly) that we become a little fanatic about perfection. It may seem that as writers we spend a very long time to gain a very small end, but we might compare our efforts with those of filmmakers. How many thousands of hours do they spend to give us just two hours of entertainment?

Most people equate revising with cleansing, with seeing to it that what is written conforms to the conventions and rules, so that the written piece can be received and judged by the reader without the distraction of faulty punctuation, poor spelling, or other errors. Such cleansing is important, but revising is a much broader process. Seldom do we write down in our first draft exactly what we meant to say. Only when we read back through our papers can we judge whether our points have come out the way we thought they did. Once we've adjusted our draft so that it says what we meant to say, we must check also to see whether there are any points on which we've changed our minds since we started writing. And finally, once we are reasonably sure of what we mean, revising also entails reading to see whether we've made our meaning clear to others.

To revise successfully, a writer must first break away—*we writers love breaks*. A day away from your paper is good, and at least an hour away is essential to writing a good paper, for the writer needs time to take off his writer's cap and to put on his reader's cap. A writer's assumptions and background are necessarily different from those of any reader, and the writer must therefore try to read from that alien reader's perspective. Much of revising lies in the writer's ability to read his writing as though he were an interested but uninformed reader. His job is much easier if he can get an honestly critical friend to read his paper. The foremost question that this reader should be asking is a question suggested by Aristotle: *Have I learned easily?* If not, why not? The comments of readers like this are often very helpful. But even if they aren't directly helpful, they may indirectly trigger new ideas for the writer. We all become fond of our own words and ideas (much as parents become fond of their own children, because they have gone to so much trouble to bring them up). But our ideas, like our children, still need to be disciplined into shape. Outsiders don't share our uncritical fondness, and they can help us sort out the best in our writing from the unnecessary.

If no reader is available, the writer should at least read her own work aloud until she is satisfied with the way it sounds. In ancient Greece, "all literature was written to be heard, and even when reading to himself a Greek read aloud" (Kennedy 4). Therefore, Aristotle took it for granted that "a composition should be easy to read or—which is the same thing—easy to deliver" (195). We in the twenty-first century often forget that words are written to be heard. But if, when we read our work aloud, we find ourselves halting or embarrassed, we should consider that embarrassment an invitation to revise:

1. We may see several places where we have hinted at, rather than specified, our meaning.
2. We may find that we need more details.
3. We may see that a briefer introduction or conclusion would better use our reader's time.
4. We may think of an introduction or conclusion which would make our intentions clearer.
5. We may see that our main point—the something that we wanted to achieve when we began—isn't clear (we may want to add an explicit thesis).
6. We may see that our coverage of issues isn't balanced and that some important matter needs more explanation.
7. We may find that a paragraph is too long and needs to be split or that several are too short and might well be combined.
8. We may find sentences that are clumsy or ungrammatical.
9. We often find that some of our sentences are not linked together well.
10. We may find that we've written lies or half-lies which we have to correct.
11. We may find clutter that distracts the reader from our message.
12. We may find that we've put our most important points in places where they'll receive little emphasis.
13. We may want to rewrite sentences to achieve a better sound or rhythm.
14. We ought to write a one-sentence-per-paragraph outline to see whether the draft makes sense, and perhaps we need to add some direction-indicating sentences that will make reading easier.
15. Most important, we ought to check to make sure that a real author comes through clearly to the reader.

In short, we "must read with an eye to *alternatives* in content, form, structure, voice, and language" (Murray, "Internal Revision" 95). When we're finished, we should have few qualms about handing this piece to a reader.

Publishing

Only now are we ready to check spelling, punctuation, grammar, and neatness. We can forget, finally, what we've said; we can now just concentrate on whether the words we're not sure of are spelled correctly. We can recheck (using the rules in Chapter 9) our punctuation, and look over the whole paper to make sure it looks clean. We don't want to leave in our work any unnecessary distractions from what we're trying to say.

Overview

We don't always spend all the time suggested here and go through all these stages as we write papers for school or reports outside school. As our writing intuitions develop, many of these steps will take place more quickly. But even with highly developed intuitions, writing is never easy, and it requires several blocks of uninterrupted time to be completed.

John Muir has said that the great thrill of wilderness exploring is that "we find more than we seek." That's the same thrill of the writing process, and that's what so often leaves us satisfied after so much work.

14

What Next?

No, I didn't like the textbook. To me, all English books rank right down there with **The Scarlet Letter.**

STUDENT

I don't think this course requires a book. This course only requires a pen, paper, and a computer.

STUDENT

I never liked to write much and I still don't like to unless it is necessary. But I think I now have more power to write.

STUDENT

This was a tough course to take while on academic probation. It involved a lot of time. Now it is slightly more enjoyable to write, but it still is a pain at times.

STUDENT

I'd still rather work with numbers but I do think I learned how to write better.

STUDENT

A blank screen isn't as frightening to me any more.

STUDENT

I feel more comfortable about writing, but I still have a lot of room for improvement. I wish I could take this class again so that I could keep improving my writing skills.

STUDENT

Few are taught to any purpose who do not become their own teachers.

SIR JOSHUA REYNOLDS

Answers to Exercises Earlier in the Book

Exercise 3-3: Magazine #1 is *Psychology Today*. Magazine #2 is *The Family Handyman*. Magazine #3 is *The New Yorker*. Magazine #4 is *Vogue*.

Exercise 7-2: In the original article Fred Reed paragraphed at 1, 4, 10, 11, 18, 25, 30, 40, and 44. A good argument can also be made for paragraphing at 6, 7, 22, 31, and 33.

Exercise 7-3: The original article reads as follows:
Guide Offers Hints to Bring Markets to Inner Cities (December 7, 1981)
      During the past decade, supermarket chains have been deserting the inner cities in alarming numbers, leaving residents without cars few or no alternatives to expensive convenience stores. The number of markets in urban areas has declined between 28 and 50 percent in Boston, Washington, and Chicago.
      Now a manual on how inner cities can maintain or bring back food markets has been put together by the Community Nutrition Institute. Using six case studies, including Santoni's Market in Southeast Baltimore, the authors offer a practical guide for establishing food coops, farmers' markets and independently operated supermarkets.
      Among the hints for saving a community store are limiting food assortment to 1,000 or so staple items and selling products that cater directly to neighborhood needs. Most people who buy with food stamps don't need appliance and camera equipment counters in their markets.
      Also suggested are Sunday hours, wine and beer sales, minibus transportation and child care centers at the market for shopping mothers. The community is urged to lobby the local government to get a low cost lease on adjacent city-owned property that could be used as a parking lot, and for resurfaced sidewalks and high powered street lights where needed.
      The guide, entitled "Food Marketing Alternatives For the Inner City," is available from CNI, Consumer Division, 1146 19th St. N.W., Washing, D.C. 20036.

Exercise 10-4:

1. In Harlem "it is possible for talented youths to leap through the development of decades in a brief twenty years. "[1]

2. In Harlem "it is possible for talented youths to leap through the development of decades in a brief twenty years" (296).

3. "This [Harlem] is no dream" (296).

4. "a world so fluid and so shifting that . . . the marvelous beckons from behind the same sordid reality that denies its existence" (296).

5. Single space the quotation, indent the whole quotation, and don't use quotation marks.

Taking Stock

Exercise 14-1
on your own

You are now finishing a course designed to help you become a more correct, more effective, and more confident writer. You certainly have not solved all your writing problems—no one ever does. But you have made some progress. Take a few minutes to take stock, now, of your current writing ability.

What kind of writer would you call yourself now? In what areas have you made the most improvement during this course? What problems do you still have as a writer? *Why* do you think you still have those problems? Can you think of methods you can use to help solve your remaining problems?

Recommended Books

In this book, I've tried to address writers who are skeptical of their own writing ability, and skeptical about whether writing can help them in their careers and in their lives. I hope now that you are less skeptical, that you've tasted the pleasure of teaching yourself and of profiting from the advice of your teacher and your classmates. I hope now that you'll take your writing education into your own hands and try to find the books that can help you learn more fully what the resources of our language are. I recommend highly:

1. A college dictionary (at least 50,000 words). Buy it used for a couple of dollars. When you don't know a word, the only way to make it part of your vocabulary is to write it down and look it up online or in the dictionary right away. No one looks up every unfamiliar word, no matter how much teachers have advised us to do so; very few of us do it as much as we say we do. But try doing it during your summers. Or for a week at a time during the school year. Surprisingly quickly, your determination will pay off in increased word and thinking power.

2. William Strunk and E. B. White's *The Elements of Style*, 4th edition (New York: Allyn & Bacon, 2000). An inexpensive, brief review of all the basics of writing, a little outdated in its references but written with good sense and humor. This book is deservedly the most widely consulted book about writing.

3. Robert Pirsig, *Zen and the Art of Motorcycle Maintenance* (New York: Bantam, 1975). Even if you're not intrigued by Zen or by motorcycles, this book is an excellent introduction to the kinds of practical and critical thinking that are so important for writers. Besides it's a good story of a motorcycle trip.

4. Reginald Bragonier, Jr., and David Fisher, *What's What: A Visual Glossary of the Physical World* (New York: Smithmark, 1994). You don't need to buy this picture book, but take it out of a library for a couple of weeks. It identifies the component parts of everything from chain saws (guidebar, guidebar nose, spark-arresting muffler) to front doors (center stile, butte stile, lock stile) to flagpoles (finial, truck, staff) to electric guitars (bridge, frets, pickguard) to fire hydrants (bonnet, hose nozzle cap, cap chain). Just browsing through this reference book will help you think more clearly and develop a better eye for detail.

Strengthening Intuition

Having taken this course, you should now realize that writing helps us remember; it helps us make sense of our experience; it helps us work out our passions and frustrations; it gives us the power to make a mark on the world around us. You now know that learning to write is—far more than we might expect—learning to understand other people. You now know that writing, not just for you but for everyone, is work, but that the satisfaction of a finished paper—well-observed, well-organized, and well-written—can make all that work worthwhile.

You have practiced many individual skills in this course, from observing to inference drawing to paragraphing to organizing to punctuating. Successful writing doesn't require keeping those skills in the front of your mind all the time. Maintaining full consciousness of your technique is more likely to backfire than to help, as is illustrated in a story told about Walter Hagen, a golfer who won many major tournaments in the 1920s and 1930s. Hagen was a notorious drinker, and in one of those tournaments, he showed up for the final round hung over, unshaven, and red-eyed. His opponent—it was match play—was a sweet-swinging, overconfident young man, and just before they teed off, Hagen said to him, "You know, you've got the most beautiful swing I've ever seen. That little pause at the top of your backswing really works. How do you do it?" By the time the young man had figured out what Hagen had done to him, Hagen had won—five holes up with four holes to play. Skills are more useful *after* they've become intuitive than they are when we remain fully conscious of them.

I hope this course has strengthened your observation, your thoughtfulness, your organization, your sense of audience, your sense of self, and your ability to bring all of these to bear on your writing. The course has been designed to help you strengthen all these skills both consciously and intuitively—we hope fast enough for you to do well in this course. But even if you haven't done as well as you would have liked in this course, your intuitions have made some progress, and if you continue to nurture and strengthen them, they will serve you well, paper after paper, presentation after presentation, memo after memo, year after year, as you navigate your challenging, enjoyable life.

Works Cited

Adelstein, Michael, "Writing Is Work." In *The Practical Craft*. Ed. W. K. Sparrow and D. H. Cunningham. Boston: Houghton Mifflin, 1978: 116–25.

Aristotle. *The Rhetoric of Aristotle*. Ed. Lane Cooper. New York: Appleton Century Crofts, 1932.

Beisanz, Mavis Hiltunen, and John Beisanz. *Introduction to Sociology*. 3rd ed. Englewood Cliffs, N.J.: Prentice-Hall, 1978.

Bernstein, Carl. "Graduation Speech from the Bottom of the Class." *The Kenosha News* 7 June 1979: 5.

Berthoff, Ann. *Forming, Thinking, Writing*. Rochelle Park, N.J.: Hayden, 1978.

Britton, James. "The Composing Processes and the Functions of Writing." In *Research on Composing*. Ed. Charles R. Cooper and Lee Odell. Urbana, Ill.: National Council of Teachers of English, 1978: 13–28.

Browne, Sir Thomas. *The Religion of a Doctor*. New York: Dutton, 1969.

Buel, Joy Day, and Richard Buel. *The Way of Duty: A Woman and Her Family in Revolutionary America*. New York: Norton, 1984.

Carson, Rachel, *Silent Spring*. New York: Houghton Mifflin, 1962.

Cowley, Malcom, ed. *Writers at Work*. Vol. 1, New York: Viking, 1959.

Crosby, Harry. "Titles, A Treatise On." *College Composition and Communication* 27 (1976): 387–91.

Davies, Robertson. "What Every Girl Should Know." In *One Half of Robertson Davies*. Harmondsworth: Penguin, 1977.

Descharnes, Robert, and Jean-Francois Chabrun. *Auguste Rodin*. Secaucus, N.J.: Chartwell Books, 1967.

Dickens, Charles. *A Tale of Two Cities*. Harmondsworth, England: Penguin, 1970.

Dillard, Annie. *Pilgrim at Tinker Creek*. Harper and Row, 1974.

Dowst, Kenneth. *Basic Writing*. Pittsburgh, Penn.: The U of Pittsburgh, 1977.

Ellis, Robert, and Denny Gulick. *Calculus with Analytic Geometry.* 2d ed. New York: Harcourt, Brace, Jovanovich, 1982.

Ellison, Ralph. *Shadow and Act.* New York: Vintage, 1995.

Faigley, Lester, and Thomas P. Miller. "What We Learn from Writing on the Job." *College English* 44 (1982): 557–69.

Farmer, Richard N. *Introduction to Business.* New York: Random House, 1972.

Finch, Vernor C., and Glenn T. Trewartha. *Elements of Geography.* New York: McGraw-Hill, 1936.

Flower, Linda, and John R. Hayes. "Problem-Solving Strategies and the Writing Process." *College English* 39 (1977): 449–61.

Fussell, Paul. *The Great War and Modern Memory.* London: Oxford University Press, 1975.

Galbraith, John Kenneth. "Writing, Typing, and Economics." *Atlantic* Mar. 1982: 102–05.

Gebhardt, Richard. "The Writing Process." *Freshman English News* 9 (1980): 19–22.

Geduld, Harry M., ed. *Filmmakers on Filmmaking.* Bloomington: Indiana U P, 1967.

Graves, Robert, and Alan Hodge. *The Reader Over Your Shoulder.* New York: Random House, 1978.

Hall, Carla. "The Radical Voice of Moderation." *The Washington Post* 14 Mar. 1983: 81.

"Harper's Index." *Harper's* Jan. 1988: 11.

Harris, Art. "The Wild Bunch, Heros Once More." *The Washington Post* 4 Nov. 1983: D1–D2.

Hayakawa, S. I. *Language in Thought and Action.* 2d ed. New York: Harcourt, Brace, and World, 1963.

Hochschild, Adam. *King Leopold's Ghost.* NY: Houghton Mifflin, 1998.

"How To Win at Wordsmanship." *Newsweek* 6 May 1968: 104.

Hyams, Edward. *The Changing Face of Britain.* St. Albans, England: Paladin, 1977.

Kearns, Doris. *Lyndon Johnson and the American Dream.* New York: Harper and Row, 1976.

Kennedy, George. *The Art of Persuasion in Greece.* Princeton, N.J.: Princeton U P, 1963.

King, Leonard. Class handout. The Maret School, Washington, D.C.

Kolb, Harold. *A Writer's Guide.* New York: Harcourt, Brace, Jovanovich, 1980.

Lash, Joseph P. *Eleanor: The Years Alone.* New York: Norton, 1972.

LeSueur, Meridel. "I Was Marching." In *Women Working: An Anthology of Stories and Poems.* Ed. Nancy Hoffman and Florence Howe. Old Westbury, N.Y.: The Feminist Press, 1979: 228–40.

Linton, Calvin. *Effective Revenue Writing.* Washington, D.C.: U.S. Government Printing Office, 1962.

Macauley, David. *The Way Things Work.* Boston: Houghton Mifflin, 1988.

Macrorie, Ken. *Searching Writing.* Rochelle Park, N.J.: Hayden, 1980.

Macrorie, Ken. *Telling Writing.* 2d ed. Rochelle Park, N.J.: Hayden, 1976.

McPhee, John. *Basin and Range.* New York: Farrar, Straus, and Giroux, 1981.

McPhee, John. *The Curve of Binding Energy.* New York: Farrar, Straus, and Giroux, 1974.

McPhee, John. *The Pine Barrens.* New York: Farrar, Straus, and Giroux, 1967.

Mitchell, Henry. "The Waugh to End All Waughs." *The Washington Post* 18 Jan. 1982: C1.

Mill, John Stuart. *On Liberty.* Indianapolis: Appleton Century Crofts, 1947.

Moon, Truman J. *Biology for Beginners.* New York: Holt, Rinehart, and Winston, 1921. Rpt 1981.

More, Thomas. *A Dialogue of Comfort against Tribulation.* Ed. Louis Martz and Frank Manley. Vol. 12 of *The Complete Works of St. Thomas More.* Ed. Richard Sylvester. New Haven: Yale U P, 1963.

Murphy, James T. *Physics: Principles and Problems.* 2d ed. Columbus, Ohio: Charles E. Merrill, 1977.

Murray, Donald. "Internal Revision: A Process of Discovery." In *Research on Composing.* Ed. Charles R. Cooper and Lee Odell. Urbana, Ill.: National Council of Teacher of English, 1978: 85–103.

Murray, Donald. "Write before Writing." *College Composition and Communication* 29 (1978): 375–81.

Pianko, Sharon. "Reflection: A Critical Component of the Composing Process." *College Composition and Communication* 30 (1979): 275–78.

Pirsig, Robert. *Zen and the Art of Motorcycle Maintenance.* New York: Morrow, 1974.

Ram, Hari. "The Path Down the Bhotia Kosi River in Nepal." In *A Book of Travellers' Tales.* Ed. Eric Newby. New York: Viking Penguin, 1985: 318–19.

Raymond, James and Ronald Goldfarb. *Clear Understandings.* New York: Random House, 1982.

Riekehof, Lottie L. *The Joy of Signing.* Springfield, Mo.: Gospel Publishing House, 1978.

Rogers, Carl. "Communication: Its Blocking and Its Facilitation." In *Rhetoric: Discovery and Change.* Richard E. Young, Alton L. Becker, and Kenneth L. Pike. New York: Harcourt, Brace and World, 1970: 284–89.

Ross, Nancy. "Guide Offers Hints to Bring Markets to Inner Cities." *The Washington Post: Business* 7 Dec. 1981: 5.

Segal, Bernice G. *Chemistry: Experiment and Theory.* New York: Wiley, 1985.

Shelley, Mary. *Frankenstein.* New York: Pyramid, 1957.

Smith, George Rose. "A Primer of Opinion Writing for Four New Judges." *The University of Arkansas Law Review* 1967.

Sterne, Lawrence. *Tristram Shandy.* Ed. Howard Anderson. New York: Norton, 1980.

Stoltz, Craig. "Doing Archaeology." Unpublished manuscript, 1983.

Taylor, Pat Ellis. "Teaching Creativity in Argumentation." *College English* 39 (1977): 507–510.

Toulmin, Stephen. *The Uses of Argument.* Cambridge, England: Cambridge University Press, 1958.

Worsley, Peter. *Inside China.* Harmondsworth, England: Penguin, 1975.

Zinsser, William. *On Writing Well.* 2d ed. New York: Harper & Row, 1980.

Acknowledgments

Harry Crosby, "Titles, A Treatise On." *College Composition and Communication.* Dec. 1976. c 1976. Selection reprinted with the permission of the author.

Robertson Davies, "What Every Girl Should Know." c 1977. Reprinted with the permission of Viking Penguin, Inc.

Paul Fussell, *The Great War and Modern Memory.* c 1975. Selections reprinted with the permission of Oxford University Press.

Rani Garrison, draft of a paper done for homework. Selection reprinted with the permission of the author.

Harry Geduld, *Filmmakers on Filmmaking.* c 1967. Selection reprinted with the permission of Indiana University Press.

Ellen Goodman, "When Grateful begins to Grate." c 1979. Reprinted with the permission of the Boston Globe Newspaper Company and the Washington Post Writers Group.

"Harper's Index." *Harper's Magazine.* c 1987. Reprinted from the Jan. 1988 issue by special permission.

S.I. Hayakawa, *Language in Thought and Action.* 2nd ed. c 1963. Selection reprinted with the permission of Harcourt, Brace, Jovanovich, Inc.

Harold Kolb. *A Writer's Guide.* c 1980. Selection reprinted with the permission of Harcourt, Brace, Jovanovich, Inc.

Ken Macrorie, *Telling Writing.* 2nd ed. c 1976. Selection reprinted with the permission of Hayden Book Company.

John McPhee, *The Pine Barrens.* c 1967. Selections reprinted with the permission of Farrar, Straus, and Giroux, Inc.

E. Ethelbert Miller, "Airport: A Takeoff on a Poem." c 1980. Reprinted with the permission of the author.

George Orwell, *The Road to Wigan Pier.* c 1936. Selection reprinted with the permission of Harcourt, Brace, Jovanovich, Inc.

Nam Pham, "Saigon, Once Upon a Time." Selection reprinted with the permission of the author.

Fred Reed, "Lean, Healthy and Forty-Five." *The Washington Post* 29 Sep. 1979. c 1979. Reprinted with the permission of the author.

Nancy Ross, "Guide Offers Hints to Bring Markets to Inner Cities." *The Washington Post*: Business 7 Dec. 1981. c 1981. Reprinted with the permission of the Washington Post Company.

Craig Stoltz, "Doing Archaeology." Selection reprinted with the permission of the author.

Pat Ellis Taylor, "Teaching Creativity in Argumentation." *College English*. Dec. 1977. C 1977. Selections reprinted with the permission of the author.

Richard Wright, *Native Son*. C 1940 by Richard Wright; c renewed 1968 by Ellen Wright. Selection reprinted with the permission of Harper & Row, Inc.

Index

CPSIA information can be obtained
at www.ICGtesting.com
Printed in the USA
FSHW022207041219
64725FS

9 780757 570148